BRAVELY, FAITHFULLY, CHEERFULLY

MEMORIES OF
ALTRINCHAM GRAMMAR SCHOOL
FOR GIRLS
1910–2010

FIDELITER FELICITER FORTITER

1910 - 2010

Celebrating 100 Years

BRAVELY, FAITHFULLY, CHEERFULLY

MEMORIES OF
ALTRINCHAM GRAMMAR SCHOOL
FOR GIRLS
1910–2010

COMPILED AND EDITED BY PAT McCORMAC

Published by
Altrincham Grammar School Old Girls' Society
March 2010

© Altrincham Grammar School Old Girls' Society, the editor and all contributors

Altrincham Grammar School Old Girls' Society
33 Pengwern Court
Longden Road
Shrewsbury
SY3 7JE

ISBN 978-0-9564592-0-6

Printed by Creative Digital Printing Limited, Shrewsbury

Front cover: Altrincham Grammar School for Girls from a painting by Pat Hodkinson, a former pupil and a member of staff in the School Art Department

Half-title page: Detail of the West Wing (formerly the New Wing 1925–1966)

Frontispiece: The Centenary Badge

Back cover: The Centenary Garden, March 2010

ALTRINCHAM GRAMMAR SCHOOL OLD GIRLS' SOCIETY
CENTENARY BOOK SUB-COMMITTEE

Pat McCormac (Compiler and Editor)
Naomi Garside
Marlen Hughes
Leila Pilkington
Susie Ripley
Pat Williamson

CONTENTS

ACKNOWLEDGEMENTS

Material for this book has been collected from many sources, the most important being the 185 former pupils and members of staff who so kindly sent in written contributions and many photographs. I am also grateful for the open access afforded to the School Archives including the *School Annals* 1915–1936, *Memories of 21 years 1910–1931*, *School Magazines* 1937–2000, *The First Fifty Years 1910–1960* and *The Insider* 2000–2008. Another fruitful source was the *Old Girls' News* 1939–2001 and the *Old Girls' Society Newsletters* 2003–2009. Also used were *A Short History of Altrincham County Grammar School for Girls 1910–1974* and *A Chronicle of Altrincham Grammar School for Girls 1974–91*, both by Myra Kendrick. In addition, many individuals and societies have been most helpful and include: members of the School who, despite their heavy workload, have been most generous of their time and consideration, in particular Diane Pullen, John Edwards, Jon Poole, Jennifer Ogunmyiwa, Lynda Abrahams, Michael Roberts for his research on Conrad Pellifex (*A Complete Guide to Heraldry* by Arthur Charles Fox-Davies), Kevin Daniell, Adi Thorpe, Pat Hodkinson, Clare Stuart and Jane Reynolds; Reith Baines (PTA); David Miller and the Altrincham History Society; Ronald Trenbath and the Bowdon History Society; Denise Laver and the Hale Civic Society; the Local History Library, Sale; *Cheshire Life*; Airviews Ltd; Linda Fowler (Glint Print); Chris Henderson (Creative Digital Printing Ltd).

I also acknowledge the generous support of Mrs Ross-Wawrzynski and the Governors, and Sally Haywood and the Parent Teachers Association without which the Old Girls' Society would not have been able to proceed with such an ambitious undertaking. Also, at the time of going to press 700 books have already been sold. Such wonderful support of a book as yet unseen must be applauded. I sincerely hope that this volume will bring you hours of enjoyment.

Special acknowledgement must also be made to two friends, the brothers Paul and Francis Engleheart, members of the Kinlet History Group which published a very high quality book in 2007 entitled *Kinlet: the Life and Times of a Shropshire Village*. The invaluable expertise gained on their project and meticulous approach to layout, colour and detail has been generously shared throughout our collaboration and made my task so much easier. Both have spent many unpaid hours working on this book and publicity material, and without Paul's computing skills it would not have got off the ground. Gentlemen, a heartfelt thank you.

Last, but not least, my husband of over forty-two years, Don, has lived with this project from Day One – 20 May 2005. Throughout he has been patient and helpful and given freely of his many talents including book-keeping, order processing, telephone answering, proof reading, chauffeur and cook.

All help has been greatly appreciated and acknowledged, but if by some oversight your name has been omitted from the list above, I do most sincerely apologise. It has been really wonderful over recent months to receive so many cards and letters of encouragement and support from 'Old Girls' spanning several decades.

Pat McCormac   March 2010

FOREWORD

Dana Ross-Wawrzynski
Headmistress

It is truly a privilege to be Headmistress of Altrincham Grammar School for Girls as it celebrates its centenary in 2010. This is a great school in every way. Those associated with AGGS, whether as pupil, parent, teacher or friend, past or present, feel a tremendous sense of pride and belonging. Each phase of the school during these hundred years has been special, and has without doubt contributed to its present success. AGGS is renowned as a centre of excellence for secondary education. Our girls leave us as articulate, outward-looking young women ready to fulfil their ambitions and play a full part in society.

I am proud that we are able to offer them a first-class academic education along with a wealth of opportunities to develop the whole person. The ethos upon which the success of this school has been built is very evident in the pages of this wonderful centenary book.

I thank the inspirational members of the Old Girls' Society for their enthusiasm and labour in compiling this fascinating record of the unique times of Altrincham Grammar School for Girls. I know that each and every one will not only find it a delight to read but will also reflect on some personal, poignant memories.

PREFACE

Marlen Hughes
Chairman of the Old Girls' Society

At the Annual General Meeting of the Old Girls' Society held in School in May 2005, we invited girls from the Sixth Form to be our Guest Speakers and talk to us about life in School in the 21st century. After their excellent presentation and over drinks and nibbles a lively conversation ensued. The girls were fascinated by the stories from the 1930s, 40s and 50s, just as the OGS were amazed at the opportunities available to the pupils today.

Sometime after this Pat McCormac phoned me up and said she thought that these memories ought to be written down and she would be willing to compile a book. What did I think about this idea? Although the centenary of the School was still five years away the Committee had been thinking about how the Society could mark this very important occasion. I invited Pat to our next Committee meeting. We listened to her ideas and immediately co-opted her on to the Committee. Originally we thought we might present a book of reminiscences to School on the anniversary of the centenary, but like Topsy and with Pat's energy, enthusiasm and organisation skills the whole venture just grew and grew. With a small budget and a tape recorder Pat and Don, her husband, have put in hours of work. They have made contact with many, many Old Girls and a few Old Boys (yes, there are some), browsed the Internet, travelled hundreds of miles from their home in Shrewsbury, interviewed Old Girls, spent hours in School and local libraries, and met members of local civic societies, gathering fascinating memories, historical facts and photographs.

In 2008 we realised that we had enough information to publish a book covering all ten decades and thought that this would be a fitting way in which the Society could mark this special occasion. Mrs Sally Haywood, Chairman of the PTA, and her Committee were also thinking of ways to mark the centenary and we all agreed that the last chapter of the book should be about the PTA-sponsored Centenary Garden bringing us "bang up to date".

Pat's vision and enthusiasm, ably assisted by Don, the support of Mrs Ross-Wawrzynski and the School Governors, the PTA, and the contributions from former pupils and staff, have made this book a wonderful record of the development and success of the first one hundred years of Altrincham Grammar School for Girls. On behalf of the Old Girls' Society I wish the School ever more success in the future. I hope you all enjoy a good read and feel a great sense of pride in our School. FFF.

INTRODUCTION

Pat McCormac
Compiler and Editor

"Let us now praise famous men, and our fathers that begat us.
Such as did bear rule in their kingdoms, men renowned for their power.
Leaders of the people by their counsel, and by their knowledge.
Such as found out musical tunes and recited verses in writing;
All these were honoured in their generations, and were the glory of their times.
And some there be which have no memorial;
Who are perished as though they had never been.
Their bodies are buried in peace; but their name liveth for evermore."

Lines taken from Ecclesiasticus, Chapter 44. This passage was read at every Founders' Day Service from the School's beginning and subsequently sung to the music of Ralph Vaughan Williams, which he composed in 1923.

I am not famous; just a very ordinary person who, like thousands before me and thousands since, benefited from a very good education, at a very good school. I thoroughly enjoyed my time of learning, and am thankful for the lifelong friendships made there, and being introduced to the uplifting world of music, art and travel and the opportunity to develop a small sporting talent.

I give thanks to Miss Howes Smith, a remarkable lady who had the foresight and tenacity to establish a school that would stand the test of time. I give thanks to the many talented, unsung but devoted and conscientious members of staff who have served the School "bravely, faithfully and cheerfully" for one hundred years.

The compilation of this book has been a labour of love and I am happy that it provides a means for many generations of pupils to record their appreciation to those "which have no memorial".

Many congratulations, AGGS, on reaching your century!

The photograph of Pat by Gary Beal was kindly sponsored by the Parent Teachers Association.

The 1910s and earlier

1820	Bowdon Lodge built
1902	Balfour Education Act
1908	Bowdon Lodge acquired by Cheshire County Council
1909	Altrincham County High School is built
1910	24 April – Miss Howes Smith appointed Headmistress
1910	4 July – official opening ceremony
1910	14 September – first pupils are enrolled and term begins
1912	12 December – first Speech Day
1914	12 February – first meeting of the Old Girls' Society
1914	24 February – Carnival fancy dress dance
1914	11 and 15 July – Chaucer pageant
1914	4 August – First World War started
1915	21 and 24 July – Chaucer Pageant
1916	19 and 22 July – Mediaeval Fair
1918	23 and 25 March – *Pilgrim's Progress*
1918	Preparatory Department moved to Edgemount, Cavendish Road
1918	11 November – end of First World War
1919	9 April – Speech Day held at Bowdon Assembly Rooms

CHAPTER 1
THE 1910S AND EARLIER

The Edwardian era heralded significant changes in society, politics, and technology. In 1901 King Edward VII succeeded his mother Queen Victoria, who had reigned for sixty-three years, and inherited "an Empire on which the sun never sets". The Boer War had ended. The Labour Party was founded. Marconi transmitted the first wireless message from Cornwall to Canada.

At this time, in the educational field, it was recognised that England and Wales were lagging well behind the newly-developed systems of the USA and Europe; some experts say by as much as fifty years. In America publicly funded secondary high schools provided personnel to run the new industries, and in Europe schools were giving priority to engineering and science subjects.

King Edward VII

Against this background Arthur Balfour became Prime Minister, and guided the controversial 1902 Education Act through Parliament. Eventually dissenting MPs, wealthy landowners and some nonconformists came to accept that, with mass education developing abroad, an educated workforce was needed if Britain was to maintain its dominant position in world trade.

The Act abolished the existing 2,568 School Boards and created 328 Local Education Areas based on existing county boroughs or county councils. These authorities became responsible for introducing new fee-paying grammar schools offering a few free scholarships, paying teachers and ensuring that they were properly qualified, and for providing the necessary books and equipment.

*Arthur Balfour
by Ellis William Roberts*

Cheshire County Council was very proactive and soon authorised the establishment of a secondary school in the thriving Altrincham area where Judge Bradbury was the chairman of the Local Education Committee and a driving force behind many educational improvements in the town. A site search was instigated which ultimately focused on Bowdon which at that time was located in the township of Dunham Massey. It was an area that had developed considerably over the previous fifty years.

The 1838 Tithe Survey showed very sparse development within the parish of Bowdon which included the hamlets of Dunham Town and Oldfield. It seems likely that the house in Field 772 in the bottom right-hand corner of the map overleaf is Bowdon Lodge, with The Beeches, later St Anne's Home, in Field 771.

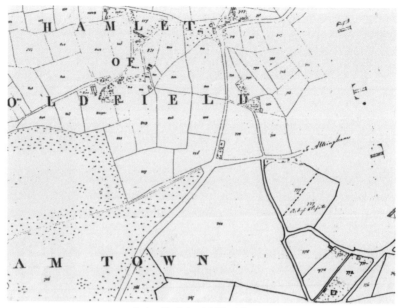

A detail of the 1838 tithe map

Bowdon Lodge was built about 1820 and occupied by Benjamin Williams at the time of the 1838 Tithe Survey. John Finnie, a retired Scottish merchant, was recorded as owner in the 1851 Census and lived there with his twenty-five-year-old wife, Hannah, from Dunham, two servants from Scotland and one from High Legh. Mr Finnie was described as a gentleman in Kelly's street directories until at least 1860. Mrs Finnie was still living there in 1878. Some time after this a Miss Dean, aged 74, from Staffordshire lived there. The Lodge was a very substantial country property with extensive grounds on a well wooded site of over

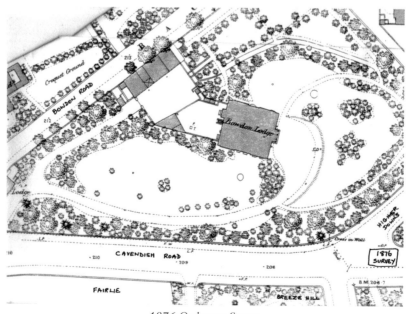

1876 Ordnance Survey

two acres at the junction of Cavendish Road (formerly Warrington Road), Bowdon Road (Back Lane), The Firs (Burying Lane) and St Margaret's Road. By the time the 1876 Ordnance Survey was completed many other large houses in their own grounds had been built for wealthy merchants from Manchester seeking a healthier and better quality of life for their families.

By the early 1900s the house had been unoccupied for about twenty-five years and was considered a very good site for a new school. The original idea to have a dual school to accommodate both boys and girls was rejected and the site was reserved for girls only. Plans were prepared by Messrs Sankey and Cubbon, Architects, of Manchester and in 1909 Messrs Gerrard and Sons, Swinton were appointed as building contractors. As building work was nearing completion Miss Mary Howes Smith was appointed Headmistress on 24 April 1910.

Mary Howes Smith was born on 2 January 1871, the ninth child (third daughter) of Colonel Joshua H

Miss Mary Howes Smith

Smith of the Royal Engineers at Halifax, Nova Scotia, where he was stationed. She came to England when very young and was educated initially by governesses. In 1885, at the age of fourteen, she attended Sutton High School in Surrey, run by the Girls' Public Day School Trust, which had opened the previous year. Whilst there she passed the Oxford Senior Local Honours examinations in 1887 and the Cambridge Higher Local Honours examinations in 1889.

In 1895 she returned to Sutton High School to teach for five years before going up to Newnham College, Cambridge, in 1900. She successfully took her Historical Tripos, Class ii, Parts i and ii in 1903 and later in 1906 was awarded an MA degree from Dublin University. (It was not until 1948 that women were awarded degrees by the Cambridge authorities. However, for a brief period at the turn of the twentieth century – 1904 to 1907 – students from Cambridge women's colleges were conferred with *ad eundem* or courtesy degrees at Trinity College, Dublin. These graduates were given the name "steamboat ladies", derived from the means of transport commonly used by them to travel to Dublin.) Smith being a not uncommon name, she adopted her second name, Howes, as part of her professional title.

In 1904 she gained the London Senior Diploma in Pedagogy and became a lecturer at the Moorfield Training College and also taught part time at Wimbledon High School, when the Headmistress, in 1906, recommended her as tutor in history and literature to the nine-year-old Princess Mary, the daughter of the Prince of Wales, later to become King George V. At the age of thirty-nine on 24 April 1910 she was appointed Headmistress of the new Altrincham County High School for Girls, and on being requested to do so continued as tutor to Princess Mary for a further four years.

The new school was ready for the official opening ceremony on Monday 4 July 1910.

Early photograph of the School

Extract from the *Altrincham, Bowdon and Hale Guardian*, July 1910

An event of unusual importance in the educational life of Altrincham and district took place on Monday afternoon, when the ceremony of formally opening the new County High School for Girls on Bowdon Lodge site was performed by his Honour Judge J. K. Bradbury, M.A., chairman of the Altrincham Education Committee, and of the Board of Governors.

The High School stands on the summit of the Higher Downs, which is considered to be the healthiest district of Bowdon. The site is considerably over two acres in area and is well wooded but open to the full benefit of sunshine. The buildings have been so arranged and designed that the main portion faces the south-west, plus ensuring that all classrooms and rooms used by the scholars shall derive full advantage from sunlight and air. The external treatment is such that it harmonizes with its ideal surroundings. The walls are faced with local grey bricks in narrow courses, relieved by vitrified, glazed terra-cotta of Doulton's manufacture. In the centre of the main frontage is placed the public entrance, through which access is obtained to the reception hall. The library and committee room, office, headmistress's room and waiting-room are entered from the reception hall, and a triple arcade leads to the large assembly hall, where seating accommodation can be arranged for over 200 scholars.

On the southerly side of the school a good preparatory department is arranged. This department consists of two very bright and sunny classrooms separated by a moveable screen, so that one large room

County High School for Girls,
BOWDON LODGE,
:: ALTRINCHAM ::

OPENING CEREMONY

On Monday, the 4th July, 1910,

At 3-30 p.m. by

His Honour Judge J. K. BRADBURY, M.A.
(Chairman of the Board of Governors).

Col. GEORGE DIXON (Chairman of the Cheshire County Council) will Preside, and

Dr. W. HODGSON (Chairman of the County Education Committee), will deliver an Address.

PROGRAMME.

HYMN   - - - "O God, our help in ages past." - - - -
PRAYER   - - - The Rev. CANON GORE, Vicar of Bowdon.
PRESENTATION OF KEY
By J. Cubbon, Esq., A.R.I.B.A., (Architect).
OPENING CEREMONY.
ADDRESS by Dr. W. HODGSON.
VOTE OF THANKS.
NATIONAL ANTHEM.

Programme for the Opening Ceremony

The Hall

can be arranged when necessary. There are six classrooms provided for the older scholars. These classrooms all communicate with the assembly hall or the gallery to the hall and the rooms are of various sizes to suit the requirements of the different classes. In addition to the general classrooms special rooms are provided for teaching special subjects. A large laboratory and lecture-room is provided for the study of chemistry and physics.

An art-room, with magnificent north light is arranged for advanced art. A music room is arranged in an isolated position for coaching singing and other purposes and special practice-rooms are adjacent. There is also a large room specially designed for instruction in cookery.

In order to provide for the comfort of scholars who have to come from a distance a comfortable dining-room, with a kitchen adjoining, has been erected, so that mid-day meals can be served to those who wish for them.

Ample arrangements have been made for cloakroom and changing accommodation, and drying chambers have been provided for wet clothing. Adjoining the main school buildings there is a good gymnasium with dressing-room, shower baths and spectators' gallery.

The whole of the school is fitted up with the most modern and approved fittings and furniture. The buildings throughout are lighted by electricity and warmed by low pressure hot-water apparatus, assisted by large open fires in all rooms used for teaching purposes. The construction of the building is fire proof throughout. The walls have a high dado of "old gold" glazed bricks and all the woodwork is selected pitch pine, toned and varnished. For outdoor recreation there are two paved playgrounds, one for junior and the other for senior scholars. There are also lawns of old matured turf, for lawn tennis or other games. A large playing field (on the Back Lawn) is situated on the easterly side of the site, where hockey and other games can be played and a terrace walk above the field gives the scholars an excellent view of the field.

The site is surrounded by shrubbery and forest tree borders and every opportunity is provided for nature study and botany. There is also a large greenhouse on the site which materially adds to the value of the instruction given.

At present the school is intended to provide accommodation for 186 scholars, or 150 girls in the general department and 36 in the preparatory.

Fortunately there was a beautifully clear sky when the opening ceremony took place and it seemed a happy augury that the sun shone brilliantly for the gathering after so many dreary rainy days. The proceedings were attended by members of the Cheshire County Council, the

The front door

County and Local Education Committees, and representatives of various public bodies and approximately 200 invited guests.

These ladies and gentlemen assembled on the front lawn facing the main entrance. The proceedings opened with the singing of the hymn "O God, our help in ages past" after which prayers were offered by the Ven. Archdeacon Gore, Vicar of Bowdon.

Mr J Cubbon then stepped forward, and on behalf of the architects, presented to Judge Bradbury a gold key, with which he opened the principal door of the new school.

In the central hall, where a temporary platform had been erected and artistically decorated with plants and flowers, the speech-making took place. Colonel George Dixon (Chairman of the County Council) presided, and supporting him were his Honour Judge Bradbury, Dr W Hodgson (Chairman of the County Education Committee), the Reverend J Grant Bird (Chairman of the County Higher Elementary Education Committee), Miss Mary Howes Smith, M.A. (Principal of the new school), and Mr Joseph Howarth (Clerk to the Altrincham Education Committee).

The Chairman, in calling upon Judge Bradbury, said his Honour was one of those who had taken a great interest in education in the county. He seemed to be the most useful member of the County Committee. They were most grateful to him for his giving up his leisure hours for the cause of education. He hoped that the school would be of the utmost benefit of the neighbourhood. It was certainly wanted; hitherto there had been no public school of such a character in the district, and it was an absolute necessity nowadays when girls had to be so well educated. There were a million to a million and a half more women than men in the country and a great number of those had to earn their own livelihood. They could not all get married; that was quite certain, and so they had to engage in various professions and enterprises. There

The Science Laboratory

The Art Room

were a large number of important posts in England which could be occupied by women, who, however, must have received the best education. There was keen competition not only at home, but from abroad, and it was essential that if girls wished to obtain the best posts they should have had the finest education possible. He hoped the people of Altrincham would take the fullest advantage of the school.

Judge Bradbury, in declaring the school opened, thanked Colonel Dixon and Dr Hodgson for their presence. Cheshire stood well in front of counties with regard to education; indeed it took a foremost place. That was largely due to the zeal and policy of Dr Hodgson, whose aim had been to see that a secondary school should be within easy reach of every child if it desired to attend. It was due to that policy that Altrincham had that new school. In a short time the district would have a similar school for boys and its education equipment would then be complete. He commended the new school to the public, first on account of the site. Everyone who resided in the neighbourhood knew the value of that recommendation and those who were visiting the place must be charmed with the beauty of the site which was ideally situated for a girls' school. The architects' design was an admirable one, the school was splendidly equipped, and provision was made for physical instruction within the school boundaries.

The Domestic Science Room

The Gymnasium

It was quite clear, however, that although buildings were important, without good teaching the premises were nothing at all. It was by the quality of the work done in the school that it must succeed or fail. The essential for success was a good staff. Above all there must be in a school of that kind a first-class mistress. The whole of the organisation planning, and carrying out of the school work really turned upon the headmistress as the central figure. They had been successful in that feature – they had an excellent headmistress. Miss Howes Smith was a graduate of Cambridge University and held an honours degree. She had had immense experience in girls' high schools. Miss Howes Smith was at the Training College, London, and was at present literary tutor to Princess Mary, daughter of their Majesties the King and Queen. The rest of the permanent staff would all hold university degrees or the equivalent. There would be special instructors in many subjects like music, art, gymnastics and domestic science.

Judge Bradbury next proceeded to say something about religious instruction which he described as a thorny subject. The Government articles provided that religious instruction

The Back Lawn

An invitation to the Opening Ceremony, 4 July 1910. Miss Florence Beckett was the Chief Librarian at Altrincham Library. She retired in 1933 after forty years' service. The Florence Beckett Lecture Hall, part of the Stamford Hall, was opened on 15 February 1934.

might be given, and the governors intended that that instruction should be given in the school. They attached importance to it, and were satisfied that within limitations – instruction must be of a non-denominational character – an effective religious instruction could be and would be given in the school.

The school would be in two departments – a preparatory school for boys and girls, who would remain up to the age of 9 years. At that age the boys would go to their own school and the girls would proceed to the main school, where they could remain until the age of 16 years or longer and prepare for matriculation at the university. The type of instruction would be drawing out and strengthening the qualities of the mind rather than the mere acquisition of knowledge. His view of education was mental training to make the mind quick and alert with clear thinking and sound judgement – an education which would fit girls for the duties of life and enable them to overcome difficulties with success. Every provision had been made for physical training. They regarded it equally important that the physical nature of children should be fully developed and brought out proportionate with the mind.

The school would be supported by fees and public grants. Taking the whole school life until the age of 16 years the fees payable on the average per annum would be ten guineas. In addition to this revenue the governors would receive very handsome grants from public sources. The Board of Education – the school would be carried on under their regulations – would make an annual grant of five guineas for each pupil over the age of 12 years. The grant of the County Committee for the main school would be £3 10s [£3.50] per annum and £3 per annum per child for the preparatory department. In addition to that the county had built and would furnish and equip the school absolutely for the governors who would not pay a penny for rent. That was a very handsome provision for education in the district.

There were many parents to whom a school of that character and quality would be a very desirable thing. As time went on it would be more and more desirable. Secondary education was only beginning in this country. Elementary education had made great strides; but in the higher grades of instruction, which required development, we were far behind Germany and the United States. Competition was getting to be increasingly keen and parents would more and more see the necessity for that higher type of education. There were many people in the district to whom an education for their children would be highly desirable but who hitherto had not been able to obtain it, because there had been no school of that class. There were good schools in the district of that efficient type but a low fee of ten guineas per annum had been unattainable in the past. Private enterprise could not provide the type of instruction at less than three times that amount of fees which would be charged at the High School. If the public of Altrincham did not appreciate that, and if they did not send their children to the school he would be much surprised and greatly disappointed.

Whatever might be the immediate future of the school he was absolutely convinced that in a few years it must be a great success. The economical conditions made that certain. He was sure in opening the school they were doing a good work for the educational life of the district.

Dr Hodgson in an address said he heartily joined in acclaiming the introduction of the school into the district. He observed that hitherto Cheshire had been badly off for schools of that kind, and not only Cheshire but many other counties. A great deal of ground had to be made up. They were commencing that day. So far as the building was concerned he did not think a better or more finely equipped place for its size could be found.

Dr Hodgson referred to the charges of unseemly extravagance which were levelled at the heads of the authorities and said that as long as there were men like Judge Bradbury, who thought more of raising the standard of intelligence than anything else, they were not likely to stand still. Therefore that day they should not be charged with having produced buildings too costly for the community. He was sure that the community would welcome the provision of that school. There were some people who had fears that they were going to spoil the beauty of the neighbourhood. He hoped when they came face to face with the school and saw the girls of the type he was sure would attend the school, they would be thankful for having such educational equipment by their homes. There is everything needed to the school and nothing redundant. He wished them God-speed and success in the use of the school.

The school opened for business on Wednesday 14 September 1910. About sixty pupils arrived for enrolment, to be greeted by Miss Howes Smith and two full-time staff, Miss Bell and Miss Riley, to be joined by Miss Wadsworth the next day, and later by five part-time visiting mistresses for French, art, gymnastics, singing and domestic science.

Miss C E Bell, one of the first teachers to be appointed by Miss Howes Smith, left School in 1920 to be married, becoming Mrs Ellis. Her stepdaughter and three daughters all attended the School. She wrote in the *Annals*:

"I HAD NEVER HEARD of Altrincham till the summer of 1910, and little thought as I drove through the busy little town that day in June that I was destined to make my home here. Seated on a bench in Central Station, Manchester, Miss Howes Smith had just offered me the post of Kindergarten Mistress in the new School, and before accepting the offer I came on to Altrincham to see the School. It was still in the hands of the builders, who were busy everywhere with the finishing touches. The hall floor was not yet laid. I was charmed with it all and with the spacious garden and the beautiful trees, and of course I decided to come.

A few weeks later I came again to the official opening on July 4th. I then felt with a thrill that I was part of a new enterprise, and was to share the joys and responsibilities of beginning a new school and to help to lay the foundations of the future.

At once we set about planning and ordering the necessary furniture and materials and that was very exciting. I had never before been able to ask for whatever I wanted!

At our first Staff meeting in September 1910 Miss Howes Smith discussed with her staff of two, Miss Riley (the Science Mistress) and myself, many of the fundamental things which, of course, are now taken for granted.

Our first morning of real school work I am afraid I have completely forgotten, but I remember that my division of the School consisted of about twenty children, aged from four to nine, and that we occupied the double classroom by Miss Howes Smith's room. It had been specially built for us and Miss Howes Smith had insisted on lower windows there so that the small children should be able to see into the garden. Our low tables and chairs did not arrive for some days, and so at first the small people knelt on ordinary hall chairs round long tables which really belonged to the dining room, and worked under slight difficulties."

An advertisement from the front page of the Altrincham, Bowdon and Hale Guardian, *July 1910*

Pat Jones, formerly Crickmore, a former pupil herself from 1939 to 1948, writes:

"MY MOTHER WAS Caroline Crickmore formerly Pickston. She was the very first girl to enrol at the new High School on the first day of that first autumn term, and was 14 years old. Some years earlier, she had been refused entry to Culcheth Hall School as the family was 'in trade' (my grandfather was a grocer in George Street) and had to travel to the rival establishment in Lymm until the new school opened in Altrincham.

She was the youngest of three children whose parents believed in education and opportunities for girls and women. When eighteen she left school and attended the Crewe County Training College. In fact all three children undertook teacher training courses, becoming head teachers. She was the youngest in Cheshire at Timperley Church of England School when marriage terminated her career until the Second World War started and her services were needed again.

Her recollections of Miss Howes Smith were not always happy ones as she once declared my mother undernourished, which was ironic considering that she was the daughter of a grocer!

My mother was always something of a fighting feminist. She fought for and believed strongly in education for girls, but what really rankled was equal pay. The fact that her brother, who was head at Mobberley School and subsequently at St John's Altrincham, received a higher salary was never forgiven and was a bone of contention for years."

Pamela Harrop, formerly Gregory, the daughter of another pupil from the very first intake, also writes:

"MY MOTHER, Elsie Gregory (formerly Yarwood), was one of the first seventy pupils to be enrolled in 1910. She always spoke very highly of Miss Howes Smith, and another teacher she mentioned was Frau Schmidt.

Mother was good at sport, especially running and cricket (she was taught by her brother to bowl overarm). She was also in the tug o' war team, but on sports day she tore the cartilage in her left knee. From that day onwards sport was banned.

She married in 1924 and was widowed in 1964. She joined the Old Girls' Society at that time as a result of meeting Joyce Kendrick, another 'old girl', at the Solicitor's Office. Mother's friends in the OGS were numerous and she enjoyed the many longlasting friendships formed from shared memories of schooldays."

Another pupil from the first intake was Kate Stevens who recorded her early memories in the *School Annals*:

"I STILL REMEMBER keenly the joy of the first day of the first term at the Altrincham County High School for Girls, a date early in September which I had been awaiting on tiptoe for about three months. How marvellous the lovely old garden seemed, with its lawns and trees and shrubbery, and how new and clean and bright and altogether wonderful the School building. Of course, it seemed vast that first day; in fact it continued to present that impression for many days, since we were so few in number.

After Prayers in the hall, when the parable of the mustard seed growing into the big tree was read, we were sent to the Art Room for a simple test in arithmetic and English. Then we went out to get to know each other and to begin the first of our long series of games in the garden. Afterwards we were placed in one of the three Forms.

What a source of delight that garden was to us all! The shrubbery seemed interminable, it was possible to travel so far without emerging from its shelter. It was just made for hide-and-seek, of which we played a very special variety which involved much stalking and many hairbreadth escapes. We also had a passion for performing scenes from the Roman History we were learning. We did it quite spontaneously, not for the benefit of any audience.

Though schoolgirls are all the same, and I suppose the life of the School goes on in much the same way from year to year, yet I feel sure there was actually some slight tincture of more than normal magic in the first few years of the new School, and I look with eyes of compassion upon those who were not fortunate enough to be present on that first day of all."

Many of Miss Howes Smith's early recollections are recorded in the *Annals*. The following selection gives an insight into her workload in those formative days.

"HOW THE NEIGHBOURS in large houses dreaded the new School, which would spoil the charm of Bowdon. They had appealed to the Government in vain. Notice boards 'To be Sold' decorated all the gardens round, and the children knew that their manners would make or mar the fortunes of the School. So wonderfully good they were that within a few months the boards were taken down, and on our first Sports Day when the School was a year old, our chief guests were our former enemies."

"YOU MIGHT THINK it unusual that for a year I had to 'answer the door' as no domestic was provided, the cook-housekeeper would only cook, and the caretaker only clean the School! My hours were from 8.45am to 9.00pm every day, as furniture, books and equipment, as well as new parents, *would* arrive by day and night."

"FOR THE FIRST two years the School settled down to solid work without any distractions except an occasional visit to Manchester to see Shakespearian plays."

"IN THE AUTUMN of 1912 the School had the experience of a Full Inspection by the Board of Education, in the person of six of HM Inspectors. The sight of the familiar face of our kind friend, Mr Trayes, HMI, broke the first shock of the phalanx of educational experts, and although some small people thought their official title was 'suspectors' their visit caused such pleasure that their departure was viewed with much regret by the girls. The report of the Board of Education gave complete satisfaction to the Governors, and we felt we then had the official approval of Whitehall."

"OUR FIRST SPEECH DAY in 1912 was marked chiefly by the absence of speeches and by a charming production of Christina Rossetti's *Goblin Market*, followed by scenes from *Pickwick*."

"JUDGE JAMES KINDER BRADBURY was appointed Chairman of the School Governors in 1910 and it is to his vision that the School owes its existence. Day by day after his long hours in Court, he came to see me. 'Fill the School and you shall have all you want,' he would say. Before he died he had the great satisfaction of seeing his desire fulfilled."

"THE CAUSE OF EDUCATION suffered a great loss through the death of Judge Bradbury in January 1913. This High School largely owed its existence to him and he had shown intense interest in developing elementary and higher education in this neighbourhood. Through his admirable judicial and arbitration work he had won a fame that was becoming known outside the North, and we are proud to think that he was, for over a year, our first Chairman. It was in the arduous task of the initial planning and founding of the School that his work was incalculably wise and far-seeing, while his encouragement and his unfailing interest in all the details of the work were of vital importance to the Headmistress at the new School. Week after week at the close of a long and harassing day in his Lancashire County Court he would come to the School to learn the latest developments, to give his help in difficulties, and to show his care for its progress and its needs. He had been a distinguished student of Caius College, Cambridge and was 10th Wrangler in the Mathematical Tripos in 1872. Then he became a distinguished barrister in the Northern Circuit and in 1900 was made a County Court Judge. But it was through his arbitration in great strikes in the North that he became known in many parts of England. On the roll of the benefactors of the School his name must ever stand first."

The First Meeting of the Old Girls of the School was held on 12 February 1914, at which the Old Girls' Society was formed and members enrolled. It was agreed that the Society should consist of past and present mistresses and old girls from the age of twelve years. It was arranged that there should be three meetings each year, one each term, and that the officials chosen from the girls should be four in number, elected annually.

"FEBRUARY 24 1914 saw our Carnival Fancy Dress Dance when the gayest scene ever enacted in the hall took place. Many scores of quaint and interesting historical and symbolic costumes were seen, and the hall festooned with garlands and hung with coloured Chinese lanterns, looked a fairyland. Great was the alarm of the tiny dancers when flash lights flared as newspaper representatives took photographs of the gay throng. A profit of £5 was donated to the funds of the School Sewing Meeting."

The Carnival Fancy Dress Dance, 1914

"THE CHAUCER PAGEANT on July 11th and 15th, 1914, a dramatic representation of the Pilgrimage and some of Chaucer's stories, adapted from the *Canterbury Tales* by ourselves, took place in perfect weather and won great praise for the beauty of the colouring and grouping, the dignity of the pilgrims and spirit of the actors, and the graceful dancing of the Maypole and country dancers.

The spontaneous burst of admiration when the mounted pilgrims first appeared in the distance and when the villagers suddenly seemed to blossom out from the overhanging trees showed that the children's efforts were appreciated. The pilgrims came from all parts to meet at the Tabard Inn, Southwark from whence they all departed on their journey to Canterbury. At each stop on the journey, pilgrims each tell a tale.

About 800 visitors came to the Pageant and the proceeds amounting to £50 from the two performances were given to the Altrincham General Hospital in aid of the building fund for the two new wings."

The Pageant was repeated on 21 and 24 July 1915 with the proceeds going to the British Red Cross Society. Every last detail was planned meticulously.

"THE NEXT FOUR YEARS were lived in the shadow of the Great War. Its tragedies and suffering were brought home to us by the many Red Cross Hospitals in Bowdon, and by the Prisoners' Camp, and made our own struggles and difficulties in that terrible time seem insignificant. We acted our Chaucer Pageant again for the Red Cross Fund."

"SINCE SCHOOL ASSEMBLED in September 1914 after the outbreak of the war, the pupils from the Kindergarten upwards and the Old Girls worked most enthusiastically to do their small part towards the many and varied requirements of the soldiers and sailors of England and her Allies. They worked both for those actively engaged in the trenches or on

Poster for the Chaucer Pageant of 1914

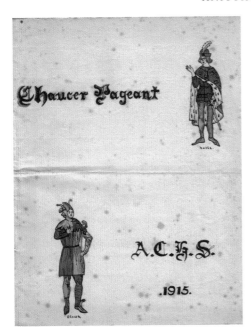

Hand-painted covers to the programme of events

the sea, and also for the many wounded who were sent back into our midst. Our first collection was seventy-seven blankets, seventy-four of which were sent to the Mayor of Altrincham for the Army, and three to the Military Hospital, Manchester. We collected and made hundreds of garments including vests, shirts, socks, belts, mufflers, cuffs and mittens, slippers and sweaters, helped in the Red Cross Hospitals, and did without all we could."

1915
Left to right: back: Elsie Benton, Iris Ward, Miss Atwool, Agnes MacDonald, Doris Watkins; middle: Margaret Dutton, E Hughes, Phyllis Hartington, Connie Meldrum; front: Joan Ogden, Sylvia Blythe, Joyce Key, Marjorie Ellison, Gladys James

The staff in 1915

"WHEN A SMALL BAND of about sixty gathered in the School Hall for prayers on the morning of September 14 1910 no one would have been bold enough to foretell that the hall would see a school numbering 195 meeting there in June 1915. That is the first outstanding feature of our history – we have grown from a school with four forms to one with eleven forms."

"FOR A LONG TIME our Prefects had no badges, and their only distinguishing mark was their good behaviour! At last, however, the needed badges appeared in the shape of silver shields embossed with a three-fold F symbolic of our motto."

"ON 19 AND 22 JULY 1916 we had a huge Mediaeval Fair organised in response to the appeal to Girls' High Schools on behalf of totally disabled soldiers in the Old Star and Garter Hospital at Richmond. The generosity of the School, parents and friends raised £380. Our School came second on the list of all the Girls' Schools in England, the first being Blackheath High School,

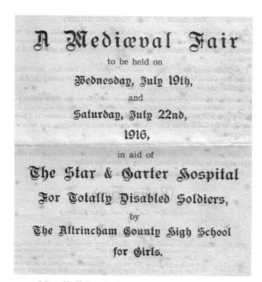

Handbill for the Mediaeval Fair of 1916

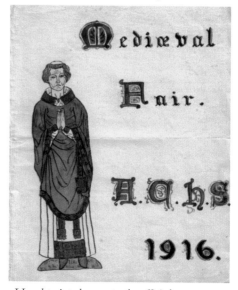

Hand-painted cover to the official programme

Pilgrims making their way to the Tabard Inn

The Tabard Inn, Southwark,
erected on the Back Lawn

London with £400. This result for a School only six years old was a cause of pride to us all."

A parent who wished to remain anonymous wrote appreciatively in the *Annals*:

"ON SATURDAY MARCH 23 and Monday March 25 1918 the parents and friends of the girls at the High School had the privilege of being present at a beautiful representation of scenes from Bunyan's 'Pilgrim's Progress'. I think the author himself would have been content with the rendering. The great sincerity and solemn pure intention of his book were felt and reproduced with a tender simplicity which seemed to one at least of the onlookers sometimes acutely beautiful. The subdued tone of the dresses against the white background exactly suited the mystical subject.

The author, by the way, was present in Cromwellian garb, and sitting solitary at the side of the stage recited the theme. The whole performance was, in my judgement, a rare success."

Pilgrim's Progress brought in the sum of over £50 for the YMCA and YWCA Hut Fund.

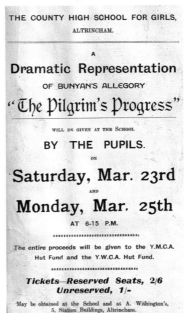

THE COUNTY HIGH SCHOOL FOR GIRLS,
ALTRINCHAM.

A

Dramatic Representation

OF BUNYAN'S ALLEGORY

"The Pilgrim's Progress"

WILL BE GIVEN AT THE SCHOOL

BY THE PUPILS.

ON

Saturday, Mar. 23rd

AND

Monday, Mar. 25th

AT 6-15 P.M.

The entire proceeds will be given to the Y.M.C.A.
Hut Fund and the Y.W.C.A. Hut Fund.

Tickets—Reserved Seats, 2/6
Unreserved, 1/-

May be obtained at the School and at A. Withington's,
5, Station Buildings, Altrincham.

On Armistice Day at the end of the First World War, Beatrice Thomas described in the *Annals* how the news was received at School.

"AT TEN MINUTES TO ELEVEN on the 11th November 1918 the Upper III was due to have a history lesson in the highest form room of all – the one among the tree tops. On that glorious sunny morning, however, when history was in the making, we decided, very rightly, that Early Britons and their customs were of no account.

We stood on our seats, on our desks, looking over the tree tops to Bowdon Church, looking for a sign, begging Miss Whitwill to see what she could see when *she* stood on a desk. While we stood, watching, something mounted up and up to the top of Bowdon Church, something that, after seconds which seemed like hours, unfurled – and at last we knew it was a Union Jack. No one could deny it now. The Upper III sprang down and out of the room. No one said 'Let's go.' No one asked permission. The door was flung open and we raced down all those flights of stairs, Miss Whitwill with us. For once, we ran on the stairs, two steps, three steps at a time, past the Art Room, the last flight now and the Upper III shot into the Hall just as Miss Howes Smith came out of her room and Miss Booth seized the bell and clanged it furiously and wildly and gladly.

Then the rest of the School came, rushing and charging, down the stairs, but the Upper III had experienced a few minutes of supreme gladness and happiness and excitement in that wild rush downstairs and nothing could quite equal the feeling again. No other part of the day could approach those minutes of realisation and expression of joy.

I remember that, after we had been turned loose into the garden to exhaust some of our excitement we had a short service. I do not remember the hymns we sang, the prayers we said, or what Miss Howes Smith said to us, but we realised then, perhaps more than ever, what the war really meant. We were silent for a few moments and the silence was broken by the quiet crying of some of the girls and mistresses for whom the Armistice meant the hopeless realisation of their loss.

When the Upper III meets again and grows reminiscent, its members still say 'Do you remember the Armistice and how we ran and were the first downstairs?' "

As the first decade came to a close, so much had been achieved. A serious work ethic had been established and high achievements were starting to flow through in academic subjects, music, drawing and needlework, but also girls were encouraged to help those less fortunate than themselves.

Annual Speech Days were held initially in the School Hall until increasing numbers made it necessary to move to the Bowdon Assembly Rooms, on The Firs.

Founders' Day was celebrated annually on 4 July to remember the debt owed to those who planned and cared for the School in past days, and to feel that they in turn must add their "brick" to the building not made with hands.

On the sporting front hockey, netball, cricket, tennis, rounders, swimming and gym all appeared on the timetable with an annual Sports Day every July.

Girls went on geographical expeditions, attended concerts and theatres, and took part in music festivals.

The building was gradually beautified with paintings and artefacts acquired to enhance the ambience, and the Library enlarged with many gifts of books from Miss Howes Smith, past and present staff, parents, and old girls.

Societies were formed – the Scientific Society in 1912 and the Literary Society in 1916. The Sewing Club also started in 1912 and made garments and toys which were donated to a needy school in Ancoats.

The 3rd Altrincham Girl Guide Company was formed in 1916 with five Patrols – Shamrock, Sunflower, Cornflower, Robins and Scarlet Pimpernel.

A War Savings Association was started.

Flowers and Fruit on Fridays (FFF) were taken to the Manchester Infirmary and Altrincham Hospital.

With approximately 350 pupils and twenty-two staff, the original building for 180 pupils was by now beginning to bulge at the seams and contingency plans had to be brought into operation to accommodate the growing numbers. In 1918 the Preparatory Department of over seventy children was moved to Edgemount, a large house not far away. Unfortunately accommodation was a problem that would not diminish over the coming years but something that successive head teachers would have to wrestle with.

An informal group taken about 1917–1918.
Those identified are Emily Newton, Irene Appleyard, Phyllis Hartington,
Dorothy Nicholson, Gladys James, Phyllis Sharpe, Nell Hawking, Joyce Key,
Elsie Hughes, Maggie Young, Connie Meldrum, Marjorie Ellison.

In the 1933 Annals *Miss Howes Smith very sadly recorded the death of Joyce Key*
(third from left, second row from front), one of a group of four sisters, who passed
away after a long illness contracted through nursing with selfless devotion her mother,
for whose sake she had given up her career as a teacher. A Memorial gift of £5 was
given by her sisters.
At Speech Day in 1944, an annual award known as The Joyce Key Memorial
Prize was instigated and was given for outstanding School Certificate results.

The 1920s

1920	School Foundation Scholarships endowed
1920	Three classes moved to Presbyterian Sunday School, Delamer Road
1921	First Form moved to Wesleyan Sunday School of Dome Chapel, Enville Road
1921/22	Games Field acquired in Belgrave Road, small pavilion erected
1923	Dome Chapel hard court laid out for tennis and netball
1925	January – New Wing opened
1925	Area of Devisdale acquired for lacrosse and cricket
1925	4 July – League of Nations Pageant
1926	4 July – League of Nations Pageant repeated
1926	Hard court laid out on the back lawn at School
1927	29 June – total eclipse of the sun – Ainsdale beach
1927	4 July – School badge introduced and House system founded
1927	School Pictorial Record
1929	14 June – Royal visit (HRH Princess Mary)
1929	20 July – Fair of All Nations
1929	Autumn term – new dining room and kitchen opened
1920s	Speech Days were held at the Altrincham Hippodrome

CHAPTER 2
THE 1920S

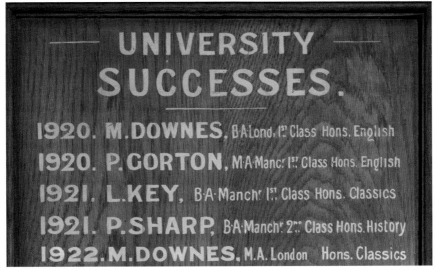

The School Honours Board

By 1920 girls had done advanced work in every subject, and many had gone on to Universities and specialist Training Colleges. There was much to be proud of with examination successes bringing distinction to the School. The first three graduates were all awarded first class honours degrees. By this time a University Foundation Scholarship had been endowed.

Miss Howes Smith wrote in the 1923 *Annals*:

> "A UNIVERSITY SCHOLARSHIP connected with a newly-founded County High School seemed a hopeless ambition in 1910, so large is the sum of money required for investment to produce even a small Scholarship, but, after ten years of anxious care and planning, the goal was reached in 1920, and a Foundation Scholarship of £20 annually was achieved. In the following year it was possible to announce that the Scholarship could be granted each year for two years to the selected candidate."

Providing sufficient accommodation for the growing numbers continued to be a thorny problem. On the expiry of the lease on Edgemount in 1920, the three Preparatory classes were moved into the Presbyterian Sunday School on Delamer Road. The following year the First Form was outhoused in the Wesleyan Sunday School of the Dome Chapel on Enville Road.

This contribution from Jean Duncan in the *Annals* tells of her impressions of her first term:

> "IN MAY 1922, I was deposited at the Dome Chapel by my sister, and I was terrified! What I would have felt like had I seen the Hall at prayers that first day I don't know. Anyhow, Miss Atkinson, in a pink and white blouse, received me with a kindly smile, and things looked

Dome Chapel on Enville Road, Bowdon. Opened in 1880, the final service was held on 21 August 1966. It was sold at auction on 30 July 1968 and later demolished.

brighter. In the one classroom I was placed between two people with whom I travelled right up the School. I remember too, that we had enormous cups of steaming cocoa at recreation and I got a distinct shock when next term we found the considerably smaller ones at school.

At drill we used to run and walk round and round outside the Chapel and great was the excitement if we could get in one more round than was requisite. On one great and solemn occasion we were taken inside the Chapel itself by 'Black Peter', the caretaker (called so because he always wore a black cardigan) to see and admire the flowers for a wedding. I was overcome with awe at the size of the palms and lilies. We were sorry when we had to leave the exclusiveness and compactness of a happy family at the Dome Chapel."

The Games Field on Belgrave Road that had been leased for some years was finally bought for the School by the County Council, but not before pressure had been exerted to accept pasture land miles away in Dunham. This suggestion was resisted and the purchase made only just in time, for the other fields around soon became covered in houses. Almost immediately afterwards a small pavilion was built and provided grateful shelter in many a shower.

In 1923 a hard court was laid there for tennis and netball. This space was enough, as long as the Headmistress's insistence that hockey was an unladylike game that overdeveloped a girl's muscles and spoilt her posture prevailed over the wishes of her games mistresses. About this time Miss Howes Smith was persuaded that lacrosse, on the contrary, would encourage the girls to hold up their heads and straighten backs and shoulders. The school began to make use of part of the Devisdale for lacrosse and cricket.

Joan Coulson, formerly Cowburn, at School in the 1920s, recalls:

"I FIRST STARTED at what was known as the Pepper Box Church and of course in HS's (as she was affectionately referred to) headship. I played cricket for College and School and later for Edinburgh College of Domestic Science. When we first started to play lacrosse we played very gently when HS came to watch us, as she didn't think it was a ladies' game.

The League of Nations displays, when all members took part, were wonderful with great effort put in by the staff."

Grace Lockett wrote in the *Annals* about Speech Day on 20 December 1923 held at 3.00pm at the Altrincham Hippodrome as follows:

"I SHALL NEVER FORGET my first Speech Day: several have passed since, when in my second term of school life, I sat with the non-prize winners, and looked on.

I wore a white blouse and a school tie, a new gymslip and two pigtails tied up with green bows (also new); indeed, I was very new myself, with little knowledge of the routine of the great community of girls to which I belonged.

At last the programme began, and the whole School rose to render Kipling's *Children's Song*. Fond parents looked down from the gallery, trying to find their own particular offspring in that sea of white and navy blue; a difficult job, when every figure standing stiffly at attention resembled its neighbour as two peas in a pod.

How I enjoyed every minute which followed! The report of the Headmistress for the past year; the prize-giving; and the inspiring address (given that year by the former Dean of Manchester, Dr McCormick).

Finally, the Head Girl appeared on the platform demanding 'three cheers for the school', and in a second I was upon my feet with the rest of them, cheering as lustily as my vocal organ would permit, for in that instant had dawned upon me the knowledge that this was 'my school', that I 'belonged' here, and had a share in it all, just as much as that wonderful Head Girl who was leading the cheers so wholeheartedly.

I went home that night glowing with the warmth of the feeling that I was included for all time in this society of good fellowship, upholding their motto of 'Fortiter, Fideliter, Feliciter'.

I have seen many speech days since then, and now the time has come when I am once more a 'looker on' – this time not an excited Lower Third but as a member of the Old Girls' Society.

Each year brings back the memory of that first Speech Day and that first great thrill of membership will remain with me throughout my life."

THE CHILDREN'S SONG
by Rudyard Kipling

Land of our birth, we pledge to thee
Our love and toil in years to be;
When we are grown and take our place
As men and women with our race.
Father in heaven who lovest all,
O help thy children when they call,
That they may build from age to age
An undefiled heritage.

Teach us to look in all our ends
On thee for judge, and not our friends;
That we, with thee, may walk uncowed
By fear or favour of the crowd.
Teach us the strength that cannot speak,
By deed or thought to hurt the weak;
That, under thee, we may possess
Man's strength to comfort man's distress.

Teach us delight in simple things,
And mirth that has no bitter springs;
Forgiveness free of evil done,
And love to all men 'neath the sun.
Land of our birth, our faith, our pride;
For whose dear sake our fathers died;
O Motherland, we pledge to thee,
Head, heart, and hand through years to be.

The great event of 1925 was the opening of the New Wing on the first day of the spring term in January. At long last all the school was back under one roof. Miss Howes Smith recorded the event in her own inimitable style:

"THE OLD RED WALL with its overhanging fruit trees has gone, and the New Wing, planned in 1913, begun in 1923, and opened in 1925, is here. Foundations were laid in the red sand, and as the walls rose blackbirds and robins built in their crevices. A long red-floored corridor, so long that a telescope is needed to identify a scurrying little mortal at the far end, with four classrooms, music and staff rooms above: another long red-floored passage with four classrooms and cloakrooms below, making a total accommodation of 420 – this sounds dull. But open wide the middle rooms below, and let the sun blaze on the southern front; look at the innumerable windows; see the frescoes on the walls, and you will feel it is something of a brick built 'Castle in Spain'."

Photographs taken during construction of the New Wing, 1923–1925

The New Wing and Back Lawn

On Founders' Day in 1925 a League of Nations Pageant was held, which was repeated again at the same time the following year. Miss R P Metcalfe, a member of staff, records in the *Annals* the purpose and the success of the event.

"To many, the League of Nations simply meant Geneva and a kind of parliament. Despite the fact that we were told of its varied activities from the Saar to Iraq, yet the League seemed an impersonal society. It was to make us realise that it consisted of fifty-five countries, each with different peoples and customs, but all united in one vision of a world peace, that the Pageant was given. The main-spring of the whole performance was the Head Mistress who conceived the plan and watched over every detail with zealous inspiration. The incongruous elements that had to be united gave some idea of the difficulties at Geneva; and our work was only achieved by the devoted effort of the whole community. The very names of countries such as Guatemala sent several back to an atlas. Every available book was searched for detail of dress and custom. No aspect of a country's life was ignored, from folk songs sung at a village wedding in Norway to the religious ceremony in India when the priest received offerings given to the idol. History provided the episode of William Tell for Switzerland and Joan of Arc for France. Thus, little by little, material was collected. It was intended that every country should show some typical characteristic; hence Greece was represented by a dance, symbolic of the arts she gave the world; and Italy chose St Francis, whose life was a practical application of the ideals of the League.

As with Chaucer of old, the stories were found, but the difficulty was to knit them together. Chaucer sent his pilgrims on

Pupils enacting an Indian religious ceremony

The gathering of all the flag-bearers of 55 nations

a journey to Canterbury; the countries of the League travelled to Geneva. Before the appearance of each nation, a herald, clad in the conventional dress of a page, announced its arrival by means of a large standard bearing its name; following the country came the flag-bearer. China, the land of ceremonial, was represented by a typical wedding scene; Panama held high a huge key that opened two oceans; Luxembourg, as befitted the smallest country, was represented by one diminutive girl in national costume. The music of the countries was represented by national songs. The trees made a fitting background to the gay colours of the dresses; and the procession at the end, when the figure of Geneva summoned the nations to the League Assembly dominated by a white robed figure of Peace, was a most wonderful sight. It was right that the Pageant should end by an appeal to the ideals which inspired the founders of the League: all nations sang together Whittier's poem:

> O Brother man! fold to thy heart thy brother;
> Where pity dwells, the peace of God is there."

By the mid-20s it had been recognised that if the school teams were to hold their own in matches a hard court at School was a necessity. But nothing came easily in those days. The Headmistress's words illustrate the task necessary to achieve the desired objective. She felt herself faced with...

"INVENTING £200. Never was there a better illustration of the old saying 'many a mickle makes a muckle.' The Fund began in February 1923 with a deposit of £1 16s [£1.80], and the promise of £20 from the County Council. Month by month for three years, sums of three shillings upwards were added, the interest varying from 6d [2½p] in 1923 to £1 5s [£1.25] in 1926. Parents, pupils and staff co-operated devotedly, the munificent sum of £65 was given by Mr and Mrs Cowburn, and in March 1926, the final £20 could be claimed from the County Council. The court was constructed and, the bill being paid, was open for play by Mrs Cowburn in the presence of the whole school in May 1926."

The Chronicle of Events, 1910–1926

In 1927 Miss Howes Smith wrote with pride, in the *Annals*, about the exquisitely worked illuminated chronicle describing the first sixteen years of the School, from the opening day on 4 July 1910.

"ORIGINATOR AND HISTORIAN, M Howes Smith. Designer and Artist-in-chief, R M Mawson. The Scribe, E Lawrence.

The Tailpiece by P James illustrates The Chaucer Pageant of 1914 and 1915. One panel by J Kendrick gives a scene from The Deluge, a Chester Miracle Play, acted in our great Mediaeval Fair, 1916. Three side panels by M Massey, N Duncan and M Clow depicts the School, the Garden, and the New Wing. Two panels by G McKerrow and M Isitt remind us of the Presbyterian and Wesleyan Churches, under whose shadow our Preparatory worked and played for years. The Headpiece, by G McKerrow, shows the League of Nations Pageants, 1925 and 1926."

School expeditions were regular occurrences to witness or take part in special events, but few required such determination and resilience as that to see the total eclipse of the sun. Miss D I Hookins was a member of staff that accompanied this party and she reported:

"ON 29TH JUNE 1927 nearly two hundred of us left our comfortable beds at the unwonted hour of 3.00am in order to catch a special train at 3.45am from Hale to Ainsdale beach, to see the total eclipse of the sun. There had been no fine morning for more than a fortnight, and so when the clouds rolled away leaving the sun visible at 5.00am our excitement was intense. All were busy with dark screens, and as we approached Ainsdale, we distinctly saw the small corner of the sun cut out, as the moon began to pass before it.

We arrived at Ainsdale at 5.30am, and hurried to suitable sand hills and produced our cameras, pencils and notebooks. A sheet was hung on the stationary bus, in order to show the shadow bars to anyone who could bear to turn away from the sun and moon at the moment of totality! Some of the girls had a thermometer to record the variations in temperature and others obtained interesting photographs and drawings.

At the moment of totality, considerable haze obscured the view, but although we saw nothing of solar prominences of which we had heard, we were all greatly impressed by the curious darkness, the cold, the stillness of the crowds and of the birds, and most of all by the corona. Most of the School saw the corona as silvery and faintly blue, but the Irish members of the staff were unanimous in declaring it green!

After totality, clouds obliterated the sun, and the School turned its attention to breakfast, after which, owing to steady rain, some went home, while more energetic people stayed to botanise. We found many interesting plants peculiar to the sand dunes, and a few of us had obtained permission to explore the bird sanctuary where we attempted to photograph a young ringed plover which had tremendously long legs and led the photographer a dance.

We saw terns and redshanks, shelducks and oystercatchers, and found nests of gulls and larks. As the rain continued we decided to return at 11.15am, even at which early hour the staff were so tired that they slept in the train! Though it was only one o'clock when we arrived home, we seemed to have been away for days!"

Founders' Day 1927 saw the introduction of the School badge, long in the planning, and the House System. The "official" description of the newly designed badge in the *Annals* reveals the extent to which meticulous scholarly research was undertaken to make sure every detail meshed perfectly into the whole.

Left: the seal of Conrad Pellifex, 1329, on which the School badge was based

Right: the School badge

"CONRAD PELLIFEX MADE THE SHAPE, and we took it for our own. This old Viennese furrier of the 14th Century solved our problem after years of search. We wanted not a circle, not a concatenoid, not a mere masculine shield, but something especially our own, which would hold our motto, a School emblem, the symbol of Altrincham, the heraldic sign of Cheshire, and symbolic decoration. His seal was an irregular hexagon with his motto round the edge; so our badge was hexagonal and has, besides our motto, the Lion of Altrincham, the Three Sheaves of Cheshire, the Lamp of Knowledge, and lastly Acorns. Perhaps these acorns will recall the saying which must ever guide those linked in School life, that 'a little thing is a little thing, but faithfulness in little things is a very great thing.'"

The House System, which was to become an institution for over forty years, was also founded on 4 July 1927. The Houses linked up staff and girls from different forms and were useful in organising games, Christmas parties, dramatic entertainments and musical events. But their greatest value was the knowledge that individual records in conduct, work and athletics brought honour or discredit to the House. Miss Coleman described in the *Annals* how the system worked and how the names of the Houses came to be selected.

"GIRLS WERE ALLOTTED TO HOUSES on reaching the IVth in a purely impartial manner – sisters being placed in the same House. Points gained by individual members for any achievement under one of the three main groups – Work, Athletics and Conduct – contribute to the aggregate of the House, the one gaining the highest score becoming holder of the House Trophy for one term. The ideal of teamwork, which has always been encouraged by our system of Form prizes, is thus extended to groups of girls of different ages, and to the widest possible range of activities.

Among many details of organisation which had to be decided at the outset, choice of names for the four Houses was the most exciting and arduous; and the symmetry and aptitude of De Massey, Delamere, Grey and Gaskell, named after two men and two women of local fame standing for Law, Liberty, Learning and Literature respectively, please eye and mind equally.

Hamon de Massey held the district round Dunham Massey (named after him) under Hugh the Wolf, the Earl of Chester in days of William the Conqueror; and was therefore one of the Normans who introduced order, discipline and justice into England. The House named after him chose as an appropriate motto *Fortis qui se vincit*, thus drawing from his career the lesson of self-control.

Henry Booth, 2nd Lord Delamere (1651–1693), was an eager politician in the reign of Charles II and James II, who stood throughout his life for the liberties of the English people threatened by the Papists, and raised a regiment of Cheshire Volunteers for William of Orange. His House has adopted his motto *A ma puissance*.

Lady Jane Grey was a learned girl who read Plato for pleasure at the age of 13, preferred reading to hunting, and became Queen after Edward VI when only 16 for a few days before her death on the scaffold. She was an ancestor of the Earls of Stamford, and thus connected with Altrincham. The House named after her was inspired by her example in its choice of motto, *Non nobis nati*.

The name of Mrs Gaskell (1810–1865) will always be associated with Knutsford, her beloved 'Cranford', the home of her childhood and early youth, the place where she was married and which she constantly visited after her marriage with the hard-working Minister of Cross Street Chapel, Manchester, and where at length she was buried. Her House adopted *Vitai lampada* for a motto, mindful that only selflessness can pass on a lighted torch to the next in the race of life, and also that the Lamp is significant in a narrower sense as a symbol of knowledge."

The very fine House notice board was presented in 1927 by Mr and Mrs Cowburn, parents of Mary. It was designed by the architect Mr Geoffrey Owen and cost £65.

Miss Howes Smith noted in the *Annals*:

"IN THE SUMMER TERM 1928, the Staff Garden shelters first made their appearance, and were followed next summer by the Roman table and bench. Here sometimes coffee reigns and sometimes corrections. The little windmill-weathervane, too, came to make the school realise which way the wind blows and where the sun rises. The sundial, a gift in memory of Mr Joe Sidebotham, one of our earliest and kindest governors, came to grace our garden; and the inscription, 'I count the sunny hours', was added to the pedestal."

Miss Coleman, a member of staff, wrote in the *Annals* about the long-awaited royal visit.

COUNTY HIGH SCHOOL FOR GIRLS, BOWDON.

HER ROYAL HIGHNESS

will pay a personal visit

to her former Tutor,

Miss M. HOWES SMITH,

Head Mistress of the County High School

for Girls. Bowdon.

"IN JUNE 1929 PRINCESS MARY'S visit to Chester, Knutsford and Altrincham seemed so crowded as not to spare her time to set even 'one royal foot' across the School threshold. Our delight was unbounded when Lord Stamford announced that 'two royal feet were to bear their owner on a private visit to her former tutor, Miss Howes Smith.' Meticulous preparations for these six precious minutes assured full use of each second; and the short time actually passed with an ordered repose which was dignified and impressive, as well as tremendously exciting. Uncomfortable days of workmen, paint and planks while the Hall was hurriedly redecorated, soon passed; patient curtseying under Miss Suffield's direction; and a full rehearsal – and we were ready at five o'clock on June 14th. Storms of wind and rain had raged all the afternoon, but the sun came out brilliantly just before that time. Miss Howes Smith and Captain Carter, the representative of the Governors, stood on the steps; behind them waited Miss Hogg and Miss Waldo (our American teacher on an exchange with Miss Whitwill), along with Kathleen Thompson, granddaughter of an original Governor, and Margaret Ellis, daughter of an original mistress; and along the length of the Hall facing the door was the school arranged in eight tiers. Outside on the lawn, in full uniform, were the Guides, and parents filled the garden. There was a hubbub of expectant voices as we awaited the warning of arrival up The Downs from a post on the garden wall, and the Caretaker was rushed up a stepladder for a last polish to the study windows. At each false alarm excitement grew and when the Royal car finally came the Guides had barely time to salute before the cars were standing at the door, and Princess Mary herself was stepping out captivating the first beholders, as all succeeding ones by her radiant smile and sheer loveliness. The Princess, followed by Miss Kenyon-Slaney, Lord Stamford, and Lord Clive, was received by Miss Howes Smith; and then Captain Carter, Miss Hogg, Miss Waldo and the two little girls were presented. The Princess spoke to each in turn, and seemed

delighted with the framed pictorial record and the illustrated chart of her journey especially done under Miss Mawson's supervision in the Art Department, both of which she accepted from the little girls. The group advanced between the pillars and many of the school had their first view, as Miss Howes Smith said 'May I present the school to your Royal Highness?' and four hundred pairs of legs bent in one sweeping curtsey and four hundred healthy young throats uttered a great cheer. Through the library they passed and as they emerged from the second door the staff were presented. Then came the hardly-to-be-hoped-for moment when the Princess turned to speak to us. I think her young hearers, fascinated by her deep rich voice and by her radiant fairness, felt a pride of ownership swelling in their hearts – for after all, England's Princess belongs to all England's daughters. Loud cheers showed

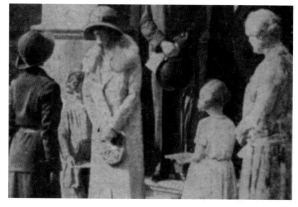

our thanks to the Princess for telling us herself of the holiday she proposed for us. Her Royal Highness then inspected the Study, pausing there for a short private conversation with the Headmistress. She smiled to see her childhood photograph on the wall. When she emerged again, the Guides saluted once more, and this time, the Princess commented on the size of the company (what a pity she cannot see our two companies now – twice the size!) – and asked for Miss Buchanan to be presented. This exciting moment was perpetuated by the *Daily News* pressman in an obliging but quite unofficial photo. Everyone was delighted with the motherly way in which the Princess put her hands on the shoulders of Kathleen and Margaret to draw them back from the cars which now approached to bear our visitors away. During the brief moment on the steps, those inside had emerged with magical speed, and were ready on the asphalt to swell the final cheers.

Her Royal Highness told Miss Howes Smith at dinner at Dunham Hall that evening how much she liked her gifts after studying them more closely; and said she regretted not having desired Miss Mawson to be presented to her. A few days later came a very charming formal appreciation of her visit in a note from Miss Kenyon-Slaney. This was followed by a signed and framed photograph of the Princess which now hangs just inside the front door as a lasting memory of the school's most distinguished visitor."

URBAN DISTRICT OF ALTRINCHAM.

SOUVENIR PROGRAMME
OF ARRANGEMENTS
ON THE OCCASION
OF THE VISIT TO
ALTRINCHAM OF

H.R.H. PRINCESS MARY,
VISCOUNTESS LASCELLES.

:: FRIDAY, 14th JUNE, 1929. ::

Official Programme.

PRICE: TWO PENCE.

The last big pageant of the decade was the Fair of All Nations 1929 which was described in the *Annals* by D M Hills, a member of staff.

"WHEN ALADDIN WANTED A PALACE he rubbed his lamp and the building sprang up before his eyes. On the hot summer's day of July 20th 1929 we rubbed a lamp hardly less magical, and the school grounds became the scene of a picturesque World Fair, in which representatives of all nations met together to raise money for the Ancoats Children's Holiday Fund. From three in the afternoon until about nine in the evening – when the shades of night drove away the last enthusiasts – we bought and sold unceasingly and entertained our streams of visitors with such success that we obtained a profit of £183, far beyond our rosiest expectations.

The general effect of the Fair was so brilliant and so varied that even mistresses and girls might well feel a little bewildered at first. Irish colleens, pig-tailed Germans, Turkish women in alluring veils, Swedes, Spaniards, Persians, Maoris in marvellous head-dresses, Russians, Brazilians, Nigerians – almost every race had answered the mysterious summons.

Visitors declared that they were dazzled by the moving kaleidoscope of colour. There were, of course, scenes from many lands, with a harmony of colour through all. In one corner was a Japanese stall hung with bright decorated lanterns, in which dainty maidens framed in blue and mauve robes with bright sprays of almond blossom sold their wares; in another, gaily clothed Italians were quickly disposing of their ice-creams; while in a third, little Dutch people were selling fruit, dairy produce and flowers.

The greatest triumphs of the Fair were, however, its processional pageants. The first took place under a blazing sky; the second amid the long shadows cast by the evening sun. As the representatives of the different countries, each with flag and standard bearers, marched across the back lawn, pausing to face the terrace at their appointed stations, the harmony of the colouring, the grace with which the costumes were worn, the charm of the episodes must have struck everyone present. Many of us realised, more vividly than before, the possibilities of the pageant as a form of art."

Miss Howes Smith viewed the acquisition of a new dining room with great delight:

"THE AUTUMN TERM OF 1928 ended with the smashing sounds of the destruction of the old bicycle sheds and roof of the covered playground at the east end of school. In the autumn of 1929 the first great event was the taking possession of the new dining hall by the school, and the installation of Mrs Collins and the domestic staff in the new kitchen. To the wonder of all, the asphalt playground seems as large, the laburnum flourishes, the path still meanders by the hedge – yet the new hall seats 200. The Old Girls ask on what site this magic building stands and all we can say is that there were two dingy bicycle sheds, which are no more. Here singers wail or warble all the afternoon, and classes are no longer given as duets with the songs below. An innovation is a small platform with a table making a miniature 'High' – the elevation to which implies sometimes the need for training in good manners and sometimes the mark of superiority."

Dorothy Toft entered the school in September 1923 as a scholarship girl from Stamford Park Council School and writes:

"MY FIRST FORM WAS REMOVE B and the form mistress was Miss Hallsworth. My school chum was Alice Harrop. I recall going by special train to Ainsdale beach to watch a total eclipse of the sun, a visit to Hale Cinema to see a film about the ascent of Mount Everest, pageants on the back lawn, the visit of Princess Mary, daughter of King George V, Speech Days at the Altrincham Hippodrome, murals on the walls of the New Wing, being taught to swim by Miss Peacock, cooking lessons with Miss Bell, Miss Whitwill's wonderful history lessons and singing with Miss Helen Anderton. I always felt Miss Howes Smith and her staff were excellent teachers – far ahead of their time – and I felt it to be a privilege to be educated at such a good school."

Above all else Miss Howes Smith kept an eagle eye on the progress and performance of each pupil in her charge, knew their individual strengths and weaknesses, and when it was needed was there to give guidance and encouragement, as shown in the following letter, which was handwritten during the summer holiday and sent to Dorothy Loft (not to be confused with Dorothy Toft).

2 Sunny Bank
Bowdon
Sep. 2. 1929

My dear Dorothy,

It was a disappointment for you I know that you had not gained a Certificate, but you will feel happier when you know that you did well in some things. You got <u>credit</u> in Cookery, & <u>pass</u> in Scripture & History. Your only really very poor subject was French & I'm afraid French of your Form was bad as you have nearly all failed in it.

But we must remember that if you have learnt to do your best you have learnt the most important lesson that School would teach you, & that this will help you to become a capable & valuable Citizen – whether you get a Certificate or not.

I am sure you will do us credit if you act in this way.

With my best wishes & sympathy.

from M. Howes Smith

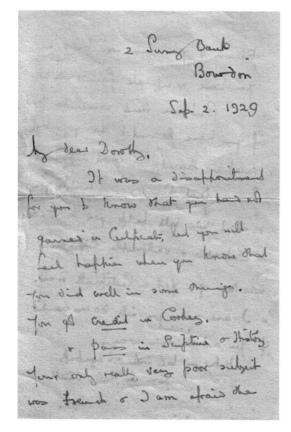
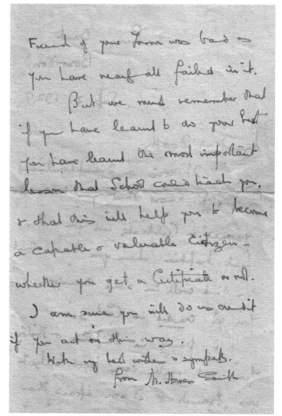

Miss Howes Smith's letter to Dorothy Loft, 1929

Towards the end of the second decade the singing mistress, Miss Helen Anderton, recorded her recollections in the *Annals*:

"WE HAD ORDERED TEA and were sitting back, suddenly becoming thoughtful. The beauty of the exhibits of Yugoslavian sculpture had pleased us greatly. Slowly my mind travelled back to a day many years ago. 'Did I ever tell you that it was here that I was interviewed by Miss Howes Smith?' 'What – at the Art Gallery?' 'Yes, we arranged to meet here.'

I now sometimes blush to think with what persistence I tried to make her believe that, although I had had no experience in school work, a class of 25 girls had no terrors for me. Anyhow, the result of that interview was – I was asked to come to school the next day to give a lesson in her presence. Before going home I scoured the town for 26 copies of a song. This proved unnecessary, for I found that the class had been entered for a competition in Manchester and that Brahms's *Cradle Song* was the test piece: as it needed finishing touches, I was only too pleased to spend my time on this. Never did half an hour pass so quickly and never did I enjoy myself more. The following Tuesday I started.

For a short time I taught in one of the large classrooms, but when the grand piano was bought I came down into the Hall and there I gave my lessons until the new dining room was built.

It was at the Hippodrome that I first realised what an accomplished musician we had in our pianist (one of our own girls). We were in great trouble at the rehearsal; Miss Howes Smith had criticised the first song severely. Our accompanist, knowing the trouble to be due to the high-pitched piano, transposed the second song to a lower key and saved us further ignominy.

I remember so well the rehearsal of *Sumer is i-cumen in* for the Chaucer Pageant. Conducting out of doors with the singers at a distance isn't altogether a joy: many of us will always remember our singing of the *Maple Leaf* at the second performance of the League of Nations Pageant. A strong breeze had the effect of turning that charming unison song into something resembling an extremely modern part-song!"

Questioner: "In which year did you come to us?"

Miss A.: "1913, dear lady, 1913."

Questioner: "Oh, that accounts for what one of the girls said to me coming up to school one day: '*Miss Anderton must have been coming to school for a **long** time , mustn't she? – she used to teach my Aunt!*' "

The Hale Cinema on Willowtree Road, closed in 1978 and later demolished. The cinema was used occasionally for School speech days and frequently for Founders' Day afternoon treats.

The 1930s

1930	Autumn term – new biology laboratory opened
1931	4 July – 21st Anniversary of Founders' Day
1931	County High Schools lose preparatory departments
1931	Speech Day held at the Regal Cinema
1932	Spring term – Hall extension completed
1933	Miss Drought appointed Headmistress
1933	Miss Howes Smith retires
1934	Union Society started
1934	First annual Christmas Fair
1936	Spring term – new hard courts at School and Belgrave Road
1936	Summer term – new playing field on South Downs Road
1936	New cycle sheds built on the school drive
1938	Small pavilion opened at South Downs Road
1939	26 July – practice evacuation of School held and gas mask drill
1939	3 September – Britain declares war on Germany
1939	Trenches and shelters built on the Devisdale

CHAPTER 3
THE 1930S

By the early thirties numbers had increased to 460 pupils in spite of the loss of all the five- and six-year-olds when the Kindergarten was closed because of a change in policy by Cheshire County Council. The struggle to provide adequate accommodation continued unabated, with building work a constant feature of school life. The autumn term of 1930 saw the welcome completion of the new Biology Laboratory, which was made out of the old dining room and kitchen. Though small, it was well equipped with benches, sinks, bench lights, a fixed lantern screen and several aquaria.

A rather surprising innovation in the same year saw the appearance of the staff in school hours in their university gowns, which astounded their pupils; but the change proved welcome and made it easier, in those days of short hair and short frocks, to distinguish between the learned and the learners!

By far the most significant event at this time was the celebration of the twenty-first anniversary of the official opening of School. Miss Coleman wrote in the *Annals*:

Altrincham County High School
For Girls.
1910-1931

Twenty-First Anniversary
(JULY 4th)

SERVICE
at
BOWDON PARISH CHURCH

Friday, July 3rd, at 5-30 p.m.
1931

Preacher:
The Rev. Canon Sandars.

"ON FRIDAY 3 JULY the whole school gathered on the front lawn, partially shaded by the acacia tree from the bright sun, for the exchange of gifts – many to the school, then to Miss Howes Smith a leather blotter and a book of original paintings of school and garden from the girls, and a shagreen trinket box from the Staff. A telegram was received from Princess Mary, 'My heartiest congratulations on the School's twenty-first birthday and best wishes for its continued prosperity – Mary.' In the afternoon, the girls had tea together before proceeding to the Anniversary Service in Bowdon Church at 5.30, when they and Old Girls, parents and Governors filled every available corner. The Rev. A Dardis conducted the service, and Canon Sandars came specially to preach. Our own form of service was used, with special significances like the School Song, the twenty-third psalm and 'Now thank we all our God' which had been used in 1910, with the great commemorative passage, 'Let us now praise famous men,' and with special prayers of Praise, of Memory, for the Future, and for True Knowledge.

The presentation of a silver salver to Miss Howes Smith

37

On Saturday afternoon came the Old Girls' Garden Party, with both cricket and tennis matches, and countless groups of talkers at School. Mr Nield's presentation on behalf of the Governors of a silver salver to Miss Howes Smith took place during the afternoon. Dinner was served later in the dining room, followed by speeches, toasts, and another presentation to Miss Howes Smith – a tortoiseshell and silver toilet set from the Old Girls.

On Sunday, a Guide Church Parade at St Margaret's was held, attended by the three School Companies, and by numbers of Old Girls and Officers. We all marched back in formation to School, past Miss Howes Smith on the front steps, giving her a full salute. From two o'clock onwards it was the turn of anyone who liked to visit us, and enormous numbers of parents, relatives and friends explored school and garden."

The Staff, about 1932
Back row: ?, Miss Colenutt, Miss Harthill, ?; third row: Miss Crowther, Miss Morrey, ?,
Miss Atkinson, ?; second row: ?, Miss Bailey (secretary), ?, Miss Hammond, Miss Attenborough,
Miss Buchanan, Miss Eagle, ?; sitting: ?, Miss Coleman, Miss Bell, Miss Whitwill, Miss Howes Smith,
Miss Anderton, Miss Hogg, Miss Hallsworth, Miss Langley

An extract of a tribute to Miss Howes Smith by Miss Coleman and Miss Whitwill on behalf of the Staff states:

" 'LET US NOW PRAISE FAMOUS MEN' says the passage that is read at School on every Founders' Day; but on Founders' Day in 1931 there is one name above all others that we wish to praise – the name of the Headmistress. Our School has built up its traditions under the rule of one dominating personality.

What blind turn of chance led to the formal opening of the School twenty-one years ago on Independence Day? Was it not merely a happy inspiration but a prophesy? For no date could be a more fitting birthday for our School. Freedom and individuality are educational catchwords nowadays, but what school is more successfully organised to provide the one and foster the other than ours which she has built?

The intimacy of a happy family was perhaps not hard to achieve in a school of sixty odd; but it is remarkable that it still persists as numbers swell eightfold. The School is now one of the largest, most flourishing, beautiful and happiest in the county. No one can deny this. The glow of colour on the walls, the health and cheerfulness of the children's faces, the spirit of friendship that pervades the whole, are so noticeable that they strike the nearest stranger who walks through the building. So the family goes on increasing and diverging, but in constant touch with us. They carry with them a love of the beauty which has constantly surrounded them in School and garden; and a will already trained in countless ways, to serve others. This is due to the head of the family.

Miss Howes Smith's success can be attributed to several qualities and powers of mind, but above all, to the great quality without which nothing of importance can be accomplished – the power to work. To estimate the number of hours of work she has given to the School, you would have to find out the number of hours in twenty-one years, for in every waking moment, and we believe also in her dreams – and some of her brightest inspirations have come to her in the night seasons – she has been thinking, planning and labouring for the School. From early morn till dewy eve you can find her at School, organising, teaching, inventing appropriate punishments for the refractory, taking temperature, discussing careers, interviewing parents, making out Board of Education returns, and doing the hundred and one things which only a Headmistress knows about. Then when she leaves the building from which all else have fled, she returns to her home, Sunny Bank, but not to sit and do nothing. Far into the night the work goes on; in the district – committees, public meetings and conferences; at home – timetables, letters and daydreams and night dreams for the good of the School.

We do not believe there is anything connected with the School which Miss Howes Smith cannot do; she can play tennis or a hymn, design the colour schemes for a play, stoke a furnace, plan a pageant, buy a swing, and receive a Princess.

Words are feeble things with which to try to thank Miss Howes Smith; we can best thank her by giving 'head, heart and hand' as she has done, and by trying to follow her example in serving our School 'bravely, faithfully, cheerfully'."

Founders' Day services were always very important to Miss Howes Smith, especially as the years went on, as a means of helping unremembering youth to realise the debt owed to those who planned and cared for the School in past days, and to feel that they, in their turn, must add their "brick" to the building not made with hands.

Another change of policy in 1931 by Cheshire County Council meant that from the autumn term no new boys would be admitted to the preparatory department in the future, and there could only be 42 girls under the age of ten years. (The last ten boys left at the end of the summer term 1933.) Even with the implementation of this change numbers had grown sufficiently to warrant moving the Speech Day venue to the Regal Cinema, newly opened in 1931, in Art Deco style, with a seating capacity of over 1500, on Manchester Road, Broadheath.

One of the boys attending the Prep School from 1928 to 1932, Ronald Trenbath, writes:

"THE KINDERGARTEN DEPARTMENT consisted of three classes: Preparatory, First Form and Second Form, with three teachers – Miss Atkinson, Miss Langley and headed by Miss Hodgson. Miss Atkinson was older and more severe. Miss Langley was young, smart and

1931: Miss Howes Smith with Toby, her Sealyham terrier. Ronald Trenbath is on the right on the front row.

Ronald Trenbath, 2009

fashionable, and owned a Morris Oxford car. Miss Hodgson was more qualified, very professional, dedicated, and would give one-to-one tuition. She left to get married.

Boys between the age of seven and ten years could attend the Prep, forming an elitist minority giving rise to male chauvinism.

School plays performed at Speech Day were of a very high standard, produced by Miss Hodgson and acted by pupils of Prep – these included *A Christmas Carol*, *Cranford* and *Rip van Winkle*. In the summer events such as garden parties with themes (Canterbury Tales, World Fair and Empire Day) involved the whole school.

Princess Mary, the Princess Royal, requested a visit to the School. All pupils and staff were instructed on bowing and curtseying (very embarrassing). My mother was invited to attend. There was much disruption of routine but we were rewarded with a one-day holiday.

Miss Howes Smith was known as HS – formidable, dominant, feared by staff, pupils, Governors and many parents, but she respected those who stood their ground. Very dedicated, she would help all those who were eager to succeed but would not tolerate uncouth behaviour. She regularly took her lunch at a table on a raised dais in the Dining Room with two members of staff and three pupils. I was one of the unfortunate pupils."

Another 'Old Boy', Stanley Dale, who attended from 1931 and left aged 9 in 1933, has contributed this poignant memory:

"I ENJOYED SPORTS PERIODS, football and cricket, although I seemed to be jinxed; cricket balls in my hands had a life of their own and went straight to the nearest window. It was so bad my father took out insurance against broken windows. Nevertheless, Miss Howes Smith, who I admired very much, showed great kindness and took me to her home several times to feed me; I was a very puny child."

Yet more construction work was underway at this time in the main school with the welcome extension of the Hall. There was much joy in the spring term of 1932 when pupils stepped for the first time on the new parquet flooring. The *Annals* record:

"THOSE FAR AWAY may like to picture the extension supported on two large pillars. A flood of light pours through the glass roof, and there are low windows, with window seats, overlooking the lawn beyond. The wall space has been covered with coloured pictures, the special keynotes being red, brown and gold. The Old Girls' Fifth Dance rejoiced in the added space and beauty."

School holidays at home and abroad had been a feature of the summer for many years, and an innovation in the thirties was the Scholars' Cruise at Easter. The first in 1932 was led by Miss Hallsworth who wrote in the *Annals*:

"WE LEFT LIVERPOOL on a typically damp and dreary April day – and our last sight of the Mersey was a massed brigade of dripping umbrellas. The *SS Montrose* was gay with bunting and fresh paint – a cheering sight even to the member of our party who had already been seasick in the tender! Perhaps it was somewhat crowded with its thousand or so passengers, but as we started we thought little of the lack of deck space and the ever-tramping feet on the companionway.

The first two days out will never be forgotten; a gale blew us down the Irish Sea and into the Bay of Biscay and the majority wished they had never seen the boat or the sea!"

Thereafter the warm sunny weather dispelled any lingering depression and the party enjoyed shore excursions in Gibraltar, Morocco and Lisbon and returned home sunburned and laden with "trophies". By contrast the departure to Madeira, Tangier and Gibraltar in 1933, this time on the White Star liner *SS Doric*, was a much calmer event. Miss Attenborough wrote:

"THE ACHS PARTY, in the charge of Miss Hallsworth, numbered twenty-eight including 4 Staff members. For some hours the boat was as steady as a rock, and we began to be very favourably impressed with our seafaring capacities until we realised we were at anchor in the Mersey waiting for the tide. Towards midnight we sailed."

In the same year Miss Howes Smith recorded:

"THE GREAT EVENT OF THE SUMMER TERM of 1933 is the appointment of a new Headmistress, who comes from her school in Surrey, with a splendid reputation. An imaginary line drawn from the Library to the Domestic Science room, beyond which no pupil could stray, left a corner so peaceful that no one could believe that the whole school was working and playing for three and a half hours while the appointment was being made. The Cambridge phase is over with the first three Chairmen (Judge J K Bradbury, Mr E J Sidebotham and Mr W M Neild), the Headmistress, and the Headmaster of the Boys' High School (Mr J S Laver), all Cambridge graduates. The Oxford phase, with the new Headmistress (Miss D M Drought), the Vice-Chairman (Mr A P Hill), the second mistress (Miss M W Whitwill), the Clerk (Mr J Sidebotham), and the new Headmaster of the Boys' School (Mr W A Hamblin), all of Oxford, will begin next September."

And so the end of an era dawned and the retirement of Miss Howes Smith was reported in the *Altrincham, Hale and Bowdon Guardian* of 28 July 1933 as follows:

"SELDOM HAS THERE BEEN more glorious weather for the annual sports of the Altrincham County High School for Girls than that experienced on last Saturday afternoon. The brilliant sunshine was responsible for a bright scene to which the colouring of the ladies' dresses was an additional effect, and to make the afternoon perfect music of a most pleasing nature was played by the Altrincham Borough Prize Band.

At the end of the events Miss Howes Smith was presented with a silver tea service as a token of appreciation from the Governors on her retirement, after having had charge of the School from its inception.

Mr Arthur P Hill, Chairman of the Governors, said it was 23 years since Miss Howes Smith was appointed Head of the School. Those who appointed her chose more wisely than they knew. They realised that they were appointing a woman of great academic learning and singular

Portrait of Miss Howes Smith

personality and charm, but they did not know, and had no means of knowing, that they were also appointing a woman of outstanding fearlessness and courage, particularly moral courage. When she was appointed the School had been recently built, and since then more than 2000 girls had been educated by her, and she had moulded them after her own fashion. During that 23 years Miss Howes Smith had given such part of her life entirely to the School. In term and vacation, in School and out, her sole thought had been the advancement of the School and the welfare of her girls. She had realised from the commencement that the first essential of any school, either for boys or girls, should be the moral welfare of the children and their good health, and that those two things must even come before their scholastic education. It was due to her recognition of those facts that the School was one of the foremost High Schools, not only in Cheshire but over a much wider area.

Continuing, Mr Hill said Miss Howes Smith had never courted popularity. She had had many tussles with the Education Authorities and the Governors and, in some cases, with the parents, but her one thought had been the well-being of the girls. She had now finished her 23 years' hard labour – a hard labour of love – and that afternoon, in those lovely grounds, they took their leave of her. On behalf of the Governors, the parents of present and past pupils, and the scholars themselves, he offered their thanks to Miss Howes Smith for all that she had done for the School. They sincerely trusted that she would be spared for many years to come, and that she would be granted the blessed gift of good health."

The heartfelt farewell from the Staff reads as follows:

"THE STAFF WISHES TO PLACE on record in this, the last *Annals* under Miss Howes Smith's regime, their appreciation of her work as our first Headmistress. Her dynamic personality and her devoted service has given the School a continuity of development doubly valuable during the critical years of growth. From her it has derived an individual character, which has founded a tradition of good fellowship, appreciation of beauty, and width of culture. In upholding this tradition we shall often think of her confident that through continued contact with the School her friendship will be a reality to past, present and future generations. We offer her our best wishes for the future leisure which she has so conspicuously earned and the work which we feel sure she will undertake."

In any discussion or debate, legend has it that Miss Howes Smith would always have the last word, so it is appropriate to record here her parting words in the *Annals*, so typical of the lady.

"AFTER THIS GOES TO PRESS, we hope for a Sports Day and a Swimming Gala; and an Old Girls' Special Garden Party and Evening Reunion as a farewell to that first member of the School who, twenty-three years ago, sat in the Headmistress's office waiting to begin those long years of happy work. Only, my dears, don't say to her, 'Now you will be able to do what you like,' or she will retort, 'That is just what I have been doing for twenty three years', and perhaps that delightful stream of thanks would end! God bless you all."

Kathleen Litherland, formerly Foulkes, recalls:

"I WENT TO ACHS IN 1923 as a child of 8. I came from a very good primary school in Ashton and did well in the exam so was put in the Lower IIIrd with 10 year olds. My form mistress was Miss Loxley. All the lower forms were in Sunday Schools around the district. The 'new wing' was being built. There were boys in the junior school – Billie Willie and John Cocker.

I went up the school in 'A' forms and took School Certificate in 1929 – a bad flu year which caused dreadful results. I was 14 then. I went into the sixth form and was there for four years. In the end I was HS's last Head Girl in 1932–3. The staff, old girls and school all collected when she retired and we pooled it all. I went with Miss Whitwill and Ella Seed to Finnigans and bought two silver coffee pots and some blue cups and saucers.

HS was a real character. She didn't care about exams but did her best to make us know about pictures and music. She bought Medici prints and good pottery for the school. Once the Emir of Afghanistan was going from Manchester to Chester so the whole school lined up outside St Margaret's Church and waved the Emir's flag as he went past. We had a League of Nations pageant on the back lawn when I was a flag bearer for Haiti. It was a hot summer so the grass was brown so brown frocks were the wrong colour and a new lot had to be made at the last minute!

We lived with Princess Mary's history notebook! She sent presents to HS and came to visit and we all had to curtsey. We were in the Hall in rows – the front row on the floor, the next row on benches, the next row on chairs and the back row on tables!

When at university I was brought back to unveil a portrait of HS at an Old Girls meeting.

(Later, I trained for teaching and married, returning to School in 1958 to teach geography – part time for 5 years, then full time until I retired in 1975 when 60. I was then Head of Geography. Mrs Delides was my boss and she and Miss Okell were very good to me.)"

The summer of 1933 was hot, dry and sunny; a newspaper headline proclaimed "Dangerous Drought Moves North". It arrived in Altrincham in September and was not the result of climate change but the new Headmistress!

At the age of 43, Miss Doris Marjorie Drought came from Farnham High School, Surrey where she had been Headmistress for eight years. She was born in Ireland, "brought up in a bog" to use her own words, in what was called Queens County and about a seven-mile drive from the nearest small country town. As a child she did not go to school but was educated at home by her father and various governesses and then spent a year or more at a finishing school in Paris. She then stayed abroad for

Miss Drought

The Lodge, home to caretakers and their families for many years

two years, for part of that time in a post with a German family. Then after another shorter period of intensive work at home she was accepted by Oxford, where she read Modern Languages and obtained a first-class honours degree. Her first teaching post was at Bedford High School for four years and her second at the Godolphin School, Salisbury.

Two more stalwarts, Mr and Mrs Collins, retired at Christmas after twenty-two years of devoted service to the School. Their place as caretaker and cook was taken by Mr and Mrs Spilsbury.

For many years various societies had existed in the School: the Art Club, Art Guild, Camera Club, Classical Society, French Society, Geographical Society, German Society, Historical Society, Hobbies, League of Nations Union, Literary Society, Scientific Society, and Scripture Union, each representing one subject. Their activities had become somewhat limited in scope, however, and by 1934 it was felt that there was a need for a new arrangement, by which the whole of the Upper School could benefit. Miss Drought suggested that the societies be amalgamated to form one, which on Miss Coleman's suggestion was called the "Union Society". It was agreed that each of the former societies should provide an entertainment once a term at meetings held on alternate Friday evenings. Thus was inaugurated the institution which would be of such value as a part of the social life of the senior members of the School. The entertainment was by no means stereotyped, with such diverse events as a visit to Manchester Grammar School to see scientific films, having visiting speakers from Manchester University; members of staff and sixth form girls gave talks, Miss Howes Smith returned to speak about her South African holiday, the visiting French Assistant, Mme Quidort, talked about France, and Miss Coleman, lately returned from America, spoke about America's National Parks. Miss Muir arranged several evenings devoted to folk-dancing and community singing; there were also charades, readings and musical plays. Last but not least Miss Bell supplied appetising teas at an amazingly small cost!

Further streamlining took place at this time with the school's charitable efforts being concentrated by means of holding a yearly Christmas Fair, organised by the Houses, the first of which made a profit of £144. Another change was introduced in 1935 as a result of a recommendation from a full Inspection by the Board of Education the previous year. From then on, girls sat on the hall floor for Assembly. It had grown beyond the endurance of the caretaker to put out and later clear away chairs for almost 500 pupils every day.

Musical activities developed with the founding of a music library and the acquisition of a new Bluthner grand piano, and in 1934 an annual House music competition was started. A choir consisting of the whole House, coached and conducted by an elected girl, performed selected pieces; and pianists representing their House, all being tested, and the best competing at the same time as the choir.

H Mary E Thompson remembers her time at School very well.

"I WAS SEVEN YEARS OLD when I first went to ACHS in 1929 – and I stayed there for my whole school life. So, I started under Miss Howes Smith who made the School in much of its essence. She was a lady of great ability and though absent-minded at times she gave us a love for the School. We always looked to see if her shoes matched, for she had on occasions worn one shoe of a pair with a different one of a pair on the other foot. But I was (young as I was) grateful for the many attitudes, ideals and sense of belonging – and the need to live, and behave and care as a pupil there. I shall never forget the 3 or so years (7-10) spent under her influence.

Miss Drought came in the year of the drought – so different yet with the same strong character, love and dedication to the School as her predecessor.

In many ways she was a shy woman but she could understand shyness in her girls – and her influence was strong and lasting. As Sixth Formers and as prefects we were expected to serve the School well and so fulfilled her expectations of service and love for the School, and that had a lasting effect on all.

Fridays – always meant flowers and fruit for the hospitals – they were taken by dinner girls. All part of the School Motto – Flowers and Fruit on Fridays – Fortiter, Fideliter, Feliciter.

I wish all Old Girls – in particular all the old Olds of my years – good health in age and happy years yet to come."

School colours for gymnastics were introduced in 1933. These took the form of two yellow tassels attached to the girdle, to replace the green ones already won for an "A" mark in deportment. (No one who had not gained her green tassels could qualify for gymnastic colours.)

Developments in the games world included in the spring of 1936 a part of the back lawn being dug up for a hard court. A little later in the year two hard courts enclosed in a chain link fence replaced the original ones at the Belgrave Road ground. At the beginning of the summer term the County Education Committee acquired the nine-acre grounds of Bowdon College on South Downs Road, for the School. Cricket in the summer and lacrosse in the winter transferred to this venue and in 1937 hockey was introduced. By 1938 the old Preparatory School at Bowdon College had been converted into a pavilion with showers, cloakrooms, kitchen and a pantry.

Because so many pupils were now cycling to school, trees were felled along the driveway towards the Caretaker's lodge in 1936, to make way for cycle sheds.

One of the new hard courts at Belgrave Road (Dome Chapel)

The sports pavilion on the playing fields at South Downs Road

Meg Smith, formerly Austin, recalls:

"IN 1929, AGED SEVEN, I moved to Altrincham High School for Girls in Bowdon. I remember it as a very happy school and enjoyed my time there. At that time there were about 380 pupils, all fee paying, some were small boys up to the age of 8 including my brother who had just moved on to the Boys High School before I joined. My sister and a cousin had been at the Girls School for some time.

Most of the time I cycled to school, which was about 3 miles from where I lived at Manor Farm in Timperley. Morning Assembly was held every morning and should you arrive late you were required to sit on the balcony instead of in your place in the hall. This happened to me rather often as I always found The Downs pretty steep and I never allowed enough time. Otherwise I travelled by bus. Sometimes we would get off a stop early to save money to buy sweets, usually gobstoppers that would turn all colours of the rainbow the more you sucked.

My first Head Mistress was Miss Howes Smith; a very elegant and kindly lady who always wore pale colours in her dress. Her large amount of costume jewellery jingled as she walked the corridors, so one could hear her coming, and you were expected to stand with your back to the wall to let her pass.

Miss Whitwill was always my favourite teacher. She taught history so well that it was quite spellbinding. We always had our own classroom and desk where we kept all our books and only moved about if it was to the Science room or Domestic Science room where we were taught sewing and cookery. Even after this length of time I can recall Miss Bell showing us how to trim an apple pie.

Our teachers never changed, they were all single ladies. They had had little chance to marry because of the huge casualties of the First World War. I always regarded them as old at that time and was amazed when my niece went to the school and several teachers were still there.

George V died in 1936 and all national newspapers were edged with black. We were told the news sitting cross-legged on the floor in the Hall.

I stayed for lunch sitting at long tables in the dining room, with a prefect at the top of each table to oversee our behaviour and table manners. She would insist that you ate all your lunch whether you liked it or not – no choice! After lunch we would be allowed out to play in the gardens which were surrounded by woods, which offered great ideas of make believe games. Otherwise whip and top, hop scotch, tick or skipping were popular substitutes. We were allowed to play tennis once we could play a decent game.

Our school song was Kipling's Children's song – 'Land of our birth we pledge to thee, our love and toil through years to be.'

The playing fields at Bowdon

Miss Drought succeeded Miss Howes Smith – a very severe but kindly lady – and being called to see her and waiting outside her door was really terrifying.

We played a great deal of sport with 5 or 6 tennis courts in the school grounds, netball on the ground behind the Dome Chapel just a short walk from the school. Cricket was always very popular, as we played one whole afternoon a week on the Bowdon playing field. With its sweeping stretches of grass and great trees it possessed a beauty rarely found in school grounds. It was next door to the present Bowdon Hockey Club.

We were often taken running in Dunham Park or on the Devisdale. We had a sports day on the Bowdon field and there was a swimming gala every summer at the local baths where we were taught to swim, walking in a crocodile down through the town to the pool each week. We took the lifesaving exams which involved diving for a brick at the bottom of the pool. The swimming pool was fairly old-fashioned, really quite small with a diving board at one end. The other part of the building consisted of cubicles where the townsfolk could come and have a hot bath. Bathrooms were few and far between then.

Miss Muir

Our games mistress was Miss Muir who was very keen on our weekly sessions of gym, and that was another area I did not excel in, always getting stuck on the horse as I tried to jump over. Our games uniform consisted of tucking our uniform blouse into our navy knickers – no track suits or leotards.

Uniform was very strict and should you be seen at any time outside school not wearing your hat (this would be a panama in the summer and a navy velour in the winter) you would be reported even by the townsfolk. We wore gym-slips and had special tassels awarded for deportment and gymnastics. Elocution was another important aspect.

May 1st was celebrated dancing round the maypole, sometimes chaotic, when the ribbons got entangled, and Empire Day was observed every year. In addition we had school outings; on one occasion we went by train to Derbyshire to visit Matlock and Bakewell near the High Peak. Another outing was by train to London for the day. We shared the train with the Boys' High School, but it was very carefully monitored with the communicating door firmly locked between the two schools.

There was great rivalry in matches between Houses and we regarded it to be a great honour to be chosen to play for one's House. Frequently I would look on the sports notice board to see if my name was on the list. I did manage to play for my House in tennis, cricket and netball, earning some 'colours'.

If the weather was hot we would have lessons in the garden under some of the trees: this was always popular, as sitting inside and hearing people enjoying their tennis could be very distracting.

I left School in the summer of 1939 aged 16, having taken School Certificate. All subjects had to be passed in one go to gain the certificate and there was no course work done beforehand."

Nancy Watkins, formerly Hale, writes:

"I WAS A SCHOLARSHIP GIRL, product of the old Bowdon Church of England School. I started at ACHS as Miss Howes Smith was coming to the end of her Headmistress days to be succeeded by Miss Drought. When Miss Whitwill, the deputy Head, was my Form Mistress, she told us one day, out of the blue, we must only marry for love. Why she said it I'll never know and I certainly never forgot it. Miss Colenutt took us for French, Miss Attenborough for German and Miss Bell for Domestic Science. Miss Whittle was awesome – I couldn't get my head round geometry; algebra I could manage a bit, and I was not too bad at arithmetic, but she told me one day I couldn't even do that.

We had two gym mistresses, Miss Muir and Miss Buchanan. We were coached to play tennis properly and had to pass a test if we wished to book and play with a friend on one of the courts after school.

It was always a lovely happy school which lives on in my memories."

With the growth in numbers, the House system was becoming unwieldy and was reorganised in 1938 into junior and senior branches. The former, consisting of the Lower Fourths and Removes, had a separate housemistress, two senior girls as head and deputy, and games captains from the Lower Fourths.

Connie Atkinson, formerly Lowe, recalls:

"OUR FAMILY MOVED FROM CREWE to the Timperley area in the summer of 1936. My father was a policeman and he was transferred to the CID at Altrincham after my eldest sister had matriculated.

The Massed Drill involving the whole School, 1932

I had passed the scholarship as it was then called and when we arrived in Timperley it took a short while to sort out a new school for me, and I was three days late starting. Miss Drought took me to my new classroom and introduced me to the other girls, and then she said, 'Shall I tell them what your father does – he's a detective.' There were a few gasps round the classroom and my face went very red.

After the first year we were put into Houses and I was in Grey. We used to have a dance in the school hall at Christmas – two Houses one night and two another. On one occasion we were doing the 'Paul Jones' – one House on the inside of the circle and the other on the outside. When the music stopped, we stopped and the person opposite you was your partner. I nearly died – Miss Drought was right opposite me so I turned and ran! Next day she sent for me – chatted to me and said she wouldn't have eaten me – so in a way it did me some good. Later, Miss Drought said I was the only person who'd gained her School Certificate having failed English, but it didn't beat me – when my children were doing their O levels I took my English again and got a grade B."

Margaret Jago was born in London, came to Cheshire aged 10, but only joined ACHS in 1937 as a very shy fourteen-year-old. She writes,

"I HAD NEVER BEEN IN A CLASS larger than ten pupils and to have 34 class mates was a real culture shock! I soon loved every minute of a busy day and every activity except lacrosse – in view of the school's reputation for the game that was a pity, but I was a hockey player and as soon as hockey was started I played for the first eleven or captained the second, but Miss Muir failed to teach me to vault any type of horse in the gym! Ten minutes of outdoor drill every morning was unexpected but physical fitness and good deportment were demanded of all of us. Miss Drought, herself, demonstrated the correct way to walk down a flight of stairs without looking down at one's feet! 'Heads up, girls!'

I stayed at ACHS for five years, leaving in 1942 to go to Bedford College, London to read Natural Sciences. I owe a great deal to Miss Sylvia Darke who came in 1937 as a new chemistry teacher and soon made a name for her high standards. High standards were the norm amongst the staff and most of them challenged us to do well. Biology with Miss Sylvia Jackson involved real specimens, 'hands-on', and I remember sixth form cycle rides to find different 'environments'. Our summer dresses were green with buff collars and cuffs, and as we approached some of the army bases she would say 'I'll go first, girls, because I'm not camouflaged.' As she loved bright colours that made sense. Miss Darke encouraged me to start Advanced – then Higher – Chemistry in the sixth form and she could be said to have started me on a very worthwhile career as a science teacher myself. In my last year at school she insisted that I went to the Altrincham Grammar School for Boys to do physics – very daring in those days!

Singing in the hall, last lesson on Fridays for the combined sixth forms, and in those days followed by voluntary attendance at the evening hymn to end the week, was taken by Miss Anderton, a visiting teacher of great repute. 'Excuse me, girls,' she would say when she needed a handkerchief which was kept in a pocket in her ample knickers. She would vanish briefly and return triumphant. She taught the whole school for the Speech Day songs and could persuade even the least musical to join in, though one of my friends who was tone-deaf had to mime her part! When Miss Porritt joined the staff in 1939 we were introduced to Musical Appreciation – a very new concept – and I was able to go to my first orchestral concert, given by the Hallé with Sir John Barbirolli conducting. By then it was war time so some of the players were in uniform, rejoining while on leave, blackout or no blackout, and trains or no trains!

I remember with delight the small group of science sixth formers who were also interested in music and in the choir, and the junior recorder band for which I played the accompaniment, let alone the House music competitions which also needed a pianist. I must have been very brave in those days. Our group was the bane of the staff room after school because we disappeared up to the music rooms in Treetops where we tried out homemade bamboo pipes, a drum, a flute and our voices, while one of us improvised on the piano! Even two floors down, it was not exactly conducive to using red pencils!

In 1939 it was decided that schools would not close for the summer holidays in case war was declared and evacuation necessary. The staff each took only two of the four weeks allowed as holiday and I was one of the team of sixteen-year-olds who cooked the school dinners under the direction of Miss Bell, the domestic science teacher. She took me on trust, as she had never taught me, and her training came in useful for many subsequent school and guide camps. Even today, I can hear her say 'Cold water for milky pans' and 'Never mix beetroot with green salad leaves' and I never have.

Of sixteen of us then in the Upper Sixth, fifteen won places at universities and the last one to Bedford College of Physical Education, so we did work hard at the more conventional side of our education. Formality in public, respect for others, politeness and consideration for the less fortunate were somehow instilled into us, probably by example rather than by rules.

Coming into this excellent school as a frightened and shy girl, teased for her London accent, I was encouraged and taught superbly, which stood me in good stead in my own teaching career. All this for £5 a term in fees and the cost of my text books."

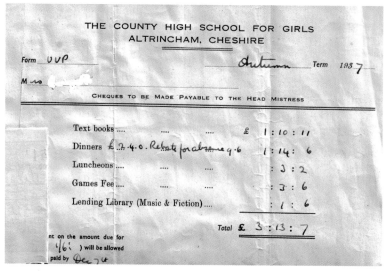

An account presented for books, meals and fees for the autumn term –
with a discount of 1s 6d (7½ p) for prompt payment

The late thirties were momentous years historically at home and abroad. The School functioned quietly and developed steadily throughout them all, celebrating the Silver Jubilee of King George V and Queen Mary in 1935; and after the death of the King in 1936 understanding the significance of the abdication of Edward VIII and the form and meaning of the coronation service of King George VI. Abroad dictators grew in power and the threat of war increased.

The first hint of war in the school records came on 26 July 1939, when Miss Drought reported that the School was subjected to gasmask fitting and drill before going home for the holidays. War had been declared on 3 September, a full week before the beginning of the autumn term, but staff were recalled early and on 7 September a local meeting of teachers "concerned with evacuation" was held, in the presence of the Director of Education, Dr Kellett. Soon the School had an air-raid warden, Mr Gregg, specially detailed to it, and air-raid practices were held frequently. Trenches and underground shelters were dug on the Devisdale for the School's use. At a practice held on 4 October the whole school was evacuated to these in five and a half minutes.

But it was many months before genuine air-raids began. Work and play, matches and examinations went on as usual, though a new charitable activity, preparing parcels of "comforts for the troops", came into being; much knitting of pullovers, socks, mittens, scarves and helmets was done. Service to others was always high on the list of priorities.

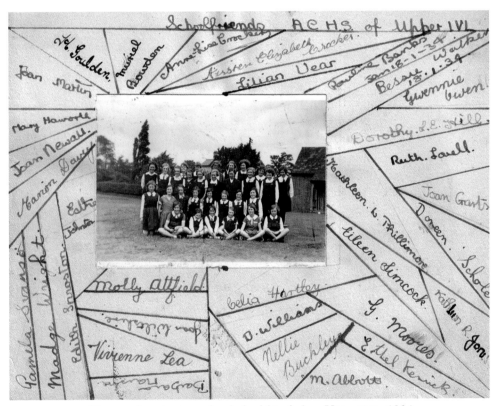

Photograph and autographs of school friends from Upper IVL, 1934

The 1940s

1940	July – Red Cross Day held at School
1940	Bombs fall in Bowdon and surrounding areas
1941	February – Dig for Victory campaign started
1941	Staff on fire watch duties at School
1941	Autumn term – farmers given help with potato picking
1942	Spring term – inter-house drama competition inaugurated
1943	American week
1944	Butler Education Act
1945	8 May – VE Day – the war in Europe ends
1945	11 May – Thanksgiving Service at St Margaret's Church
1947	School holidays abroad resumed
1947	December – *Hiawatha* performed at the Garrick Theatre
1949	The 1st Lacrosse XII competes in the National Schools Tournament in London
1949	The 1st Tennis VI competes in the Aberdare Cup at Wimbledon

CHAPTER 4
THE 1940S

In May 1940 the "phoney war" ended when Germany invaded the Low Countries. As a precaution the Education Authorities brought in revised attendance patterns, but otherwise life at school continued almost normally.

In July a display and sale was held to raise funds for the Red Cross and was described in the *School Annals*:

The Finnish Harvest Dance

"A DIMINUTIVE JUNIOR, carrying a Red Cross flag, led the figure marching, which was followed by exercises and folk dances. The Finnish harvest dance must have been difficult, not to say dangerous to perform, as the dancers were burdened by villainous-looking rakes and scythes. After the disappearance of these lethal weapons the juniors carried out an interesting and charming ballet.

In the interval the guests patronised the cafeteria, the ice cream parlour and various stalls. At one of these, a gentleman who had the welfare of the Red Cross more at heart than the claims of previous customers, nearly auctioned a pile of cakes which had been reserved and set aside.

After a vaulting display and Senior drill the display terminated in the school forming itself into a red cross by the sudden appearance of hitherto well concealed red and white handkerchiefs.

By the proceeds of the display together with money raised during the term by tennis tournaments and competitions, the Red Cross was richer by nearly one hundred and thirty four pounds."

The Senior Drill display with Miss Muir

The night of 28 August was disturbed with air raid warnings locally and the majority of girls did not go into school the next day until 10.00am. On the nights of 29 and 30 August heavy bombing occurred in Hale and Broadheath, with some bombs falling on Bowdon and Knutsford. Later on in December, Altrincham and Timperley were bombed.

The effect on the lives of the Staff and girls is described in the following selection of memories, the first from Joyce Rhodes, formerly Bullivant.

"EARLY ON A SUNNY September morning nearly seventy years ago I set off on a fifteen-minute cycle ride, schoolbag on my back and gas mask slung across my shoulders. I was on my way

Staff members on this photograph include:
Back row from left, Miss Davenport (5), Miss Whitwill (7), Miss Muir (8)
and on the front row, Miss Mary Bell (1)

from my home in Lower Peover, to my local station at Plumley to catch the 8.04am Cheshire Lines steam train. At the station I was to meet an older girl who would take me on the train to Hale. After a journey of twenty minutes we had a ten-minute walk up to my new school. As we got to the top of Cavendish Road I saw the gilded words 'THE COUNTY HIGH SCHOOL FOR GIRLS, BOWDON. HEADMISTRESS MISS D. M. DROUGHT M.A. (Oxon)' glistening in the sunlight on the imposing oak notice board inside the iron school gates. The year was 1940. I was ten years old and would walk through those gates every school day for the next eight years.

So the day began, but not before we had changed into our 'house shoes' – lightweight black – in an effort to keep the school floors as pristine as possible. Prayers in the Hall were taken with serried rows of girls sitting cross-legged on the polished parquet floor overlooked by each form mistress sitting on a chair in the central aisle adjacent to her form. Certain mistresses were renowned for their changes of hair colour over the weekend and it was a matter for intense speculation as to what 'Monday's colour' would be. As Miss Drought swept in from her study at the side of the Hall, her black gown flowing behind her, all immediately stood in respectful silence. After a hymn, prayer, bible reading and notices we filed off to our form-rooms to the accompaniment of a march played on the grand piano.

Lessons were 'talk and chalk' with information written up on a large blackboard fixed to the wall with a shelf at the bottom to hold various coloured chalks. Everything was laboriously written up on the board and then copied into our exercise books for future reference. At the end of each lesson the blackboard was cleaned with a duster by the blackboard monitor.

During the turbulent and traumatic times of the Second World War teaching was frequently interrupted by air raid drill or air raid warnings. Three consecutive rings on the school bell signalled these events: leave everything, line up, file to cloakroom, put on coat, take haversack – containing 'iron rations' (dried biscuits) – and gas mask from peg and proceed in strict formation out of the school grounds to the Devisdale where air raid shelters had been dug out on the former playing fields. Ironically the Devisdale had been requisitioned by the Army and was an ack-ack (anti aircraft) gun site. Quite a diversion for His Majesty's forces to watch tribes of girls trudging to the shelters whilst they were scanning the skies for any intruding enemy planes. So we descended into our dark, dank and extremely dismal places of safety. We sat on wooden benches along either side of the shelter until the 'All Clear' sounded its monotonous blast before returning to our form-rooms.

It was a marvel, being wartime, that with supplies severely rationed there was always a nourishing school dinner for us. Not that we particularly thought so at the time. A staple diet of mince, mash and mushy peas followed by rice pudding and rhubarb on some days with fish pie and cabbage on a Friday followed by sponge pudding and custard. Stew with potatoes, swedes and carrots was another dietary delight. Oh yes, I remember jam tart too. No choice. We ate what was put in front of us and the words of the Grace delivered by Miss Drought before each meal 'For what we are about to receive may the Lord make us truly thankful' had real significance.

Amazing too that our parents somehow managed to find enough clothing coupons for the school uniform though, of course, it meant that our casual wear was very much restricted. For winter we wore navy serge gymslips with box pleats from top to bottom, tied round the waist with a navy girdle fastened in a bow at the back. The gymslips had to be a maximum of two inches from the floor when kneeling, and were altered to meet this criterion by means of adjusting two buttons across the top of each shoulder thereby dropping the length as we grew upwards. White blouse and school tie underneath the top half and navy serge knickers with elastic round each leg below the belt. These knickers doubled up as shorts for gym and games due to clothes rationing. Our legs were kept warm with either fawn ribbed knee socks with green bands on the turnover or lisle stockings. My grandma knitted my knee socks from cotton yarn as, unlike wool, it was not 'on coupons'. Wide elastic garters kept them from slipping down and simultaneously promoted the future development of varicose veins. Black lace up shoes, navy blazer, navy raincoat, navy velour hat with a ribbon in the school colours sewn right round the brim and an elastic band under the chin to keep it on, completed the ensemble. Optional summer uniform was a regulation cotton dress, white ankle socks, green cardigan and a straw panama hat. Hats were compulsory at all times when travelling to and from school. Hair styles too were strictly monitored with collar length only allowed if tied back in bunches or plaits.

Top: Evelyn Forster; left: Joan Gilman; right: Joyce Bullivant

It goes without saying that the school had a fine academic and sporting record. Whilst all staff were totally dedicated, twinned at the top for me must come Miss Porritt and Miss Anderton, with both of whom I enjoyed a lifelong friendship. Their combined skills and empathy imbued in me a love of music and singing that has taken me to so many places and made me many friends. 'Andy', a mysterious and magical musician who, though unmarried, wore a fabulous dress ring on her wedding finger which always intrigued us. She had close links with the Schumann family, with whom in her younger days she had shared her affinity for music, and from whom she received this ring. Along with Miss Porritt she led us to success in music festivals. Not for us sitting in a stuffy room until it was our turn to compete: Andy always found us somewhere in the fresh air to wait and fill our lungs so that we wouldn't 'go

Miss Porritt and Miss Morrey, 1943

flat'. I well remember a time when we were competing at Chester Town Hall and were taken out on to a balcony to gulp in the fresh air. I also remember that we won! We sang *The Lotus Blossom doth Languish beneath the Splendour of Noon* by Schumann and *Spring doth let her colours fly* by Hugo Wolf. Miss Porritt, as always, accompanied – an art much underestimated. Together they masterminded the staged musical production of *Hiawatha's Wedding Feast* which the school presented for six nights in 1947 at the Garrick Theatre, Altrincham, from 1–6 December. The scenery and costumes were all made at school.

Another extra-curricular activity was the annual School Fête when a Saturday in the summer was given over to fund-raising. Afterwards, girls had to make an appeal for money raised to go to their particular good cause and proceeds were then divided up according to the voting. I remember making my appeal in front of the whole school for some of the money to go to the restoration fund of my local church at Lower Peover which was being ravaged by the death watch beetle. I was lucky and did get a sizeable chunk but the NSPCC came very low on the list and though Miss Drought had to stand by the voting she made it quite clear that the needs of children should always come first. Food for thought indeed. In passing I also recall one of her oft-used pieces of advice: 'Girls, never agree to anything containing the word etcetera.' I have always remembered that and acted accordingly.

My school days passed happily, though they were by no means 'the happiest days of my life' as the old adage goes. I have recently disposed of my School reports in an effort to reduce the clutter in my drawers. They brought much mirth to my children, especially seeing such candid comments as 'I have had many girls who cannot draw but I have never had a girl who will not draw' – Miss Turner (art); 'I do not know how Joyce can study this for 4 years and know so little' – Miss Furness (maths). On the other side of the coin I gathered in prizes for subjects that really interested me, particularly English and history, and still recall the expression on Miss Bell's face when informing her that for my domestic science prize I had chosen *English Social History* by G M Trevelyan. I was of course expected to choose *Mrs Beeton's Cookery Book* – the Delia Smith of her day.

So what elements of my education have sustained me through my life? Above all, three Latin words on my school badge: FORTITER, FIDELITER, FELICITER. Not meaning much to me as a schoolgirl, now in my eightieth year I am still proving their relevance. They form a constant reminder of the privilege it was to attend The County High School for Girls, along with my two sisters Ruth (who became Deputy Head Girl) and Janet, under the stewardship of Miss D M Drought MA (Oxon) and her dedicated staff."

Permilla MacLaren, formerly Johnson, recounts:

"AT THE AGE OF FIVE I sat a very simple test to see if they would accept me, and in September 1934 at just six years old I entered the school by the very imposing steps and the very heavy front door where I was met by the Head Girl, Alice Chorley, who later, when I was fourteen, was my biology teacher. She took me to Form Two where the teacher was a lovely gentle lady called Miss Langley. In my first year at school I was in awe of everything, morning prayer, milk in a little bottle

Miss Colenutt, Miss Atkinson, Miss Langley, 1943

with a straw and a chocolate digestive biscuit, big girls wearing badges of prefects with coloured girdles and tassels on the back. The next year I moved up into Lower Third with Miss Atkinson, another very kindly lady, where I was introduced to sewing. We made a doll's crib out of a wooden tomato box, painted it and lined it and made all the bedding by hand. Another year and up into Upper Three. Miss Davenport, as I remember, a young and very modern-looking lady, pretty strict. There we made a small needle case showing the different embroidery stitches. I still have it in my sewing box today, over seventy years later.

Mr Spilsbury, 1936

Then up again to the BIG school, a class called Remove where we were joined by a lot of girls from other schools and the serious stuff started. I remember my introduction to French with Miss Colenutt. We had to take a small hand mirror to school and look at our lips so that we would learn to exaggerate them like the French do, and we learnt a song *Sur le Pont d'Avignon*.

During the war days we knitted squares for blankets, collected paper, made do and mended, but in spite of clothing coupons we all went to school in full correct uniform. When you had outgrown an item you took it to Miss Seed, a very tall lady who dealt with all sorts of things; one was school gardens, helping Mr Spilsbury, the school caretaker, and another was exchanging uniform for a larger size when necessary.

Other vivid memories are of domestic science, with Miss Bell, whom we all worshipped. We learnt to clean, wash, iron, cook with a limited amount of rations available, and make Christmas pudding sweetened with carrots to save sugar. I still refer to my cookery book 'Cookery and Nutrition', with its royal blue cover. In my last year at school I volunteered for fire watch which meant you slept overnight on mattresses on the floor in the Staff Room. The Staff Room had always intrigued us when standing outside the door with its dark green curtain covering the window – wondering what went on in there – and now at sixteen I was allowed to go inside!

Miss Seed, 1943

So many memories with ten years at one school, my only school. It certainly moulded me for the rest of my days."

Sybil Norcott, formerly Shacklady, tells of her rebellion and the eventual successful outcome:

"HOW DIFFERENT THE CHANGE from a village school which had a dark green curtain dividing the babies from the older pupils to being in Miss Langley's form, each with our very own desk. The journey to ACHS was at first very tedious, having to cycle to Dunham Massey station, take the train to Broadheath, bus to The Downs, then walk up the hill to my new school.

It was in this form in 1938 that 'House Beautiful' was introduced to us. Prefects visited the classroom each week, never on the same day, to check every desk for neatness and judge the flower arrangements, giving marks throughout the term. Mum loved her gardens at the farm and I was lucky enough to be able to take flowers, sometimes exotic ones, and had been taught at home how to arrange them. With Miss Langley checking our desks, and flowers in each window, the 'House Beautiful' picture took pride of place on our wall many times.

The following year we all moved next door to be delighted by Miss Atkinson's reading, in many and various intonations, *The Wind in the Willows*. It is still my favourite book because I can still hear in my mind Ratty, Toad of Toad Hall, and the evil characters. On to Miss Davenport and a room in the New Wing. School was beginning to be more serious. Homework had to be on time! We had different members of staff for many more subjects. I have to admit I had favourites; I loved geography with Miss Hallsworth, sport with Miss Muir, biology with Miss Chorley. Poor Miss Chorley, she only had to mention some grub or caterpillar and with the help of Dad, who was a great naturalist, next day she would be presented with a live specimen.

When I was twelve Mum became almost bedfast and I learnt to bake and cook, even churn butter. I was now allowed to cycle the ten miles to school, and having sorted out home before leaving, sometimes fell asleep during a lesson if it was not a favourite. This was the time rebellion set in and I was considered just plain naughty. A hiding place was the Dome Chapel for I played wag, truthfully to have a sleep.

Domestic science was the subject I loved the most. Miss 'DomSci' Bell used to swap recipes, for Mum was a super cook, having been brought up by an aunt and uncle who managed the 'Home Farm' for Lord Sefton. She was expected to help in the kitchen when the Seftons entertained royalty. It was my dream to become as good a cook. This was shattered when Miss Drought said I must choose another subject as I could learn to cook at home and my father was paying for my education. Music it had to be instead of my dream – hence the rebellion.

I can't say how often I sat on one of those straight-backed chairs outside Miss Drought's room waiting to be chastised. I remember well the time she told me, 'You are a complete failure, a total disaster.' My confidence was shattered. In contrast, Miss

Miss Whittle, Miss Whitwill, Miss Drought, Miss Bell, 1943

Whitwill's approach to my naughtiness was completely different. There was a play at the Garrick Theatre and a pal and I knew about the matinée on a Wednesday. Helen Cherry, Brian Rix and Joan Sanderson were in the cast, so off we went. Little did we know that Miss Whitwill was sitting a few rows behind us. Next day we were 'invited' to her room. 'Where were you both yesterday afternoon?' 'We went to the Garrick, Miss.' 'Well, be naughty my lambs, but always tell the truth. Off with you, but never again,' and she patted us both and smiled.

I did achieve my dream but by a different route – through the WI. I became the youngest National Federation of WIs' judge in cookery and preserves at the age of twenty, and went on to become a National demonstrator. Perhaps some of you remember ITV's *Farmhouse Kitchen* in the days before autocues and when we did our own chopping and preparing without helpers, in readiness for the live programmes. My proudest moment was being chosen to demonstrate at Earl's Court with the Queen sitting in the front row.

Thank you, Miss Bell, for those early years, for if I ever say 'Aerate it well' when making pastry, there is usually someone in the audience who asks 'Did you go to ACHS when we had two ounces of flour and one ounce of fat in one of those huge yellow mixing bowls?' 'Yes, I did.' "

Miss Drought noted in 1941:

"AT THE REQUEST OF MR YATES, the Regional Agricultural Officer in Manchester, parties of about 30 girls each day went to help with potato lifting at farms near Warburton and Knutsford. Each girl worked for 6d [2½p] per hour and most of them worked 7½ hours a day. Some mistresses went round the farms day by day to see how the girls were getting on."

In 1943 she noted:

"IN THE SUMMER HOLIDAYS parties of girls worked on farms at Knutsford, Tabley and Plumley potato and pea picking. Others went to Dunham Massey, Broadheath, Rostherne,

Little Budworth, Timperley, Statham, Ormskirk, High Legh, Altrincham and Evesham. Altogether they did the equivalent of 825 days work."

Marian Wood writes first hand about war work on the land:

"IN THE SUMMER OF 1941 senior girls worked on Brunt's Farm at Knutsford, mainly on harvesting early potatoes. Starting at 9.00 am, joining the workforce of mainly young mothers from the village, work continued until 4.00 pm with a break for lunch. We provided our own picnic lunches and much envied were the proud owners of Oxo tins to carry them in. If for some reason work continued until 6.00 pm you were given a meat pie for sustenance, through some Ministry of Food dictum. One or two girls continued working at Brunt's over weekends in the autumn, helping to harvest turnips for cattle feed and to lay tile drains."

Brunt's Farm, Knutsford, 1941
Back row: ? , Joy Hellier, Betty Eltoft; middle row: Peggy Spruce, Joan Pickford, Joyce Jackson, Olga Ranson;
front row: Deirdre Wilson, Dorothy Bonson, Dorothea Fletcher, June Lawson, Marian Wood,
Joan Smith, Peter Brunt, Robert Brunt, Bunty Pycroft, ? , Barbara Brunt (farmer's daughter);
seated: Keith Scott

Some other memories from Marian are:

"AS A VERY NERVOUS ten-year-old I led the parade at Speech Day on to the stage at the Regal Cinema as winner of a bursary, considered more important in terms of promise than all the other awards. Mrs Bromley-Davenport, a very large overpowering eccentric personage and wife of the Lord Lieutenant, was the presenter. After that nothing at ACHS was ever as terrifying.

Firefighting lessons were held after school and on one occasion Miss Muir 'accidentally' showered DMD (as Miss Drought was affectionately known) whilst demonstrating the use of a stirrup pump.

The years at ACHS were made memorable by some inspirational teachers: Miss Darke and Miss Wood in science, Miss Porritt who gave me a lifelong pleasure in classical music, and Miss Whitwill for superb history lessons. Compared with other schools we were provided with a well-balanced education so that whichever direction we took after school the basic raft of subjects were all in place."

Miss Muir, Miss Davenport, Miss Chorley,
Miss Turner, 1943

Many others who were at School in this era, Betty Wilkinson, Margaret Bone, formerly Phillips, Dorothea Parker (Fletcher), Pat Jones (Crickmore), Winifred Lang (Searle), Iris Cooper (McEvoy), Jean Wearne (Morton), Brenda Harrison (Lawrenson), Joyce Wilkinson (Allsop), Lorna Gartside (Farquhar-Young), and Jean Frith (Ferguson) have all written recounting similar memories and tributes, with Anne Davies (Lambie) additionally painting a delightful picture of her first visit to School in May 1938:

> "THERE WERE MASSES OF WALLFLOWERS in the beds under the windows on either side of the front door and to this day the scent of these flowers recalls that spring afternoon. There was a bowl of wallflowers on the table in the library where I took the examination for entrance to the Preparatory Department, and the whole atmosphere was warm and friendly – a pleasant change from the rather austere Scottish school which I had attended. I must have acquitted myself reasonably well, for the next day I was installed in the Upper Third under the care of Miss Davenport. Later that year Margaret, my sister, aged seven, entered the Second Form. The two little girls from Scotland were made very welcome."

Margaret Dunton, formerly Pybus, recalls:

> "I STARTED IN 1936 when I was seven and remember when going for an interview the previous year I had to read a passage. I was very anxious about my expression not realising they wanted to know if I could read at all!
>
> When the war came both the bombing and seeing Manchester burning quite upset me so my parents took both my sister and me to Llandudno, and I went to school at Loreto Convent in 1940 for two or three years. That school was very different – not academic – but concentrated on etiquette and music and has given me much to compare since.
>
> On my return to Altrincham I continued to the Upper Sixth and became deputy Head Girl. Miss Porritt and Miss Anderton stimulated my interest in music so I nearly took this up as a career, but decided medicine was a better bet and music could be a lovely hobby, which it is to this day. Miss Drought took Assembly each morning and I can hear her saying some prayers so beautifully in my mind now. I think we were very fortunate to have her. I also remember Miss Whitwill, the Deputy Head, and a very forceful character. Miss Whittle taught me maths, which I loved, and Miss Chorley biology. As I wanted to read medicine I had to do science A levels, so having no members of staff to teach these subjects, two of us went down to the Boys' School for chemistry and physics.

Margaret Dunton,
2009

> I can remember in the Lower Sixth getting hold of a double bass which I played most lunch times and encouraged friends in the form to sing with me like *Mammy's Little Baby Loves Shortening Bread*. I was then summoned to Miss Drought's room to be told they wanted to make me a prefect but I would have to stop this nonsense – so I did!
>
> Thinking about all these pleasant memories makes me feel how fortunate I was to have had such a good education in spite of the war."

JULY 1947 – UPPER VI

Margaret Moxon, Barbara Lewis, Veronica Byers, Gillian Knight, Audrey Gardner, Winnie Searle
and Gwen Hallam
Joan Maddison, Shirley Proctor, Barabara Mountfield, Dorothy Harrison, Joan Bexon, Margaret
Pybus, Audrey Willis, Margery Moore and Sheila Ridley.
Betty Ridgeway, June Beswick, Ruth Duncan – Miss Drought – Mary Titterington, June Beattie
and Jane Marsh.

Like Margaret Dunton, June Marshall, formerly Beattie, transferred to a boarding school in Llandudno from 1940 to 1942 and she remembers:

"WHEN I CAME BACK TO ALTRINCHAM there were many new pupils from the South whose parents had been moved out of London as Government and other employers were decentralised.

Three things I recall particularly – doing our School Certificate in Treetops while the school celebrated the end of the war in Europe with patriotic songs going on below – joining the largest sixth form ever – and going with Margaret Pybus to the Boys' School for chemistry for Higher School Certificate. This was an innovation and great fun!"

Win Kent, formerly Nuttall, describes her contribution to the war effort:

"IN DECEMBER 1942 we were asked to volunteer to help at Altrincham Post Office with the Christmas mail and I reported for duty thinking I would be sorting mail, but oh no, it was actually delivering the cards and parcels. I remember going with the post-lady on the train to Timperley and then walking down Riddings Road to learn the route I would do on my own from the next day. The postbag was very heavy and I did it all Christmas week, including Christmas morning when the dinner had to be delayed until I arrived home."

Joyce Molyneux, formerly Ormerod, remembers wartime too.

"AN 'AMERICA WEEK' WAS HELD when we were all expected to study American history, geography and literature and produce a folder of the consequent work. As a result I can still recite the greater part of Lincoln's Gettysburg address!

But we were young and the war didn't dominate our lives and the School had so many other interests to offer. Greek dancing was in fashion and we all had to flit across the hall floor in our little green

Win Kent, 2006

Joyce Molyneux, 2000

dance slips once a week. Then there was the obligatory daily drill on the hard courts behind the school, conducted by an energetic Miss Muir, and sometimes skipped by less energetic and hardy pupils! I did, however, enjoy the organised snowball fights arranged by Miss Muir, during the exceptionally harsh winter of 1943.

Unfortunately the war restricted out-of-school activities, but for a while there was a school Guide group of which I was a member. The only school trip I recall was a visit to Oxford with Miss Boshier and I was completely overcome by the magnificence and beauty of the colleges and came home with the absolute determination that that was where I wanted to be.

As for our academic education I could not have attended a better school. My father had already given me a burgeoning love of history and this was fully stimulated by Miss Whitwill's fascinating lessons – I can still see her swinging the sleeve of her gown to indicate that the answer had something to do with money. The other teacher who most influenced me was Miss Jean Cole who encouraged me to write and gave me a lasting love of English literature. I have been eternally grateful to them both. Without them and the other excellent staff who taught me I would never have achieved my place at Oxford at the end of the war.

ACHS was a gracious school in every way. Good manners were insisted on and good posture too – I was extremely proud to receive my green deportment tassels from Miss Drought, herself a very stately Headmistress. She presided daily over a full school assembly and, as she was Irish, we all learned *St Patrick's Breastplate* to sing on 17 March. She could be very stern, but behind the austere face lurked a sneaky sense of humour. One day I was summoned to her study after the regrettable misdemeanour of skipping the singing lesson with a friend one Friday afternoon – we were found on the market ground by Miss Morrey! After giving us a fearful reprimand she couldn't resist a positively cheeky grin as we left the room. The main buildings were gracious as well, more solidly built than the average modern school. I was hugely impressed, when I first attended, by the magnificent Hall: its acoustics are dreadful, but its tall windows overlooking the terrace and rear lawn are as splendid as I have seen in any school. All in all I owe ACHS and its staff a huge debt of gratitude. I am sure that it has benefited hundreds of girls since my time and will continue to do so long into the future."

Brenda Lomax, formerly Millet, recalls other aspects of the war effort:

"ONE EXTRA-CURRICULAR ACTIVITY developed by Miss Muir and Miss Hallsworth was gardening. As part of the Dig For Victory campaign a sizeable plot was cleared on the playing field at South Downs Road. With her usual thoroughness and energy 'Jock' Muir held meetings of a small band of those willing to turn up at weekends to help in such tasks as double digging, fertilising, planting out, weeding and harvesting. This led to growing vegetables for school meals which were

Miss Ashworth and Miss Cole, 1943

welcomed as our diet was much in need of improvement.

Every term each one of us was weighed and measured by Miss Muir in the gym. If someone lost weight letters were sent home, and it turned out that many people were still hungry after lunch at school. Dear Miss Morrey (my maths mistress at that time – great fun as she livened the lessons with funny stories from a book of jokes!) declared that after school lunch she felt in need of a good hunk of bread. After that things improved a bit – as far as the poor cooks could manage on the

Lunchtime outside the New Wing, 1942.
Brenda Millet is on the left on the back row.

rations allowed. However, when a visiting speaker came to talk to us all one day about the plight of people suffering cold and starvation in occupied Greece, and another person told us about the effects of the Malta blockade, these were very sobering thoughts and made us realise that so many others were much worse off than us.

Evacuees from a Manchester school shared our premises for a time. Suzanne in our form and her little sister came as refugees from Czechoslovakia. Many girls must have had fathers or brothers in the war – and when Liverpool and Manchester were badly bombed, people close to home were affected. Later, when the 'doodlebugs' descended on London and the south, we met up with a new wave of evacuees.

Later US troops came to be camped on the Devisdale, and once an American officer came to talk to us about life 'over there'. Need I say he was a very popular diversion (and had a strong Texan accent).

During winter, with fuel shortages, the heating of school became a problem. We ourselves were kept warm with many activities – gym and games, and daily drill involving much marching and counter-marching. Miss Seed busied herself with raking the lawns, groundsmen being in short supply. Indoors all the staff wore their academic gowns, beneath which Miss Whitwill declared she had layers and layers of woollen garments which could always be peeled off if necessary. There were extra-severe winters and Altrincham's George V Pool froze long and hard enough for us to learn how to skate."

The Dig for Victory campaign was taken very seriously and enormous amounts of produce were harvested and used to supplement school dinners. Areas of ground were set aside on the playing fields at Bowdon and Dome Chapel and cultivation started in February 1941.

Elizabeth Clow records in the *School Magazine* for that year that by October their efforts had yielded

"CABBAGES 900 LBS, cauliflowers – a few, lettuces 700, peas 60 lbs, sugar peas – on trial, runner beans 94 lbs, broad beans 33 lbs, kohlrabi 50 lbs, carrots 100 lbs, beetroot 100 lbs, turnips 80 lbs, potatoes 560 lbs, marrow 330 lbs, tomatoes 20 lbs, and herbs. Still to be harvested: cabbages, savoys, Brussels sprouts, kale, broccoli, swedes, carrots, turnips, beetroot, potatoes, parsnips, artichokes and spinach. Members of the School may be justly proud of this result in the garden's first year of existence, and the knowledge that in so short a time the country's food production has been so increased in our part of the world."

Miss Hallsworth, 1936

In 1943 the *School Magazine* records:

"MISS HALLSWORTH AND MISS MUIR, with the aid of 36 helpers, have provided us regularly, several times a week, with vegetables from the school garden. Nearly 1500 lbs of cabbage have been supplied this year already, and at our Harvest Festival there were eighteen varieties of vegetables which had been grown at School."

Jean Clark, formerly Horner, recounts:

"WE KEPT RABBITS on the playing fields by the Dome Chapel. One day these creatures disappeared only to reappear a few days later at lunch time. Miss Drought gave us a lecture about food shortages and we were ordered to eat our rabbit stew and be grateful. Every mouthful choked us and to this day I have never again eaten rabbit.

Miss Bell, domestic science, was a favourite of mine. I remember the vivid yellow dried egg which, strangely enough, I got quite used to. I also think of the time we made Christmas cakes with sago as one of the ingredients – they were absolutely ghastly. Dear Miss Bell also taught me to sew. Who can possibly forget making the green knickers with elastic around the legs? I never wore mine – one size fitted all! I also knitted a one-piece woollen bathing costume – no bikinis in those days. Disaster – the first dip in the sea at Llandudno and it ended up round my ankles!

I enjoyed being in the school choir and Miss Porritt was an excellent teacher. She joined the school in September 1939, at the same time as me, and was always elegantly dressed in navy blue with matching court shoes. We didn't think much about fashion in those days, being eleven years old, but she seemed to stand out in the crowd."

Isobel Watson, formerly Parker, remembers:

"IN SEPTEMBER 1939, the very month and year war was declared, I began my schooling at ACHS. Miss Atkinson was my form mistress and I remember her as a big, very kind, Irish lady who read us Irish folk tales. When the laburnum tree was in flower she took us into the garden to draw it in pastel – a medium we normally never used. I thought this was wonderful – my very first experience of outdoor sketching!

Miss Drought, the Headmistress, was also Irish and she and Miss Atkinson were always presented with a posy of shamrock on St Patrick's Day. Miss Drought was an excellent Headmistress – strict, but fair and very ready to talk to you and praise you when you deserved it! After we assembled in our form rooms for the register we marched into the Hall for Prayers – always taken by Miss Drought. She chose some of the loveliest prayers ever written by St Ignatius Loyola, Thomas à Kempis, Erasmus and from the *Book of Common Prayer*. Looking back I think she had a real feeling for the beauty of language; the lesson was always taken from the Authorised Version of the Bible.

At the beginning of the war girls from other lands would appear; some stayed for the duration, others disappeared as mysteriously as they had arrived. There was Eva, a German Jewess, a girl of about fourteen, clever and placed in a top stream. I don't think anyone really got to know her; she was billeted on two elderly spinster ladies who lived across the road from my home. Ginette came from Belgium – she was in my form, eight or nine years old and very pretty. She curtsied when spoken to and on receiving anything from an adult – the staff were charmed by her manners and she was liked by us all. Finally we had three girls from Guernsey who remained at school for the duration of the war – Jean, who became a close friend, Moira and June – I liked all three.

The war affected the school in many different ways. First there were the air raid warnings: our departure to the air raid shelters, all 500 of us, was a most orderly affair. Miss Whitwill, in tin hat and mackintosh, would stand in the middle of the road as each form crossed over to the Devisdale. As you can imagine the first thing we did on getting into the shelter was to eat the chocolate from our iron rations! There was a paper shortage and in every new exercise book we pencilled one line at the top and two lines at the bottom of every page. Periodically gas masks had to be checked during lessons. I never heard the staff complain. Most of them had to haul out their old bikes to come to school (no petrol for cars, except for Miss Porritt who lived some distance away in Wilmslow). I can see Miss Whitwill now, her bicycle basket weighted down with thirty essays, swaying dangerously on hers!

The war even affected, but in a pleasant way, our mid-morning Swedish drill on the hard court with Miss Muir – as we marched we sang the war songs of the Tommies – in particular I remember *Pack up your Troubles in your Ol' Kit Bag*.

War or no war, our school ran like clockwork and as I look back I am amazed how nothing appeared to disturb the smooth running of the place. Our education never suffered and was second to none. Perhaps due to the war the staff remained much the same. My favourite teacher was Miss Whitwill. She was a remarkable person and a gifted teacher and in her hands history came alive (it wasn't a case of boring dates and wars, as so many of my contemporaries spoke of their history lessons). Starting with the Anglo-Saxons and the monasteries we studied the different reigns and were given an all-round picture of each one of them; not only did we look at the kings and queens, their wars and the way they governed but we heard about the outstanding people of their day – soldiers, sailors, explorers, writers, philanthropists, artists and architects, musicians and actors. As you can imagine she held our attention completely. I never forgot the advice she gave me when I left school to start my training to be an art teacher – 'Remember, firm but friendly.'

Miss Jean Cole was another very inspiring teacher. I loved her lessons and I can remember everything we studied with her – literature of every type, from Kipling's poem *Boots*, *Pride and Prejudice* and Stevenson's *Travels with a Donkey* to *Romeo and Juliet* and *She Stoops to Conquer*, and enjoyed them all. I remember her telling me never to waste my time reading rubbish – those were her exact words. I was *very* sorry when she left. Her sister Nancy joined the staff shortly afterwards to teach Latin. Almost overnight we enjoyed the subject, though I was never good at it. She was a 'live wire' and seemed such a happy person.

Music played an important part in our school lives. We started every session with singing exercises, scales and arpeggios, Miss Anderton teaching us how to breathe correctly and use our voices. I have loved the *Messiah* ever since we sang parts of it – another highlight much later was Coleridge-Taylor's *Hiawatha's Wedding Feast*, which we performed publicly. I look back and think how fortunate we were to have a professional singer to introduce us to a wealth of lovely music.

Isobel Watson, 2008

But to go back to my very early days – we learnt to read music with Miss Porritt, but I was glad when aural training gave way to playing the descant recorder. Miss Porritt arranged for Carl Dolmetsch to come to talk to us and to play his various recorders. Later he gave several public concerts combining strings, recorders and percussion. Miss Dunnington, who was the leader and conductor of the Northern Women's String Orchestra, came to School to teach the 'string' pupils – for a while I was one of them. I loved the violin and she was a super teacher and a very nice person.

I loved art, especially in the early years with Miss Turner; she was a gifted teacher, giving us imaginative subjects to draw and paint. We worked in a purpose-built art room with a small room off it containing a sink, the palettes, powder paint and brushes. Good reproductions of the Old Masters and other artists were hung throughout the school. I especially remember Breughel's *Village Wedding* in one of the New Wing's form rooms and Holbein's *Ambassadors* behind the platform in the Hall – such a good way of introducing children to great art. In my career as an art teacher I haven't come across this very often in schools or colleges.

Finally, I have always loved books and reading, and to go to a school which had its own lending library was almost too good to be true – aged ten I haunted the place. I went right through the animal section, took each *Children's Encyclopaedia* out in turn, and the discovery of George MacDonald's *The Princess and Curdie* and the *Princess and the Goblin* was like finding treasure."

Inger Serb, formerly Larsen, recalls:

"SCHOOL DURING THE 1940s was school during the war. The lawn tennis courts faced the threat of being dug up unless we could show that we could reach the Devisdale at a trot within a certain time. The Devisdale won and two semi-buried Nissen huts covered in grass became our shelters. I only remember one visit made to them when we sat inside on long benches. It was cold, dank and smelly and our feet were nearly ankle-deep in water.

I volunteered to dig for victory on the Bowdon playing field and remember the vegetable allocated to our form was my least favourite – Brussels sprouts – which were harvested in the frost and cold of winter.

We also did knitting for a Norwegian ship. One morning at prayers Miss Drought announced that School was adopting a Norwegian merchant ship, *SS Erviken*. 'We have a Norwegian girl in the school,' she said. 'Where is Inger?' I stood up. 'You are Norwegian aren't you, Inger?' 'No, Miss Drought,' I replied, 'I am English.' At this the whole school dissolved in laughter and henceforth I was known as English Inger. We sat after school on summer evenings on the front lawn knitting things in grey wool for our ship's crew. My best effort was a pair of knitted wristlets – not something you see nowadays! – but I like to think they kept a seaman's wrist warm in the cold of the Arctic winter.

We were very lucky during the latter war years as we were able to go to Saturday matinées at Manchester Opera House where we saw Donald Wolfit in many Shakespearean roles, and Sadler's Wells Ballet with young dancers who were later to become world famous. Also our first taste of opera – and I have had a love of the theatre ever since.

Looking back I realise how fortunate we were during those years. Although aware of the horrors of war and the loss of fathers and brothers, at school we were privileged to be in a safe and secure environment which gave us continuing stability during those difficult years. Thank you, School."

Annette Page was at School for two years before being auditioned by Ninette de Valois in Manchester and awarded a scholarship to the Royal Ballet School in 1944. In 1950 she became a member of the Royal Ballet Touring Company (then known as Sadler's Wells

Annette Page in Swan Lake

Theatre Ballet), rising to be a principal ballerina with the Royal Ballet Company (Sadler's Wells Ballet) in 1955. Her roles included *The Firebird*, Princess Aurora in *Sleeping Beauty*, Odette–Odile in *Swan Lake,* Giselle, Lise in *La Fille Mal Gardée*, Juliet in *Romeo and Juliet* and *Cinderella*. In 1957 she married Ronald Hynd, also a principal of the Royal Ballet, and they were unique in that, as a married couple, they danced all the great classical roles with the company.

Annette recalls her time spent at ACHS:

"I EITHER WALKED OR CYCLED to school every day and particularly remember my form mistress Miss Atkinson, who was very sweet, Miss Davenport and the inspirational Miss Porritt for music. Although I was only there a short while, it was a very happy time at a very caring school. I send my congratulations to the School in its centenary year and every good wish for further success in the years to come."

Doreen Walmsley, formerly Garner, recalls:

" 'OWZAT?' As a rookie umpire, I gingerly raised my index finger and waited for a cry of protest from Miss Muir. None came. Miraculously, I had got it right.

It was a hot, sunny day in 1942. Miss Muir was taking the Lower Fourth for cricket on the South Downs Road playing field. I didn't really like cricket then. The ball was so hard! But Miss Muir insisted we learned all the fielding positions and the rules of the game. In 1945 when I went to watch the Victory Test at Old Trafford between England and Australia I understood what was going on. My great love of the game was born. I have been hugely grateful to Miss Muir ever since.

We wartime pupils were very patriotic, knitting gloves and scarves for the men on board our adopted ship, remembering them in our prayers. It was a desperately sad morning when Miss Drought broke the news at Assembly that the *SS Erviken* had gone down, all lives presumably lost. We had to learn to cope with such tragedies. Later, we adopted another ship *SS Cefn-y-Bryn*. In May 1945 our prayers were answered: hostilities in Europe drew to a close.

As I left school in the July, the protective nets were coming off the windows, the shelters on the Devisdale were abandoned. School was no longer a High School, but a Grammar. It was all going to be so different, but I felt sure the heart of the school would remain the same. I do believe it has."

Doreen Garner and Betty Unsworth, 1946

1944 was a landmark year in the field of education when the Butler Education Act came into being. The Act, named after the Conservative politician R A Butler, made secondary

Miss Drought

education at a grammar school, technical school or secondary modern school free for all pupils. To assess which pupils should attend which type of school, the Common Entrance Examination, or 11+, was introduced. The Act renamed the Board of Education as the Ministry of Education, giving it greater powers and a bigger budget, ended fee-paying for state secondary schools and enforced the division between primary (5–11-year-olds) and secondary (11–15-year-olds) that many local authorities had already introduced. Compulsory prayer was introduced into all state-funded schools on a daily basis, a feature that remained until this clause was amended in 1988.

The Act was not implemented until 1945 as much advance preparation was required. The effect on School was a change of name to Altrincham County Grammar School for Girls. The junior department closed and no more girls were admitted under the age of eleven years. The junior school staff were gradually absorbed into work with older pupils. Fees were abolished.

A snippet from Miss Drought's annual letter to the *Old Girls' Society News* shows how School was developing and settling back to normality after the war effort. She wrote:

"1945 OPENS WITH 580 GIRLS, too many for comfort. There is a need to rent a large room at the Congregational Church next door into which we might overflow for aural training and singing lessons. Now that the black-out has become a dim-out we have been able to revive the Union Society. We had an Irish evening recently at which we laughed a great deal and enjoyed ourselves very much, as we still do in our school where faces may change but the spirit of friendliness remains the same."

Some particular highlights recalled by Shirley Hill were:

"PREFECTS' INVESTITURE WAS HELD on the first Tuesday of each term. After a reading from Romans and Bunyan's Pilgrim hymn, Miss Drought gave the prefects their badges saying to each in turn, 'I give you this badge in trust and I believe that you will serve the School Bravely, Faithfully and Cheerfully.'

We had an inter-form wild flower competition; each week, every form had to produce different flower species with correct botanical identification. I remember guiltily nursing one stem each of butterwort and a wild orchid back from the Lake District – but it was all in the name of science and for the prestige of LVA.

Union Society meetings for senior girls were held every other Friday when, after tea, we had talks and discussions on a variety of subjects. I particularly remember two meetings: one on blood grouping and transfusion and the other on Louis Pasteur and the beginnings of the science of microbiology.

A small group of science sixth-formers went to the Boys School for chemistry and physics and some of the boys came to us for botany and zoology. The latter two were my favourite subjects. I enjoyed the microscopy and dissection work but my worst memory of these is the overpowering smell of dogfish in formalin. At least it prepared me for my eventual career as a pathologist but thankfully the formalin was not then combined with dead fish.

I was very pleased and surprised that when I went up to Cambridge and talked to girls from a wide range of private and state educational backgrounds, none had happier memories or more gratitude and admiration for their school than I had."

Shirley Hill

In November 1947, unusually, Miss Whitwill wrote the annual letter to the *Old Girls' Society News* explaining that,

" THIS YEAR I AM WRITING the News Sheet letter instead of Miss Drought. The reason for this innovation is a very simple one – Miss Drought has a great many things to do and very little free time in which to do them. I have very few things to do and a great deal of time in which to do them. Miss Drought's lack of free time is largely owing to the cantata *Hiawatha's Wedding Feast* which is the all-absorbing interest at School at the moment, and which 147 of the VI's and UV's are performing at the Garrick Playhouse in the first week of December. Of course the brunt of the work falls on Miss Anderton and Miss Porritt for the singing, Miss Midgley for the dancing and Miss Colenutt for the miming, but every mistress has a finger in the pie and Miss Drought all her fingers and thumbs involved; but we hope and expect that she will pull out a grand plum for the School.

Now, why I have so much free time is a different story. Playing in a hockey match for the Staff against the 1st XI, I most foolishly fell down and broke the neck of my right femur. So here I am, encased in plaster and forced to be inactive for three months, and glad to be whiling away some of the time writing to you."

In 1948, Miss Drought resumed the correspondence with the Old Girls' Society:

"MOST OF YOU WILL HAVE HEARD of our production of *Hiawatha*. It was a great success from every point of view – artistically, socially and financially. We cleared over £100 which is to be spent on a cine-projector for the School. The *Hiawatha* fund is providing half the cost and the Cheshire Education Committee is generously paying the difference. We hope that it will be a source of much pleasure and interest to all our girls.

We have regretfully said goodbye to Mrs Jones, our secretary, who with her husband has gone to Hull, where he has a teaching appointment. Our new Secretary, Miss Rowbotham, travels here every day from Marple. She works hard and cheerfully from morning to night to make the wheels of administration run smoothly. One of her many tasks is to help check the new equipment which keeps arriving from the Ministry of Works and which will one day find a place in the new kitchen and dining room to be built at Belgrave Road. At present the storing of ovens, potato peelers and boilers is a problem and there is no sign of any new building to house them in."

Hiawatha's Wedding Feast

Joyce Bullivant	Margaret Hacking	Margaret Ellis
(Iagoo)	(Paupukeewis)	(Chibiabos)

Yvonne Navratil, formerly Bertin, recalls:

"I HAVE SO MANY HAPPY MEMORIES of my years at ACGS, from Lower Third to Upper Sixth, and then they finally had to throw me out! What I lacked in ability I made up for with enthusiasm. I joined everything that was offered, be it sports, music, or societies. Music was my first love; Miss Porritt my idol and mentor. What a wonderful teacher and role model she was. I owe my career to her teaching example and became a Music Consultant for the Ottawa Board of Education, Canada, responsible for writing and implementing music curricula throughout the system. I was also the conductor of the Ottawa Children's Choir for many years, and still do cameo performances to this day.

My happiest and most fulfilling memories centre around music. Performing *Hiawatha's Wedding Feast* at the Garrick Theatre in 1947; donning our 'war paint' and costumes at school and going by coach loads through Altrincham, waving our tomahawks at the people en route!

I remember being dragged by my future sister-in-law, Ludi Navratil, to play in the orchestra for the Altrincham Boys' Grammar School production of *The Mikado* when I had had just a few lessons on the viola. Another great learning experience! Also, very fond memories of music-making on occasional Saturday afternoons at Miss Porritt's lovely home in Wilmslow.

I should mention my frequent encounters with Miss Drought. They weren't funny at the time, but I now look back on them with affection and amusement. I had a healthy respect for DMD, or 'Droughty' as we called her. I occasionally found myself outside her door, eyes heavenward, waiting for the 'come in' sign to light up. One incident I remember very well. I broke a window throwing coke (the fuel kind!) from one pile to another outside the old dining room. Mr Spilsbury, the caretaker, was not amused and sent me for a suitable punishment. I waited in trepidation for some time outside 'The Door' as DMD was having her afternoon tea. When finally admitted she listened to my tale of woe and, after some thought, said that two shillings should be my contribution towards the replacement of the window, you have been punished enough, sit down and have a biscuit!

She had a great sense of humour too. She once wrote a note to my parents that I kept for a long time, and I quote, – 'Dear Mr and Mrs Bertin, This morning Yvonne was weighed, along

70

Hiawatha, *1947*

with her class, and it was found that she had lost 2 lbs. Maybe this is an occasion for rejoicing, which I thought I should let you know.' I loved the school, the fun and the laughter, the friendships made and kept over the years. The school motto Bravely, Faithfully, Cheerfully has served me well all my life."

Dorothy Paddon, formerly Rennison, remembers

"BEING OVERAWED ON MY FIRST DAY in September 1946, by the size of the building, and the great front door which we were *not* to use, also the big, airy hall where daily assemblies, concerts and speech days were held. The numerous pictures on the walls were a pleasure. I can still recall one of a classical statue of Hercules – even at aged eleven I was impressed. But our attempts at Greek dancing (yes, this was the 40s) were less impressive.

Miss Whitwill's history lessons inspiring her 'lambies' to imagine the 'tramp, tramp, tramp of the Roman armies'. And later, for A level with fewer sound effects the English Civil War – a story which still holds the imagination.

These years – the late 40s & early 50s – were still in the grip of post-war food rationing. Although omnivorous, I had to draw the line at 'Pom', the glutinous instant mashed potato of those days which was served up regularly. I would secrete it in a

Wilmslow, late 1940s
Standing: Mrs Porritt, Ludi Navratil, Miss Porritt,
Yvonne Bertin, Delia Fuchs;
sitting: Sheila Carr, Leonie Lonsdale

Dorothy Rennison

handkerchief under the table, but disposal was a problem, and laundering the hankies later a sticky challenge.

We studied comparative religion with Miss Drought in the Sixth – 'Philosophy of the Good Life' by Archbishop Gore and 'windows were opened upon the world'. What a wonderful bishop she would have made in a later century! How lucky we were to have school days so full of interest and fun, thanks to the loving care of Miss Drought and all her staff."

So many of these memories have also been recalled by others: Annette Nixon, formerly Bailey, Margaret Christie (Hacking), Gillian Wilkes (Knight), Doreen Evans (Lucas), Joan Davidson, Maureen Irwin (Jefferson), Mary (now Maerjele) Allcock (Buckley), Mary Missen (Davies), Margaret Burrows (Christianson) who said,

"LIFE GRADUALLY BECAME EASIER as the years progressed after the war and I remember with gratitude all the outings we had. Miss Porritt and Miss Anderton took the Choir to Music Festivals, and Miss Muir and Miss Whitwill took the lacrosse team to the All England Schools Lacrosse Tournament at Merton Abbey, London. We had a grand day of lacrosse and then another day or two sightseeing in London. Lord Altrincham met us at the Houses of Parliament and we were taken up Big Ben and walked behind the clock face. We visited Covent Garden for the ballet one evening and another evening we were taken to the theatre for *The Happiest Days of Your Life*. What sports Miss Muir and Miss Whitwill were! Another memorable weekend for the 1st Tennis Six was when we played in the finals of the Aberdare Cup at Wimbledon, no less!"

And finally... for this decade the last word is reserved for Miss Zena Walkley, member of Staff (later to become Second Mistress) from 1946 to 1966, who writes about her early years in teaching:

"I REMEMBER THE SCHOOL where I embarked upon the happiest years of my teaching career. The war had just ended. There were very few books in the Book Room, there were amazing syrupy steamed puddings produced by a delightful Swiss cook, there were dense clouds of blue smoke in the Staff Room. I admired the parquet floor in the Hall (never mind the splinters!), I loved the Virginia creeper on the main building (never mind the wasps!), I learned the quaint names of the teaching spaces – Treetops, the New Wing (patently not new!) and settled down to the responsibilities of full time teaching.

In 1946, if you were 21 years old, you were either old beyond your years because of involvement in the war drama played on the world stage, or young for your years because of the restricted life the war had imposed. I fell into the latter category and was overwhelmed by the seemingly larger-than-life personalities who dominated the school, Miss Drought, Miss Whitwill, Miss Colenutt, Miss Muir... I can still see Miss Drought moving to the

Aberdare Cup team, Wimbledon
Back row: Ann Swire,
Pat Fakes (captain), Sheila Carr;
front row: Sheila Derbyshire,
Peggy Lowe, Margaret Christianson

edge of the hall platform after prayers, to boom out bits of social education: 'No flowers are better than dead flowers!'; or 'You should smell as though you are not there!' One day there was advice on the decorous way to deal with plum stones at school dinner.

As a raw recruit who had had only four years of impoverished (though rigorous) secondary education, I marvelled at the riches of the curricular and extra-curricular activities on offer, and the quality of teaching. I admit that it was no fun on Friday afternoons trying to teach a recalcitrant class in a balcony classroom in competition with three forms singing together in the hall below, but whatever the frustration, I acknowledged the girls' good fortune. Musical treats were not restricted to school. There were trips to Chester for the competitive festival, and tickets on offer for Hallé concerts where Glorious John Barbirolli was wielding his baton. On Friday evenings many of the staff and perhaps a hundred senior girls stayed for the Union meetings – shared jam sandwiches and polite conversation before a programme put on by staff and girls. There were delightful evenings when girls spoke uninhibitedly about their first ventures abroad in war-torn Europe. And weighty ones for instance when Miss Porritt proclaimed the Five Great Bs: Bach, Beethoven, Brahms, Britten, (I've lost one!). And who like me remembers Miss Whitwill's revelation of her passionate admiration for Abraham Lincoln!

To present-day school girls so many things of which I might write will seem tame; but to an age group still starved of warmth and colour even modest pleasures gladdened the heart. Miss Gowland, biologist, supervised every year the planting of bowls of daffodils – one for each class. Woe betide any who allowed them to wilt! They were lovely and cheered Miss Cole who so wittily judged the Tidiness and Beauty Competition. (Again I hear Miss Drought: 'Every form reflects its form mistress!' How I shrank within myself.) To a school member of this century just back from China perhaps a weekend trip to Stratford-upon-Avon to see two Shakespeare plays from the 'gods' will not seem exciting but, thanks to the support of a long-suffering colleague, even I as organiser remember these exhausting excursions with pleasure, despite the Youth Hostel beds! Miss Drought came with us once: 'A bawdy play, *Cymbeline*,' she said.

All so long ago! What I write is dangerously self-indulgent – possibly inaccurate – though true to my fond memories. The reader should be grateful that I put an end to their unravelling."

Miss Walkley, centre, chatting to Carole Formilli, formerly Newsam, left, and Christine Barratt (Needham) at the Class of '51 Reunion, 2002

The 1950s

1950	June – new dining room completed at Belgrave Road
1950	September – role of sub-prefect abolished
1950	30 December – Miss Howes Smith dies
1951	General Certificate of Education introduced
1951	May – Miss Drought's portrait painted
1953	July – Miss Drought retires
1953	September – Miss Okell becomes Headmistress
1953	Autumn – purchase of Breeze Hill completed
1954	First American Field Service scholarship awarded at ACGS
1955	March – 21st anniversary of the founding of the Union Society
1955	September – forms renamed
1958	November – Breeze Hill ready for occupation
1959	18 December – Miss Whitwill retires

CHAPTER 5
THE 1950S

In the early 1950s an excellent aerial view of the main school was taken showing a fine building set in wooded, well manicured grounds, with grass tennis courts to the front and three grass and one hard tennis court on the back Lawn.

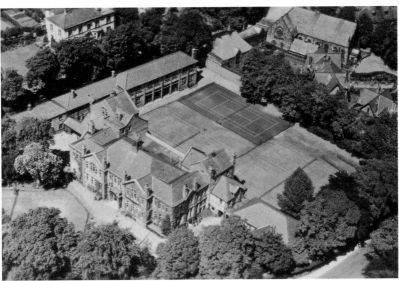

At long last the problem of meeting a fourfold increase in demand for School dinners in the late forties in an efficient and orderly manner was solved. The building on the Dome Chapel field on Belgrave Road was ready for use and all the equipment for the new dining room, which earlier had been carefully squirreled away in cellars, store cupboards and every conceivable hidey hole at School, had been retrieved and by June 1950 was installed and in full working order. The interior walls were painted by girls from the middle and upper school, with illustrations in modern style inspired by Kipling's *Just So Stories* and *Jungle Book*. The old dining room at the east end of School was converted into a music room.

Left: the dining hall and Dome Chapel

Right: in front of the dining hall: Pauline Watson, Anthea Howes, Anne Finlinson, Maureen Luce, Elisabeth Andrew; kneeling: Marion Delaney, Glenda Silverwood

An innovation in the autumn term was for all members of the Sixth Form to be formally invested with Sixth Form Authority, each receiving a badge and sharing the Prefects' responsibilities. A Head Girl, her deputy and fewer full prefects were appointed, but the office of sub-prefect was abolished, as their place was in effect taken by the rest of the Sixth Form.

The Staff, 1951

Back: Mrs Hull, Miss Walkley, Miss Muir, Miss Gowland, Middle: Miss Smith, Miss Crowther, Miss Whittle, Miss Yorston, Miss Porritt, Miss Mottershead, Mrs Goldsmith, Miss Bowen, Miss Walmsley, Miss Mary Bell; front: Miss Colenutt, Miss Baker, Miss Davies, Miss Qualtrough, Miss Puckle, Miss Saunders, Miss Davenport, Miss Atkinson, Miss Richards, Mrs Blackborough, Miss Robinson; seated: Miss Whitwill, Miss Drought, Miss Bell

On Saturday 30 December 1950, within three days of her eightieth birthday, Miss Howes Smith died suddenly in her home at Sunny Bank, Bowdon. Miss Drought wrote the following memorial for the *Old Girls' Society News*:

"IT IS HARD TO REALISE that one whom we have known so long as part of the very life of our School is no longer with us. Her zest for life, her intense interest in Art, Literature, Geology and in many other activities of the mind, but above all the interest in people will make her memory ever green in our thoughts and affection.

Miss Howes Smith often spoke of the Princess Royal with deep affection and there is no doubt that the affection was returned with interest. The Princess wrote to Miss Howes Smith every year for her birthday. She invited her to occupy a seat on the Royal Household stand for the Coronation in 1937 and was kind and thoughtful for her to the end of her life.

As the Princess outgrew her schoolroom days our School grew in size and scope and demanded all Miss Howes Smith's time and energy which she lavished on the School with rare generosity and enthusiasm.

In the seventeen years after her retirement in July 1933 Miss Howes Smith continued to live at Sunny Bank, Bowdon. She had not intended to finish her life so near to her beloved school, but the prolonged threat of war during the 1930s had kept her from moving south on retirement to be near her sister. She felt she should keep a place for her sister to retreat to if need arose. So the years passed and she remained a near neighbour and constant visitor to the School.

She made one long eventful journey to visit her brother in South Africa and she took up the study of Geology. During the Second World War, she worked hard for the Red Cross Library and used her artistic gifts in making soft toys which she sold in aid of war charities. She came regularly to Old Girls' Reunions until her health failed and visits, letters and cards from Old Girls in many parts of the world were an abiding source of interest and pleasure to her.

Perhaps the greatest tribute her successor can pay to Miss Howes Smith is the realisation that the School owes to her its distinctive character, that 'something' which makes it different from other schools. In its very buildings there is a graciousness which may not always be practical but is certainly lovable. Within its walls there is much to interest children, beautiful pictures, colourful plaques, gay flower vases, little figurines in the library as well, all remembered and loved by the Old Girls.

When we think of Miss Howes Smith's love of beauty it seems fitting that the memorial to her initiated by Old Girls, Staff and other friends should take the form of a Prize for Art, to be given to members of the School taking up Art as their career."

In the same edition of the *Old Girls' Society News*, Miss Drought also had this to say:

Miss D M Drought MA
by Arnold H Mason RA

"WHEN I LOOK BACK on the past year the other event that stands out in my memory is the painting of my portrait. The thought was Professor Waller's, a governor of the School. Then a Committee was formed with representatives of Governors, present Staff, Old Girls, and members of the Sixth Form. The Committee must have worked very hard, but I suspect that Miss Whitwill worked hardest of all, as she was Secretary-in-Chief.

The artist, Mr Arnold H Mason, arrived in the afternoon of 24 May 1951. He took one look at me and said: 'I think I shall require a larger canvas.' He then set to work in Room C because of the east light, and in an incredibly short time, the portrait was finished on 2 June. I found all this a most interesting experience. I enjoyed watching the artist at work and seeing in a mirror the picture coming to life. I was impressed by his integrity, his skill in research after truth. The picture was presented to me at a reception held on July 11th in the School Hall. Nearly 200 guests were present and the artist came specially from Chelsea for the occasion. The picture as a work of art is an abiding source of satisfaction to me."

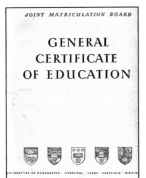

The cover containing the
GCE certificates

In 1951 the major public examinations taken by fifth- and sixth-formers had changed their names and format: School Certificate, Matriculation and Higher School Certificate were superseded by the General Certificate of Education.

On 23 July 1953 Miss Drought retired and Miss Whitwill wrote as follows:

"MISS D M DROUGHT was Headmistress for twenty years from 1933–1953. The School under her leadership gained the reputation of which we were rightly proud. How did she achieve her results? There are so many sides to her fine work and character that it is difficult to assess them correctly. There is a Headmistress who won the respect and affection of Staff and girls and set an example of service to the community; the scholar and teacher giving to her classes a love of learning; the organiser producing out of the conjurer's hat that miracle of a timetable, not by waving a wand or uttering the word abracadabra, but by many hours of concentrated thought and patience. Then there was the sincere Christian giving to our morning prayers a real meaning and value; the wise and understanding counsellor to whom the parents came for advice – which they usually took!

To the outside world there was the public servant, welcomed on many committees of an educational or social nature, and a much sought after platform speaker, inspired rather than flustered by the sight of an audience.

But to me the dearest memory is not of the imposing presence playing its important part in the life of the neighbourhood, but of the warm-hearted human being, never too busy to listen to the troubles of young or old, always ready to seek out a solution for our problems, and doing innumerable acts of kindness, both great and small, of which the world never knew.

All members of ACGS who worked under Miss Drought owe her a great deal of gratitude for all she did and all she was."

Miss Drought with her suitcase on the front steps with Miss Whitwill

Miss Drought was presented with a suitcase from the School, an umbrella from the Upper Sixth and an antique chest of drawers and electric toaster from the Old Girls' Society. Miss Drought moved down to Rudgwick in Sussex where she shared a house with Miss Davies, the Senior English mistress who also retired at this time.

Yet another long-serving member of Staff, Miss Atkinson, retired after thirty-two years of kindness and merry humour, teaching initially in the Preparatory Department – it is known that some quite venerable fathers proudly claimed to have been among her 'Old Boys' – and later on she looked after the juniors in the Removes.

Subsequently Miss Drought wrote to the Old Girls:

"I EXPECT MOST OF YOU have heard that I was 'hung' last summer! My portrait was exhibited at the Royal Academy, Burlington House. I was invited to the Private View and taken round the Exhibition by Mr Arnold Mason. It was a very pleasant and interesting experience and revived my gratitude to the donors of the portrait. It narrowly missed being put on the train which was involved in the accident at Harrow last month, but it is now safely back in the School Hall and hangs by the door of the lending library.

The portrait was reproduced with those of two other Headmistresses in the *Times Educational Supplement* and found its way into The Masters' Common Room of my brother's school. He came up to a group of masters who were looking at it and one of them, pointing at me, said, 'I wouldn't like to work under that one.' I hope the members of my Staff did not share that sentiment. I certainly enjoyed working with them."

Following Miss Drought's resignation at the end of 1952 nine candidates were interviewed for the post of Headmistress on 31 March 1953, when Miss R G Okell was appointed. On 1 September she took up the appointment. Miss Whitwill wrote:

"MISS RUTH GRACE OKELL has come to us, or rather come back to us, after years of experience of the best kind. She started at ACHS in 1912 as a five-year-old child and when fourteen transferred to Queen Ethelburga's School, Harrogate, a School with a fine reputation in work, games and standards of behaviour. She then spent three years at the Bedford College for Women, London, and became a BSc of London University with 2nd Class General Honours in Botany, Chemistry and Zoology. She began her teaching career at St Brandon's Clergy Daughters' School, Bristol, and after four years there returned to Queen Ethelburga's as Science Mistress. Five years later she became Head of the Science Department at Doncaster Municipal High School and in 1943 was appointed Second Mistress. For the last seven years Miss Okell had been Headmistress of Selby High School with such good results that the Selection Committee had no doubts when in March they asked her to come to Altrincham.

No one could have been better equipped by experience, intellectual gifts and social graces to become Miss Drought's successor. From the very first moment she ceased to be a stranger and had already endeared herself to us, above all by making us feel that our School and our traditions are precious to her."

Miss R G Okell

Whilst all these momentous changes were taking place, life at School continued as normal. Margaret Dunn, who started in September 1949, recalls her experiences during the early fifties – memories shared by Brenda Blackwell, formerly Moore, Ann Quinn (Jago), Marjorie Bottomley (Peers), and Barbara Tristram (Venables):

"I BEGAN IN REMOVE A, with at least thirty girls from primary schools in the Altrincham area, including my best friend Margaret Hearn who was Head Girl in 1955–56. Uniforms had been purchased from Grierson's on The Downs and Henry Barrie's in Manchester and duly labelled with Cash's nametapes. Clad in new clothes, carrying satchels and shoe bags and wearing hats, we entered the portals of ACGS. We had arrived! The next seven years were to stand us in good stead for the rest of our lives.

The size of the buildings, corridors, passages, so many rooms, so many pupils, so many staff was overwhelming. However, our initial apprehension was soon allayed by our form mistress, Miss Kathleen Colenutt, in whose capable hands we felt safe. Coco, as she was affectionately known, was small in stature, with beautifully groomed white hair, head held high,

Bowdon Downs Congregational Church. The entrance to the schoolrooms is from Bowdon Road.

and always dressed stylishly. She taught us French and I remember acting out the French alphabet on the front lawn amongst the trees under her direction. Our French lessons often took a dramatic turn; Miss Colenutt had close connections with the Garrick Theatre in Altrincham.

Every three weeks we took a picnic lunch to school as dining room accommodation was at a premium. In June 1950 the new dining room on the Belgrave Road playing field came into use. Sitting 'on high' was a daunting experience for a first-former. However, we were soon put at ease by Miss Drought. I suppose it was similar to meeting the Queen!

Back row: Brenda Moore, Stephanie Chadwick, Wendy Huggett, Diana Blakemore, Miss Walkley, Jeanice, Margaret Irvine, Jocelyn Massey; third row: Ruth Ashcroft, Dorothy Winterbottom, Ruth Ross, Alwin Medford, Christine Gregory; second row: Susan Hunter, Barbara Venables, Monica Ferguson, Joyce Harris, Margaret Dunn, Christine Applewhite; front: Margaret Hearn (Head Girl), Margaret Shannon

The Upper Sixth, 1956

Christmas time was always exciting with the Prefects' Entertainment, carol services, form parties and the annual Christmas Fair. Miss Gowland and Miss Muir, assisted by girls, decorated the gigantic Christmas tree which after the end of term was donated to the local children's home. Small groups visited local nursing homes to sing carols to residents.

On the first of May, a May Day celebration was enacted. In 1950 Remove A provided the maypole dancers (I was one of them) trained by Miss Dennett and Miss Muir. Remove B provided the Queen and Remove B Parallel the cushion-bearer.

On February 6th 1952 King George VI died. The whole school assembled in the Hall where Miss Drought announced the sad news. A short service followed. Two days later we listened to the radio broadcast of the Queen's accession. We were entering a second Elizabethan age. The following week we heard the broadcast of the King's funeral. 1953 was the Coronation Year. We enjoyed an extended Whitsun holiday, and each girl received a red propelling pencil with a gold crown on top. The whole school saw the film *A Queen is Crowned* at the Hale Cinema. In the July of that year Miss Drought retired.

Our education was broadened beyond the classroom. Visits were made to local cinemas to see such films as *Everest*, *Great Expectations* and *Julius Caesar*. I was also fortunate enough to be one of a group who saw Alicia Markova and Anton Dolin in *Giselle* at the Opera House in Manchester. Frequent visits were made to hear the Hallé Orchestra conducted by Sir John Barbirolli at the Free Trade Hall. A weekend was spent in October 1955 in Stratford-upon-Avon accompanied by Miss Walkley. *Othello* and *Much Ado About Nothing* were seen. In addition, the Union Society, open to senior girls, provided further excursions into the arts and science.

In the Upper Sixth Miss Walkley became our form mistress. She was an inspirational teacher, serene, compassionate, and with a keen sense of humour. Every English literature lesson was a delight; it was a pleasure and a privilege to be there. I studied Latin and Greek with Mrs Hull, a scholarly and exceptional teacher. To staff of this calibre I am much indebted.

With many school friends I enjoyed three house parties which Miss Baker helped to run. We called it 'going to camp' although our accommodation was not in tents but at boarding schools. The first two were at Alverstoke and Swanage and the third in Clevedon. We experienced Christian fellowship during an action-packed holiday.

When I entered ACGS in September 1949, I knew that I was going to enjoy school life there. I feel proud to have worn the gold and green of the uniform and the school badge bearing the motto *Fortiter, Feliciter, Fideliter*. How fortunate I have been to have experienced education in its broadest sense at ACGS."

House Party, Clevedon, 1958
Back row: Margaret Hearn, Eileen Shore, ?, Hillary Twiss, Diane ?, Penny Gaddum; middle row: Elizabeth Brayshaw, Margaret Dunn; front row: Kathleen Dunn, Sheila Peacock, Miss Baker, Marjorie Peers, Jean Parker, Joyce Harris

Phyllis Stuffins, formerly Smeaton, also recalls with affection and gratitude all the staff members mentioned in this account.

By 1953, with 594 pupils on the roll, the Cheshire Education Authority acquired the use of Breeze Hill, a mansion standing in its own grounds just across Cavendish Road and opposite the main gates of School. Conversion plans were drawn up to have cookery, needlework, art rooms, and some Sixth Form study rooms there together with a peaceful garden and a tennis court for the enjoyment of seniors. This welcome addition would then release accommodation in the main school to be converted into much-needed biology and physics laboratories. The keys were handed over by the previous owner, Judge George Preston Rhodes, a governor of the School, in 1954. However, the property was very damp and there was trouble with dry rot which led to extensive re-flooring throughout. This caused serious delays to the completion of the adaptations.

Patricia Brunt, formerly Davies, writes of a life-changing experience during a maths lesson:

"I AM SO GRATEFUL to have had a grammar school education. It was life-enhancing. It provided the basics of mathematical awareness, appreciation of literature, languages, knowledge of the world and its peoples through the sciences and my particular love of geography. Then there was sport – anything and everything in my case – and music with choral and madrigal singing. But that was not all, as staff members had a huge and individual influence too. One day springs to mind.

Miss Morrey (maths) bustled into the classroom of thirteen- and fourteen-year-olds and asked what day it was. She was appalled that we, as grammar school girls, did not know it was Budget Day! So we had half a maths lesson on government, budgets and the hard-won right to vote, and our duty to vote was made very clear to us. One half-hour of a teacher's time made a life-long impression. A day without a newspaper and political comment is a day lost."

Breeze Hill, 1957

School holidays abroad once again became a regular feature of Easter or the summer holidays. Margaret Simpson, formerly Shannon, recalls a memorable visit to Italy:

"SO DAN BROWN cracked the Da Vinci code in 2005? His research failed to discover that ACGS had been and seen circa 1955! There is no underestimating the avant-garde nature of exploration engendered by such a school.

It was the first European tour since the war and involved senior pupils and staff that Easter vacation. Destination – Lago di Como. Travel – by train: Manchester–London–Channel (not Chunnel)–north-east France–Basel. *En passant*, the memory of a smart Swiss breakfast lingers yet: red and white checked tablecloths spread on tables on the platform, hot croissants with cherry jam and real coffee with warm milk – so refreshing after bunks on racks overnight. Thereafter train through Switzerland, true *Sound of Music* stuff, and finally Italy.

Among the trips was one to Milan with an official visit to see the painting: Leonardo's unique masterpiece on the refectory wall of the Convent of Santa Maria delle Grazie – *The Last Supper*. Schoolgirl impressions? A bit vague in colour, the picture is or was much deteriorated through his use of an experimental oil medium.

Italy, 1955
School holiday led by Miss Titterington and Miss Baker

Table arrangement not unexpected, but what is impressive are the seemingly real attitudes of each disciple. All in all a great sense of age, Gospel Truth and that was that. Pity about the cut-out door head at the base of the painting, caused by Napoleon's troops on horseback at a later period. From our point of view no evidence of shadowy figures, no secrets, not a whiff of sacrilege and nothing of a code. So there, Dan Brown!"

Joyce Borland, formerly Harris, recalls other aspects of life at school in that era:

"HOW CAN ONE EXPRESS the gratitude for all that ACGS gave to us and were the happiest days of one's life? Seeds sown then matured as our lives developed. In geography lessons taught by Miss Atkinson we heard about her travels to Lake Titicaca and the Atacama Desert. A desire to visit those places was fulfilled in 2003 and 2005 – a dream since the early fifties.

How I enjoyed being wild flower monitor, again starting a hobby of botany which I still enjoy and am now sharing with my granddaughters.

As a child from a non-musical family I appreciated the opportunity of school music lessons, the choir and music festivals – and those lovely triangular chocolate biscuits sold before choir practice on Thursdays. Besides morning assemblies, and RE lessons, the school had a great influence on our Christian life with the summer holidays to Christian fellowship 'camps'. One school activity I really valued was the hymn and short service at close of school on a Friday evening for anyone who wanted to attend.

In May 2006 I visited Dalemain House near Ullswater and there, in the nursery, was a framed copy of *The Children's Song*. 'Land of our Birth, our Faith, our Pride...' Tears well up when I think of how we all sang this at school; the most poignant occasion being on my last day at Altrincham County Grammar School for Girls in 1956."

In 1954 Monica Jones, formerly Ferguson, was one of only twenty-five British students awarded an American Field Service Scholarship, the first time pupils from this country had been invited to take part. She recalls:

Monica and Charlene on Graduation Day

"IT IS OVER FIFTY YEARS since I read a small notice on the board by the old staff room door, inviting girls to study for a year in the USA. Applicants were expected to write an essay explaining how it would benefit them and also the community with whom they would live. Lucky applicants were invited for interview at the American Embassy in Grosvenor Square, and then, if successful, had to wait to be 'matched' with a family in the US.

My AFS year started with an Atlantic crossing of twelve days and three days' orientation in New York, at AFS HQ, on 55th Street, and included a visit to the new UN building: then an overnight bus to Chicago and a train to IOWA!

I stayed with Mr and Mrs Deal and their daughter Charlene, my new seventeen-year-old 'sister', living in Ottumwa, Iowa. It was an amazing experience. The exchange rate was $8 to the pound and I had $12 pocket money a month; a hamburger was about 25 cents and I tasted Coca-Cola for the first time! I was the only 'foreigner' in a 3000-pupil High School; most of them had never seen the sea, never mind met someone from another country. I was received with great kindness everywhere and hosted by many groups old and young, and I hope they learnt something about England and the British way of life. Academically, it was relatively easy to fit in because of the structure of American education. Even so, it was very fulfilling to graduate at the end of the year – a particularly memorable occasion. Charlene and I are still in touch and we have visited each other many times. I have attended various Reunions in Ottumwa over the years, most recently to the 50th and still with the 'Travelled Furthest' prize.

Genie Nash and Monica signing autographs at the front of School

Genie Nash, a summer student from California, came to ACGS in July 1956 and impressed many of the young English girls with her personality, American accent and style of dress. Subsequently, several ACGS girls have won AFS scholarships.

Because my year away fell during A levels at ACGS, I had to return to a new peer group in the Upper Sixth and attempt to catch up. However, it was an experience of a lifetime for me and I do thank my parents and Miss Okell for letting me go into such an unknown world."

Two friends from schooldays who now live on different continents still occasionally meet up: E Anne Taylor, formerly Cooper, and Irene De Sanctis (Critchley), who lives in Los Angeles. Anne recalls:

"I PASSED MY SCHOLARSHIP to attend ACGS in 1950. I had attended Lymm Parochial School and not many of us 'local yokels' got the opportunity to attend such a school. I was fortunate enough to be in Remove A, and Miss Davenport was my form mistress. We had some really good teachers, Miss Whitwill, the Deputy Headmistress, Miss Whittle – the Senior Maths Mistress – to whom I seemed to respond, and Miss Muir, the Games Mistress (well – she was a law unto herself). I wasn't very sporty, but can remember at the ten-minute morning drills marching across the hard tennis court singing *Perfect posture* to the tune of *Frère Jacques*!

I am still in touch with one of my school friends, Irene Critchley, who now lives in California. We last met in Mexico at my youngest daughter's wedding in 2002."

Irene De Sanctis, formerly Critchley, has written:

"My MOST AMUSING MEMORY from being awarded the retired Miss Drought's School Prize for Scripture was the fact that my choice of prize was considered unfit for a sixteen-year-old! I chose *The Cruel Sea* by Nicholas Monsarrat and I guess that the language contained therein was too mature. Such words as 'damn' were just taboo! So I went for *Reach for the Sky* by Douglas Bader. No wonder I was an airline stewardess for twenty-four years."

Irene De Sanctis with former tennis champion Vic Sexius

Pam King, formerly Jolley, Mary Perry (Lewis), Christine Beverley (Cashmore), and Janet Stukins (Wilkinson) have similar recollections to Jennifer Hickling (Nuttall), who writes:

"I HAVE MANY HAPPY MEMORIES of my days at the Grammar School. There was the biennial drama festival with early morning rehearsals. Trips to Chester to sing at the musical festival, art lessons with Mrs Pat Cooke, but most of all Miss Porritt and her piano-playing in the morning, especially the massive chords at the beginning of *Sing Aloud! Loud! Loud*! Then for Advent the large star would always appear above the piano in the Hall covering the light, and the excitement of Christmas, with carol books instead of hymn books, had begun."

Christine Barratt, formerly Needham, is certain that she would not be the person she is today without experiencing the following, in no special order:

"BIG KNICKERS. Before Bridget Jones was even thought of we were wearing huge navy bloomers with elastic round the top of the legs as well as the waist. They were big enough to store hamsters in, and one of my fondest memories is of 'Jock' Muir keeping her hanky in hers, which were worn beneath her pleated shorts.

Miss Whitwill was tremendous. She would sweep into a class in her gown and with one movement would switch off all the lights, intoning '*wasting England's money.*' Miss Porritt was cool and was somehow connected with the Lifeboat Society, thus exhibiting some personal glimpses. Miss Anderton was eccentric and loveable, conducting the choir with such verve that often the lacy modesty bit covering her cleavage would come astray and she had to fish down her front to retrieve it. I can still see her urging us to smile while we sang.

Mrs Hull was a bit dashing as she was married. She is now Dr Hull, and even more dashing with stunning modern jewellery and an impeccable manicure. Miss Gowland (botany) was young, beautiful, pale and interesting. Both she and Dr Hull have been to our 'Class of 51 reunions' – which is how I know about the jewellery and manicure – as has Miss Walkley whom I worshipped and who instilled in me a delight in and respect for the English language which bolsters me daily.

Then there were Tinkerbell and DomScibell, both Miss Bells, the first teaching music and the second domestic science. I still roll pastry out in a circle inching it round so there is no waste. I still wring out my dishcloth in DomScibell's wonderful fashion so that it is almost dry.

Mrs Cooke, Miss Edwards, Mrs Kalpakdjian, Mrs Hull, 1957

Tinkerbell's piano lessons could be heard trickling down the stairs from Treetops, where I learnt to torture a violin. Was I the only member of the school orchestra who played with her bow a fraction above the strings so that no-one would hear how bad she was?

Miss Drought will never be forgotten. She was the link between the old days and the new, in her shoes with pointy toes, in her office which was furnished, I thought, more like a small drawing room. Off it was Miss Rowbotham's office which she inhabited with Barrie, her little Scottie dog. Miss Puckle, the Matron, deep-bosomed, and a walking advert for her sponge puddings, was often to be found there too.

I took A level art on the sole grounds that Mrs Pat Cooke was an unorthodox warm teacher. I often use the calligraphy skills I learnt from her. She knew L S Lowry and claimed that when one walked round Manchester with him people with heads shaped like onions would spring up in the crowds.

Why I took speech training I shall never know and for some reason I never asked. I remember sitting on a bench in the sun under the library window reading Shakespeare to whoever taught me. This and the debating society may have led me to win national competitions twice for my hospital later on. My first talk at the debating society was about canoeing. I had never been in a canoe, but it was quite well received, so maybe ACGS also taught me something about overweening self-confidence.

ACGS taught me more than how to wring out dishcloths, roll out pastry, 'talk proper', walk gracefully, speak French and do calligraphy. It was exactly right for the culture of the time. It gave us the environment to grow and develop, experience a range of activities, and appreciate a structured yet enabling education. It played a great part in making me the person I am today. I'm comfortable in that person, and for that comfort I owe the school an enormous debt of gratitude."

Brenda Dodge, formerly Eno, writes from a warm and sunny Costa del Sol:

"I WAS ONLY AT THE SCHOOL from 1951 to 1953. Many memories spring to mind: Miss Drought stopping her Austin Seven in the middle of the main street in Altrincham, completely oblivious of the queue of traffic behind her as she wished to speak to a pupil walking along the pavement; Miss Whitwill calling us 'lambies' and Miss Smith (French) demonstrating the tango, as it had been performed in the play she had recently seen, during our last lesson before exams to help us relax."

Marion Hicks, formerly Ferguson, recalls:

"ONE DRAMATIC MEMORY was being collected into the School Hall on 6 February 1952. We were solemnly told that King George had died and that Princess Elizabeth, who was up a tree in Kenya at the time, had become Queen Elizabeth II. Another distinct memory was my first and last visit inside the staff room at the end of my school career. Two of us had been sent to transcribe the next year's timetable to paper from a huge multi-pocketed fabric and card frame. This was in the pre-computer era.

Miss Gowland taught me biology and this led to a university education and a husband, an initial career, and a lifelong interest in the natural world shared by my husband. Appreciation of ACGS has grown through the years. Lessons in the timetable included French and English for scientists, discussion for the general knowledge paper, musical appreciation, civics, playing and hence understanding cricket. These were all frustrations to a teenager but have proved to be valuable lessons for life.

I must confess to being delighted to read my name on one of the entrance hall boards on a first visit back after over forty years. This must have been put there in the days before so

*1952: centre row: Miss Rowbotham and Barrie,
Miss Robinson, Miss Bowen, Miss Storer,
Miss Muir, Miss Walmsley*

many pupils achieved their degrees. Like so many of us I owe much to those grammar school years. Thank you ACGS."

Shirley Winstanley, formerly Barton, recalls:

"I ARRIVED FEELING VERY NERVOUS on my first morning. I had come from a small school where the Headmistress warmed our morning milk for us on a chilly day! I made a friend as soon as I sat cross-legged on the hall floor. We were welcomed by Miss Drought – a lady with a kind smile and her hair in a bun. Assembly in the Hall most mornings was to become a real pleasure.

All teachers were excellent – my favourite being Miss Whittle. Mathematics lessons with her were the best. Science and biology with Miss Bowen came a close second. In her high-pitched Welsh voice she insisted we repeat experiment details time and again but her persistence got results. I was engrossed in a class of hers when a wasp crawled down my collar and stung my back. She very kindly took me to the sick room and administered a soothing lotion. Many a time I think how lucky I was to have such a good grounding in education at ACGS."

Ruth Callaghan, formerly Moston, remembers:

"HAVING CUT MY LITERARY TEETH on the Enid Blyton stories of Malory Towers, when at the tender age of eleven I learned I was to go to ACGS, I believed that I was to enter a kind of day school version yet have the same adventures which the boarders experienced. Well, it wasn't quite like that but there were some tenuous similarities.

One of the most enjoyable and worthwhile things for me was the strong music element, with such expert teachers as Miss Porritt (Kipper), Miss Anderton, Miss Bell (Ding Dong as opposed to DomSci) and their great enthusiasm for their subject. We sang the most romantic love songs with Miss Anderton conducting, her amber beads swinging to the beat and her 1930s pointed, buttoned shoes tapping the rhythm. We sang of *The Young May Moon*, *Linden Lea*, and *The Roadside Fire* to name but a few, and had a really good grounding in choral singing. Who could forget the school song *Land of Our Birth* or choir practices in the Congregational Church Hall next door where I remember singing *Where Corals Lie* and *Let us Now Praise Famous Men*?

I did get the opportunity to play the grand piano in the hall on two occasions when I won the solo piano competition for the inter-house music festival and so scored a few points for my House, Gaskell.

All I can say now is, 'Great School', 'Great Friends', many of whom I am still in touch with and some I see regularly. Thank you ACGS."

Aileen Winstanley, formerly Littler, recalls her visits to London:

"IN 1956 AND 1957 we went to London for the All England Schools Lacrosse Tournament. We stayed at the YWCA on Eccleston Square. On our first visit we went to see *The Pajama Game* at the London Palladium. I remember that *The Mousetrap* was in its fourth year. Today, in 2009, it is celebrating its

*Miss Anderton and Miss Porritt,
1952*

Lacrosse 1st XII, London, 27 March 1956
Back row: Gill Marsh, Aileen Littler, Jean Mackie,
Jean Marshall, Juliet Freeman, Pat Allbones, Margaret
Powell; front: Ruth Dyson, Margaret Shannon, Dorothy
Winterbottom (captain), Janet Smith, Joan Chappell

fifty-seventh year! We saw the Queen distributing Maundy Money at Westminster Abbey. We ate at one of the Lyons Corner Houses, which were very popular at the time. We didn't do very well at the tournament and we had to wear school uniform all the time, including our visit to the theatre, but we all enjoyed the experience as it was a first visit to London for some of us.

All girls were arranged into Houses and if we were awarded House colours, it was announced at the end-of-term service, and we embroidered the first letter of the sport for which we had won an award on to one of the corners of the House ribbon sewn on to our gymslip. All-round House colours were represented by a chain stitch border around the ribbon, and an embroidered star in the centre represented House colours for work. Junior School colours were a yellow and green striped ribbon which was sewn on to the navy girdle of our gymslip. The Senior Half School colours were a green ribbon – wider than the junior one – and full School colours merited a green girdle."

Jennifer Elston, formerly Rampling, recalls:

"LOOKING BACK TO THOSE DAYS between 1951 and 1958 my main memory is of the lovely Hall and the small office in the corner by the Headmistress's room where the secretary, Miss Rowbotham, sat by her typewriter with her little Scottie dog. In the opposite corner of the Hall was the little library where the new portrait of Miss Drought was to be installed. Miss Drought was a gentle lady and I am always pleased we, the 1951 intake, had that time under her guidance before her retirement in 1953.

I remember two special teachers. Miss Porritt instilled in me a lifelong love of classical music, and I am also deeply grateful to Miss Whitwill: she gave me an interest in history which has been a pleasure through my life.

Always when I hear the hymn *The day thou gavest Lord is ended* I am back in the School Hall on a Friday afternoon at home time with my satchel beside me on the floor – and, I have to admit, with a lump in my throat. It was so 'un-academic', but it was one of the things which made Altrincham Girls Grammar School just that little bit different."

Sue Abbott, formerly Saunders, had a long daily journey to School which caused similar difficulties to those recalled by Julia Wilson (Carter), who remembers:

"THE NORTH-WESTERN BUS from Congleton to Knutsford passed our farm at 7.45 every morning. This rattling old bus saved me from going to Sir John Deane's at Northwich as the County decided taxi fares to send me there were too expensive.

Our history teacher, Miss Whitwill, was one of my heroes; 'heroine' is not strong enough for such a powerful

Jennifer Elston and Miss Pollitt,
Class of '51 Reunion, 2002

Miss Yorston, Miss Dedman,
Miss Jackson, 1957

personality. Her lessons were always full of drama – I remember her lying on the desk to indicate death, and shaking the pockets of her gown to imply 'money bags'. But all my teachers had a great influence and were memorable characters: Miss Gowland with beautifully detailed drawings in botany and the intriguing Miss May who taught scripture and dropped hints of an interesting past and encouraged me to think for myself about the 'Wisdom of Solomon'.

The school acquired Breeze Hill and we in the Sixth Form enjoyed the privilege of small rooms and the chance to discourse with our peers, unsupervised. Teachers were always willing to give up free time after school and I benefited from extra help with Latin which I had missed out on earlier in my school career and I also tried some Greek with Miss Yorston.

Being a prefect was a great honour – we took life seriously and imposed school rules about wearing berets, even after you got off the train! Eating in the streets was not allowed! I was happy at school and remain eternally grateful not only for the education but also the encouragement and guidance I was given. I am so glad that North-Western bus service meant I could go to ACGS."

Eileen Shore has happy memories to recount:

"WHEN I FIRST WENT TO ACGS I think I had some fear about the sheer size of the place. But if I had those fears they certainly did not last. I remember that first pre-entry meeting with Miss Drought in her study with two other new girls, Joan Chappell and Karen Rowe, and the opportunity to look round the school. Very different from my previous school that consisted of two rooms and three teachers.

Miss Drought seemed to want to get to know us as individuals and it was the sense that the individual mattered that was the hallmark of ACGS. But the individuals collectively made up the school in which there was a high expectation of each one. Perhaps it was the quiet sense of order that pervaded the school that helped to give us a sense of purpose.

We were summoned by bells – going in bell, get ready for Assembly bell, into Assembly bell, bell for drill, bell for break, bell for lunch, as well as bells for the change of lessons. In the Sixth Form to be on a rota for the ringing of those bells gave one a strange sense of power. The movement of the whole school silently into assembly was the epitome of order and organisation. In silence we waited for Miss Drought and later Miss Okell as she walked the short distance from her office to the platform. A reading, a hymn, a prayer and notices. The notices told us of achievements in sport, in music, of academic success, of events that would help to fuel our minds – all helping to build up our aspirations. Sometimes there was reference to some misdemeanour – there was no excuse for not knowing what was not acceptable behaviour.

1958 poster from the Delamere House
notice board. Artwork by
Christine Needham

As regards my contemporaries, it has been good to meet up with many of them at the 'Class of 51 Reunions'. There are others of whom I wonder what has happened to them in their lives. But whatever we have done I think we all have happy memories of ACGS and value the grounding and confidence it has given us."

Catherine Merrell, formerly Shaw, remembers with pride:

"I LOVED THE HOUSE SYSTEM and was delighted to receive my green petersham ribbon to sew on to my gymslip to show I was in Delamere. The House system enabled so many of us to compete in many areas – I particularly remember the Drama Festival held at Bowdon Assembly Rooms. We did the trial scene from *The Merchant of Venice*. I was Shylock and thus began my lifelong love of drama. I also became Head of Delamere House.

Catherine Merrell (Mayoress of Trafford 1997–98) and Judy Sutherland

I adored the music, the swimming, the sports practices – was there ever a day when I didn't stay behind for something? Another strong memory is of wet lunch hours when some brave soul would put on ballroom dancing records in the Hall and we would learn to dance. It was great to be able to do the foxtrot, waltz and quickstep and the joys of doing the square tango with a member of the Senior School! All so innocent and we learned so much.

On leaving school I was awarded the A P Hill prize for Services to the School and it was with a tremendous sense of pride and gratitude that I took the train back from London to enable me to stand on the steps of the platform in the Hall to hear Miss Whitwill announce my name for the last time.

A wonderful school, wonderful atmosphere and I made some wonderful friends."

Judy Sutherland, formerly Rocca, recalls:

"I STARTED MY ACGS CAREER IN 1951 and loved it from the very first day. One of my great memories is of our class putting on a production of *Cinderella* at Christmas. Cathy Shaw was Cinderella, I think Elise Wilkinson was the Prince and Eily O'Callaghan, now sadly deceased, wrote the music. We had enormous fun with that. I also remember the feeling of superiority of being able to go through the front door when one had reached the Sixth Form, helping at the Boys' School Gilbert and Sullivan productions and singing in the school choir. '*Ready Porritt!*' Miss Anderton would intone – what a wonderful inspiring pair they were.

So many happy memories – I feel I can never repay the debt I owe to the School because it did its best for me, and although I didn't work hard enough the grounding it gave me has stood me in good stead all my life – and without being sentimental, what better sentiments could one have than those expressed in the school hymn by Rudyard Kipling?"

Marjorie Horncastle, formerly Higgins, writes:

"MY FIRST THOUGHTS ABOUT Altrincham County Grammar School for Girls were a good two years later than most. 'Late as usual' do I hear you say? I was an intake into the upper thirds in 1952, having just moved from Yorkshire.

My belief that I definitely was on the wrong side of the Pennines began straight away when I entered the New Wing. 'Ah, New Wing', I thought. 'I am used to this newness,' as my

Lower Sixth, 1957
On the terrace steps with form mistress
Miss Whitwill

previous school was very modern, spacious and set on an open hill. 'This'll be nice,' I thought expectantly. Imagine my horror when I was led down a long, dark, narrow corridor. 'I'm in prison!' We went into a classroom and I was allocated a desk, an old, small splintery desk set in a very narrow aisle. I felt I needed to reduce by 50% to fit in.

I had further setbacks when I learned a little more about the school. For instance, 'Where are the hockey fields?' I asked naïvely. Disbelief when told they were twenty minutes walk away!

And then! My first break-time when we had drill! I thought they were kidding – but no – out we all went in our blouses and knickers, never mind the weather, into long straight rows on the tennis courts. Instructed to do all the various exercises and contortions demonstrated and woe betide you if you tried to skip one. 'Drill?' I mused. 'For what or whom are we drilling?' What paramilitary organisation was I being schooled for?

I gradually adapted and eventually I came to love the school, with all its foibles. The Sixth Form was the best because you chose your favourite three subjects to study and you had some privileges – not many, mind. Oh – the pleasure of getting into a skirt instead of a gymslip. And why, anyway, is it called a gymslip? No-one to my knowledge ever did gym in it. Miss Muir would have had a fit!

Well, there we are – a few memories. My abiding ones are of music. This love will be with me for ever and I owe my place in Portsmouth Choral Union to Miss Porritt. Also I loved history and all the arts but the greatest gift the school provided was friends, and the seeing and meeting up with them still gives me great joy."

Marlen Hughes, formerly Brine, recalls many experiences:

"GOING TO WEMBLEY to watch Miss Webster playing hockey for England and the tremendous roar when England scored. Ringing up on Saturday morning to see if matches were on or off. The horrid black, itchy bathing costumes worn during swimming lessons at Altrincham Baths and the yellow cross you sewed to your costume when you could swim a length. The thick and thin discs we had to carry in those green purses and drop into boxes in form rooms as a punishment for naughtiness. I seemed to lose a lot. Speech Days – would your mother's hat embarrass you? Science lessons doing experiments – I was particularly fascinated by the way mercury rolled and rushed across the lab bench if it escaped! Reading Chaucer and Shakespeare aloud in class and being introduced to Hardy, Dickens, the Brontës, Jane Austen and Gerard Manley Hopkins to name but a few, by Miss Gourlay.

Making short, puff, choux and cold water pastry, rollmop herrings and being told to 'Clear as you go, girls' by Miss DomSci Bell. Being taught how to paint a tree and the art of perspective by Pat Cooke. Being greeted at the beginning of each Latin lesson '*Salvete O puellae*' by Mrs Hull and we responded '*Salve O magistra.*'

Learning about the geography of South America and being taught about glaciation, corries and coombs by Miss Brown: we thought she was so glamorous. Lessons in Breeze Hill, huddled round a fire on freezing winter days, gazing at the amazing William Morris-like wallpaper instead of concentrating. Overtaking Miss Whitwill, in her little car on Broomfield Lane, on our bikes.

Becoming a prefect. The wonderful silver gilt badges we wore pinned to our ties – I don't think we realised how valuable they were. The Prefects' Entertainment at the end of term, the enjoyment of watching it and the fun in taking part. The Prefects' Quiz, daunting when you had to answer the questions, and difficult when responsible for compiling the questions and marking the papers.

The special friends I made at school who have remained very precious to me throughout my life. I loved school and feel I had a wonderful all-round education thanks to the care and dedication of the staff.

Thank you to all those ladies who stalked the corridors in their black gowns, taught us, told us off and encouraged us. Happy memories of ACGS."

Some of the Prefects, 1959
Back row: Delohne Webbon, Alison Rampling, Delsia Gowing; middle: Marlen Brine, Ann Robinson, Janet Bowden; front: Penny Gaddum (Deputy Head Girl), Judy Rocca, Elizabeth Brayshaw

Just a few personal memories from your compiler, Pat McCormac, formerly Allbones, for I belonged to the 50s era.

"I WAS KNOWN AS PAUL from the second day of my ACGS school career. My very proud father had made me a new pencil box *par excellence* with P. Allbones emblazoned boldly in full technicolor across the lid to use at my new school – a school he knew I had set my heart on attending from being very small. My peers shortened my name immediately and that was that.

I have shared in many of the memories recounted in this chapter, so my contribution will be short. I enjoyed my schooldays and joined in almost everything – sport being my favourite – lacrosse, netball, cricket, tennis, rounders – with School matches most weekends. On one occasion when raising funds for the lacrosse team to go to the London tournament, we ran an evening jumble sale in the Hall. At the due time, I went to open the front door to let the public in and was almost knocked over in the rush. Literally hundreds of 'professional jumble-sale ladies' were gathered outside sensing rich pickings. We were not streetwise but they were! Enough to say that a few minutes later I was just in the nick of time to save the school barometer from disappearing for ever. A visitor had managed to remove all but the last screw holding it to the wall in the vestibule inside the front door. Phew.

Quite apart from academic challenges faced everyday at School, my horizons were constantly being widened across a broad spectrum in the field of music, art, cookery, foreign travel to Italy and Switzerland and current affairs. I enjoyed it all! Thank you everyone for your support, guidance, laughter and camaraderie. And to School… congratulations on a first-class century and all good wishes for the next hundred years."

Miss Kathleen Pollitt taught PE from 1954 to 1964 and shares a memorable recollection:

"I RECALL FROM TIME TO TIME listening to the sound of the choir practice as the tennis team practised on the grass courts outside the music room. The music from *Hiawatha's Wedding Feast* is permanently lodged in my mind, and I have the LP still!"

Delsia Hann, formerly Gowing, recorded the following observations about her first year at School in 1953 in her diary:

> "I WAS VERY PROUD when I was chosen to be prefect of Remove B. In the first year we did not go to Speech Day but we heard the girls practising for it. The end of the Christmas term was very exciting for there were many entertainments. There was the Christmas Fair to which every form contributed; we did the Christmas Post. Three sacks were put up and cards would be posted to anyone in School for a small amount of money. On the Fair Day we had to deliver them. We all enjoyed the Christmas Party which was held in school time. There were seniors and mistresses helping. We played games and danced, then went along to Dome Chapel for tea."

Union Society, 21st birthday party, 18 March 1955, Dining Room, Dome Chapel
Amongst those present were Miss Okell (President), Miss Baker and Mrs Evans (Vice-Presidents), Miss Whitwill, Miss Colenutt, Miss Puckle, Stephanie Chadwick (Head Girl), Elizabeth Plummer (Deputy Head Girl), Sylvia Walton, Hanne Holmes, Angela Leech, Anne Hodgkinson, Jennifer Hartley, Pamela Buzza, Joyce Taylor, Jennifer Studley, Margaret Hunter, Maureen Coop, Christine Applewhite, Ruth Dean, Christine Wright, Ruth Horrocks, Norma Rowen, Frances Downes, Judy Howard, Margaret Dunn, Margaret Massey, Barbara Armstrong, Judith Burdett, Patricia Davies.

In 1954–55 the Union Society enjoyed an excellent twenty-first season during which nine full meetings were held. The Earl of Stamford spoke about Lady Jane Grey, one of his ancestors. Other topics included Holidays, Food, Canada, Christmas, Wagner and the Bayreuth Festival, a French evening, a Youth Club evening, and on 18 March 1955 a twenty-first birthday party – its 176th meeting. A wonderful birthday cake was baked by Miss Puckle from ingredients collected by the senior forms, iced by Lower Six B, and adorned with twenty-one candles. Miss Baker, the senior Vice-President, read the toast of 'The Union Society' sent by Miss Drought and the reply was given by her successor as President, Miss Okell.

In the autumn term of 1955, old form numbers were abandoned, though many still referred nostalgically to the first forms as Removes and the seconds as Lower Fourths. At this time there was a record number of 602 girls at School, a fact which made the heartfelt cry to start work on Breeze Hill more frenzied than ever.

Beryl Hopkins, formerly Rowbotham, recalls:

> "MISS OKELL WAS A 'NEW GIRL' at the same time as me. Was it her doing to change the names of the classes? I know it came as a surprise to me to move from Remove B Parallel to IIA the following year. She introduced me to biology – still the love of my life. I hated Latin at school

and was terrified of Mrs Hull, but the grounding became invaluable to my botanical career and my vocabulary increased tenfold!

My first ever trip abroad was with the school to Brienz in Switzerland. We travelled there by overnight train – no berths – and no sleep! We went swimming in the freezing lake and everyone but me had a 'civvies' costume. I had taken my ACGS black woollen one with a Yellow Cross on it.

Over fifty years on I am still best of friends with Kay Hestermann, formerly Longshaw, even though she studied languages and has lived in Germany for nearly forty years."

And now an explosive report from Pat Bottrill, formerly Larsen:

"HOW MANY OLD GIRLS can say they left school with a BANG! For those of you there in the summer of 1958, do you remember the fire brigade coming because someone had blown up the fume cupboard in one of the science labs? How pleasant it was standing outside on the back courts in the fresh air whilst the incident was dealt with! I confess it was I, and several others, who inadvertently mixed the wrong substances when we were supposedly making soap.

I left school that summer (one could say under a cloud or fume) and departed from the Lower Sixth to commence cadet nursing training at Leicester Royal Infirmary. I had really wanted to be a PE teacher, and had participated in all the school teams in a variety of sports. I went for an interview at I M Marsh College of Physical Education and failed the medical as I had a 'bent arm' from a fracture some years earlier. A doctor considered this would mean I would not be fit to catch children in gym classes! Returning to school full of disappointment, I was summoned to Miss Okell's office, and asked what I now intended to do. As I had no other career in mind she suggested (strongly) that I had better go and be a nurse. Finding that I could start training at sixteen years old, I departed for Leicester at the end of the summer term of 1958.

I had a wonderful nursing career, and despite my 'bent arm' managed to lift patients and carry out all nursing duties without a problem until I retired in 2001. I was awarded an MBE in 1997 for Services to Healthcare and a Royal College of Nursing Fellowship in 2004. Although initially aggrieved at how a doctor had changed my life's direction I have never regretted taking Miss Okell's sound advice. I treasure the Old Girl's Society gift that I was awarded on leaving, a book token with which I purchased my first nursing textbook, now long out of date but still in my possession, at the princely sum of two guineas (£2.10).

Pat Bottrill MBE with her family at Buckingham Palace

The overall memories of my schooldays at ACGS are essentially very happy ones and the discipline we were instilled with has held me in good stead ever since. My links with Altrincham continue as my married daughter lives there with an eight-year-old who may follow in my footsteps, and also those of her great-aunt (Inger Serb – Chapter 4) and aunt (Tina Serb – Chapter 7). With this in mind I follow all the published results of school in the exam league tables and am so proud of seeing School going from strength to strength."

The Revd Ann Wood, formerly Robinson, writes from Canada:

"MY FIRST DAY AT ACGS was not in September to join all the other first year students at eleven years of age, but two years and a term later, in January 1954 at the age of 13¼ years. In

December 1953 my parents moved to Timperley and this meant I had to change schools – a daunting prospect for a young girl.

On my first day, accompanied by my mother, I arrived at the School's imposing front door and was welcomed by Miss Okell. She sent word to Mrs Hull, my form mistress, that I had arrived, and soon three girls came to collect me. I can recall to this day seeing one very tall girl (Pat Allbones: 'Paul'), one very short girl (Julie Napier: 'Squib'), and one in between (Christine Needham: 'Seedy') coming towards me. Miss Okell introduced us and they took me back to Upper

Robbie, Seedy, Squib, Paul,
Class of '51 Reunion, 2002

IVA to meet everyone. On the way to the classroom, I was immediately given the nickname 'Robbie' which stuck with me all the way through school and beyond.

I soon felt 'at home' in the new school surroundings with my new friends. I liked School and have a host of happy memories which included: cycling to School; playing hockey and taking part in tournaments in the School 2nd and 1st XI teams. I sang in the school choir and vividly remember our choir practices with Miss Anderton and Miss Porritt and taking part in many choral musical events both in school and in choir festivals. I was somewhat intimidated by Miss Whitwill in history lessons as she swept into the classroom in her university gown half off one shoulder but I have always remembered her repeated phrase 'the swing of the pendulum', as it related to events throughout history.

I enjoyed most subjects and decided to go into the sciences – particularly zoology and botany. One highlight of our senior years was the trip we made to the Marine Biology Station at Milford Haven, Pembrokeshire, for a week. Some of us stayed an extra year in the Upper Sixth and this led in 1959 to my attending the University of North Wales, Bangor, influenced in my choice of university by our zoology teacher, Miss Dedman, who had not long graduated from there herself. We were given some special privileges in the Upper Sixth years, one of which was studying in the recently acquired Breeze Hill. Here we also put on plays on the back terrace.

Happy days, not to be forgotten, the legacy of which is still with us in our late sixties!"

Lesley Boxer, formerly Gill, has an unusual maritime experience to relate:

"I THINK THIS MEMORY goes back to my first year in the summer of 1955, when about six of us used to play at the Dome Chapel field, before or after we had lunch in the dining hall. Down by the netball courts on the left was a line of lime trees and they were very good for climbing! We used to pretend one particular tree was a ship and several of us used to climb to different

Madrigal group, 1959
Susan Holmes, Delohne Webbon,
Roslin Williams, Anne Schofield,
Miss Anderton, Brenda Talbot,
Ann Robinson, Carole Crowther,
Janet Bowden

heights depending on how confident we were. I didn't make it to the top (one who did was Valerie Levi who was unfazed by a huge oak that she used to get me climbing by the Bridgewater Canal in Timperley). We spent many hours that summer up this tree and we were either not spotted by the teachers or they sportingly left us alone."

Kathryn Turrell, formerly Brown, recalls:

Valerie Levi and Lesley Gill

"MOST OF MY MEMORIES of ACGS are fragmentary: morning drill, the purple ribbon of Gaskell House, the gold lion wallpaper in the Hall and other such trivia, but the constant thread I remember most clearly was the singing and the unexpected delight with which it enriched my schooldays. It began with my first Carol Service and my amazement that choral music could be so beautiful and that we could sing carols in Latin as easily as we sang in English; and it continued with memorable church services, concerts, and in 1958 the trip to record carols for a Christmas programme on Granada Television.

We sang some wonderful music; I am sure I am not the only pensioner who can still remember most of the words of *Kubla Khan* and I still prefer the setting of *Brother James's Air* to any other version of Psalm 23. I still bless the musical tradition of the school for giving me such pleasure and know that each time I hear the haunting words and music of the lovely *Coventry Carol* I shall be transported back to school and to 1954."

Rae Morven Rickwood, formerly Jones, followed in her mother's footsteps and writes:

"MY MOTHER ALICE JONES, formerly Begent, went to School before me and we even had the same cookery teacher, Miss Bell, and Miss Anderton for singing. Despite Miss Whitwill's best efforts I failed history and was requested to drop Latin as I would compromise the pass rate! But I learnt to walk not run, sit up straight in the front row, and '*not waste my talents*'. My fondest memories were the school plays because I loved dressing up; going to Knutsford Fair in my American tan tights and white pointed shoes with my best friends from ACGS, and dancing to Victor Sylvester's records in the school hall when it rained at lunch time."

Margaret Collins, formerly Oxley, writes:

"I HAVE FOND MEMORIES of the School trip to Switzerland accompanied by the wonderful Miss Titterington, and had a great time. I ran out of cash for food on the way home so ate nothing but grapes for hours!"

Kathleen Leigh, formerly Tomlinson, shares similar sporting memories to those of Bridget Beggs (Chadwick) who recalls:

"AS A KEEN SPORTS PERSON and under the expert tuition of the Misses Muir, Pollitt and Webster, ACGS had a great deal to offer me. Tennis, netball and hockey (with some rounders and lacrosse) all occupied many hours of my time, during the week and on Saturdays.

The music department, driven by the tremendous enthusiasm of Miss Porritt and Miss Anderton, occupied even more hours of my time, and way back in 1955 I was the first clarinettist to join the school orchestra. There were no transposed parts for a clarinet so I had to write them out for myself. Modern parlance would call it 'fast track' learning!

Academically, I know that I could have been more diligent, but life was very enjoyable in a caring establishment and it set me up to tackle the adult world 'Bravely, Faithfully, Cheerfully'. Thank you ACGS!"

Miss Patricia Gilbert, a member of staff from 1957 to 1961, writes:

"IN 1957 I WAS WORKING as a pharmacist, being assistant manager of a chain of chemists' shops in Bristol, when I realised that I wanted to be a teacher. The first copy of *The Times Educational Supplement* I obtained carried an advertisement for a chemistry teacher at ACGS, so more in hope than expectation I wrote to the Headmistress. As it happened Miss Okell was due to attend a head teachers' conference in Cardiff so I received a reply inviting me to have tea with her at her hotel. Consequently the wheels were set in motion and I was offered the post.

I could not have had a better introduction to teaching or school life in particular than that given at ACGS under the Headship of Ruth Okell. The head of the science department, Barbara Gowland, was so very supportive as were the other senior members of staff.

I remember with fondness the laboratory assistant Mrs Blackborough, without whose help I would have floundered in those early days. She once had to leave the laboratory, shoulders

Miss Titterington and Miss Gilbert, Switzerland, 1958

shaking, shedding tears of laughter and mopping her eyes at my efforts to draw a frog on the blackboard! I soon became fully involved with extra curricular activities, in particular helping with the Union Society, escorting school holidays and participating in staff *v* school matches.

One memory stands out – that of producing a staff entertainment for the pupils. It was my version of a popular TV programme at the time called *Emergency Ward 10*. I had members of staff in bed in a ward – one swathed in bandages so as to be unrecognisable. The highlight was the entry of Miss Anderton, the senior music mistress held in much awe by pupils, dressed as a ward cleaner (rollers in hair beneath a turban) singing *Que sera*. She took much persuading to take part but her appearance was received ecstatically by the audience!

After leaving ACGS to tour Nigeria as a trainer for the Girl Guides Association I had a teaching appointment in Stockport, four years in Hong Kong as Senior Mistress at the Forces Education Authority Secondary School and then a post as Senior Mistress at Exmouth School in Devon. I finally retired in 1988 as Head Teacher of a school in Oswestry, Shropshire."

Marion Ketteridge, formerly Delaney, Head Girl in 1962, remembers:

"IN THE EARLY YEARS I grew up with Miss Colenutt as form mistress of 1A, French teacher, and raconteuse of wartime fire-watching episodes; Miss 'DomSci' Bell's cookery – '*I'll have no finger cookery in my class,*' lessons in scrubbing pine tables, polishing knives, and laundering a range of fabrics – rayon, for example – with care.

Later on there were Mrs Hull's Latin lessons, her good humour and imperturbable calm when confronted by ignorance, a misdemeanour, or a fit of giggling – 'Really, Marion, that is extremely tiresome of you.'

We had marvellous hymns all year round – *He who would valiant be* meant prefects' investiture, and *O valiant hearts*, Remembrance Day; before exams, *Nearer and nearer draws the time* produced significant glances; *Not forever in green pastures do we ask our way to be, but the steep and rugged pathway may we tread rejoicingly* – did we have any idea what this might entail?; Founders' Day and *Let us now praise famous men*; and Christmas with carols from the Oxford book.

I could go on but will end with thanks for so many memories, to good friends and stalwart staff."

Staff v Girls Netball, 1959
Girls: Ann Brocklehurst, Margaret Davies,
Pat Allbones, Elise Wilkinson, Pat Larsen,
Carole Crowther
Staff: Miss Kemp, Miss Pollitt, Miss
Newbrook, Miss Webster, Mrs Eglin,
Miss Gilbert, Miss Schaffer

Judi Robinson, formerly Holland, recalls:

"HAVING COME FROM another grammar school at the age of thirteen, it wasn't easy to make friends or settle into constructive academic work, but I did. My happiest moments were spent in the art room at Breeze Hill with Mrs Pat Cooke. She was ahead of her time with a change of hair colour every week and change of stocking colour every day from red, through to black and all possible hues in between. I don't think it went down too well with the older members of staff. When I was sixteen she was only about twenty-three, so we got on really well and she made my school life very happy. Her maiden name was Gerrard and she lived very near to L S Lowry in Mottram in Longdendale as a little girl. In fact I came in one day half way through a Radio 4 play about his life and he was talking to a little girl called Pat Gerrard. I had the impression that she became a pupil of Lowry and her work in many ways reflected that. I did get my Art O Level thanks to Pat."

Miss Okell noted,

"ON THE 16TH AND 17TH JULY 1958 the Vs and VIs performed *Hiawatha's Wedding Feast* by Coleridge Taylor at a memorable concert at School and distinguished guests in the audience expressed their admiration for the performances. The feat of learning 56 pages of words and music was astonishing in itself, but to hear such words of praise as '*worthy of the Free Trade Hall*' proves that despite the distractions of all the usual end of term activities, the girls can still rise to the occasion. The proceeds of £83 from these concerts paid for a flute, viola and clarinet for loan to school musicians and some money was sent to aid child refugees in Austria."

At long last in November 1958 Breeze Hill was transformed. The two forms whose entry had been deferred in September (a situation that even *The Times* had commented on) joined the four already at School, bringing the total on the register to 720. Miss Okell commented in the *School Magazine*:

"THE NEW ART AND CRAFT ROOM has ample floor space, windows on all sides and excellent new furniture. The Housecraft Room downstairs is alas smaller than anticipated but is gay and has a certain homely appeal whilst the three small classrooms, though remote, are proving useful for senior lessons."

Mottram in Longdendale Church
by Pat Cooke,
on display in the Staff Dining Room

Orchestral rehearsals for Hiawatha's Wedding Feast *conducted by Mr Kenneth Duckworth.*
The players include Jill Coop, Sheila MacDonald, Valerie Thompson, Anthea Howes, Phyllis Beswick, Marion
Delaney, Susan Clegg, Janet Williams, Rosalind Johnson, Lalage Thorne, Janet Bowden, June Crabtree, Elizabeth
Nelson, Jennifer Reed, Julia Reynolds, Bridget Chadwick, Susan Cunliffe.

On 18 December 1959 another era in the School's history came to an end when Miss Mary Whitwill retired after forty-three years of devoted service. Born in 1892, she joined the school in 1916 after taking an MA at Oxford University. She was the Head of the History Department and for thirty-four years Senior Mistress. In 1927 when the House system was introduced she chose to be House Mistress of De Massey because 'its name had the longest history.' Miss M R Bell and Miss Colenutt, who had both known Miss Whitwill for over thirty years (forty in the case of Miss Bell), wrote knowledgeably in the Golden Jubilee publication *The First Fifty Years.*

"THERE ARE MANY OF US who knew Miss Howes Smith, and many more who know Miss Drought and Miss Okell, but everyone knows Miss Whitwill.

For thirty-four years and through three 'reigns' she has been Senior Mistress in the School, where, in the course of time, numbers have ranged from 250 to over 700. Her task has not been an easy one. Over 4,000 girls have passed through the school since its opening, yet Miss Whitwill is able to recall so many of them and has kept in touch with a countless number, for she possesses extraordinary insight into the capacity of those she has taught. How often we hear Old Girls recall the inspired teaching and drama which brought to life the historical incident or character she was describing!

There are many facets to this interesting personality. She has an amusing and perceptive mind, a Churchillian love of tradition, an abhorrence of anything slovenly, and a passion for fresh air – who has not seen the look of anguish when she entered an ill-ventilated room? She is not easily hoodwinked by sins of omission, though minor failings are viewed with tolerance and understanding.

The unity of the Staff and the friendly atmosphere of the Staff Room are remarked upon by every newcomer. These qualities have been fostered and encouraged by Miss Whitwill who herself sets a high standard of competence, friendliness and graciousness, giving help willingly to the uninitiated and smoothing out the mistakes and difficulties of the more experienced. She has the quality of approachability quickly appreciated by all of us.

Her enthusiasm for games is well known. De Massey House so frequently urged on by her often held top place in inter-house matches. This has been achieved not only by prowess on the field but by her infusion of keenness and zeal.

By all this and by much more Miss Whitwill will be remembered. She will be greatly missed. With deep sincerity we wish her a fond 'bon voyage' into retirement at her home in Somerset."

At the Staff farewell party she was presented with a gold wristlet watch, and she gave a Parker Knoll chair to the staff room. On her last day she was presented with a brooch (a cluster of garnets) from the School. On 6 January 1960, at an Old Girls' Society Reunion with 120 members present, including Miss Drought, she was elected as Vice-President, her portrait, recently painted by Mr Frederick Deane, was hung in the Hall, and after a tribute by Miss Ella Seed she was presented with a camera, case and projector from the Old Girls' Society.

Miss M W Whitwill MA
by Frederick Deane

The 1960s	
1960	March – *The Zeal of Thy House* performed
1960	2, 3 July – Old Girls' Golden Jubilee Weekend
1960	4 July – 50th anniversary of Founders' Day
1960	19, 20, 21 July – Golden Jubilee concerts
1960	September – House system ended; games awards changed
1960	18 November – Golden Jubilee Speech Day, Free Trade Hall
1964	4 July – 50th anniversary of the Old Girls' Society
1964	July – *Hiawatha* performed
1964	14 September – work started on the East Wing
1965	September – new prefect system introduced
1966	26 October – formal opening of the new East Wing
1966	December – *A Happy Prince* performed
1967	July – The Misses Anderton, Colenutt and Okell retire
1967	September – Miss Jackson becomes Headmistress
1969	4 July – Miss Okell's portrait hung

CHAPTER 6
THE 1960s

The Zeal of Thy House
Jill Coop, Christine Parkinson, Elizabeth Thompson, Julia Partington, Susan Huggett, Janet Dawson

The fiftieth anniversary of the founding of School was celebrated in style with four main events in 1960. The first was a production of Dorothy L Sayers' play *The Zeal of Thy House*, which dramatises the restoration of Canterbury Cathedral after it was destroyed by fire in 1174. This fine play about building and rebuilding was chosen because it suggested a hopeful looking forward, an appropriate mood for a school growing and vigorous as it reached its half-century.

The play was performed in the Hall on four evenings, 31 March, and 1, 4 and 5 April, by two separate casts, each playing for two evenings. Miss Colenutt was the producer, Miss May the stage manager and Mrs Cooke designed the settings and costumes. Miss Okell wrote:

> "PARENTS AND OTHER VISITORS are not likely to forget the colourful and dignified action of the play, set against a background of crimson and gold, or the atmosphere of dedication that prevailed."

The Golden Jubilee programme

The second major event was an Old Girls' weekend. On Saturday 2 July the Old Girls' Jubilee Dinner was held in the Hall and attended by three hundred Old Girls and four very brave Old Boys. Extracts from the School Magazine for 1960 written by Shirley Bowler and Mary Fecitt of the Lower Sixth describe the proceedings as follows:

"AFTER THE GUESTS WERE WELCOMED by Miss Okell, Miss Drought said grace and the guests sat down to a delicious four course dinner. Later Miss Whitwill as Toast Master introduced the speakers who represented each of the five decades of School's existence. Through their reminiscences ran the thread of the steady growth of the School's tradition against a background of historical events, changing social conditions, and changing fashions in dress and behaviour. Miss Ella Seed, herself a former Head Girl, member of staff, gardener during the Second World War, and still the collector of National Savings, who had never severed her ties with School, proposed the

WELCOME   by MISS R. G. OKELL

* *

Toast

THE QUEEN

Speakers

1910-1920   MONICA LUNT
                 (Broadbent)
1920-1930   BEATRICE GREENHOUGH
                 (Thomas)
1930-1940   ALICE CHORLEY
1940-1950   HILARY SHUARD
1950-1960   STEPHANIE CHADWICK

Toast

THE SCHOOL

                 Proposed by ELLA SEED
        Response by MISS D. M. DROUGHT

Toast Master : MISS M. W. WHITWILL

Jubilee Dinner order of events

toast. She attributed the success of the school to the work done by its three Headmistresses, who each contributed in her own special way to its character and well-being. School was never impersonal. The claims of the individual were recognised and each one was called upon to give of her time, thought and energy in serving the school. In reply to Miss Seed, Miss Drought (with no aspersions to the verbal comedy suggested by their surnames) spoke of the undeniable character of the School, with all its customs and its traditions which make everyone feel part of it.

Opportunity was then given for chat and what a noise ensued! Time was of no consequence; husbands and taxis waited patiently outside, but no-one seemed anxious to leave. An atmosphere of joy and thankfulness for the past mingled with wishes of success and happiness for the future of the County Grammar School for Girls, Altrincham."

The next afternoon the School ran an Open Day to enable Old Girls and their families to retrace their steps of old round the buildings and grounds, and enjoy a leisurely Sunday afternoon tea with old acquaintances – both former pupils and staff.

The third event was the special service of thanksgiving and re-dedication for the School held at Bowdon Church in the evening of Founders' Day itself, 4 July. An account of the proceedings reported in *The Altrincham, Bowdon and Hale Guardian* was as follows:

Golden Jubilee Dinner, 2 July 1960
Miss Whitwill, Miss Okell, Miss Drought,
Miss Colenutt, Miss Walkley, Miss Holderness

"ST MARY'S CHURCH, Bowdon, was packed on Monday, when hundreds of pupils, parents and Old Girls of Altrincham County Grammar School heard the Bishop of Chester, the Rt Rev Dr G A Ellison, preach at a special service celebrating the School's golden jubilee.

The jubilee was a time for reminiscences, for both old and young, said the Bishop. For former pupils, it provided an opportunity to assess whether they were putting into proper use instruction they had received in the past, and the use to which it would be put.

It was a time, too, for present pupils to look back on how people had striven on their behalf over the past fifty years. 'Look back in order that you may judge what should be done in the future', added Dr Ellison."

The next memorable Jubilee event was a series of three concerts on 19, 20 and 21 July. Valerie Thompson of the Lower Sixth noted:

"AS WELL AS PIECES performed by the orchestra conducted by Mr Duckworth, there were various choral works sung by the choir and some junior forms, ensemble and solo works. These widely contrasting items created an atmosphere of unity as everything followed smoothly; everyone seemed anxious to give of her best.

Each of the concerts ended with a performance of Coleridge

Altrincham County Grammar School
for Girls
Golden Jubilee
Thanksgiving Service
At the Church of St. Mary, Bowdon
(Bowdon Parish Church)
Monday, 4th. July 1960. at 7.15 p.m.
Please be seated by 7.5 p.m.
Admission by ticket only

Admission ticket for the
Jubilee Service

Taylor's *Kubla Khan* which Miss Porritt gained permission to arrange for female voices and two pianos. The performances inspired both the singers and the audience and on the final evening all members of the choir were sorry that they were singing the work for the last time. Miss Anderton conducted with the sympathetic skill and ability her experience had given her, and the choir was ably supported by the two pianos played by Miss Porritt and Mrs Chadwick."

The Form and Order of
the Service for

THE FIFTIETH ANNIVERSARY

of the Foundation of

THE ALTRINCHAM COUNTY
GRAMMAR SCHOOL FOR GIRLS

Monday, 4th July, 1960
in Bowdon Parish Church

Programme for the Jubilee Service

Miss Okell was unable to be at the last concert as she had been invited by the Queen to attend the Garden Party at Buckingham Palace.

One of the longstanding traditions became a casualty at this time. The House System had become untenable because, with increased numbers – now over 700 girls – and the need for some lessons to overlap into the dinner hour, it was no longer feasible to arrange house meetings involving girls from many forms. For the seniors, opportunities for art, drama, music, sport and other pursuits were provided by the activities of the Union Society and the younger girls now had hobby groups – in many cases mentored by senior girls.

Some adjustments to the School's games awards were introduced in 1960. The Full Colours for Seniors, and Junior Colours for outstanding play during the season were retained; the recipients in the Seniors receiving enamel brooches, the Juniors green girdles. The Half Colours previously awarded to Seniors were replaced with Commendations whereby the names of girls who had played to the full extent of their ability, given their services willingly at all times and reached a generally good standard in any of the teams were recorded.

Another link with the past was severed at the end of the summer term with the retirement of the senior domestic science mistress, Miss Bell, born in 1892 and appointed to the School in 1920. Generations of girls have reason to be thankful for the training she gave them, for the fastidious and methodical example she set and for her kindly and personal interest.

A Golden Jubilee Speech Day calls for very special treatment and what could be more appropriate than to celebrate it in an impressive building like the Free Trade Hall in Manchester, a hall whose proportions would accommodate not only the whole school, but

Dr Ellison, Bishop of Chester, with Miss Drought, Miss Okell and Canon Low after the Jubilee Service

parents and friends as well. To be allowed to hold the ceremony in this hall was a great honour for the school and it was fitting that the guest and speaker, Dame Mary Kingsmill-Jones, DBE, JP, MA, should herself have been the first woman to be Lord Mayor of the city. The events of the evening were recorded in the *School Magazine*:

"AS SEVEN O'CLOCK APPROACHED on November 18th, tension mounted and as the buzz of excited conversation ceased, Miss Okell and her guests came on to the platform which, since the morning, had been gaily decorated with colourful plants and flowers. Members of the Sixth Form presented button-holes to the guests and a surprise bouquet to Miss Okell.

Mr Freeman, the Chairman of the Governors, welcomed

Dame Mary, and all parents and friends. He spoke of the school's progress during the last fifty years, of the increase of importance of grammar schools, and paid tribute to the school as a whole, mentioning with gratitude the secretarial and domestic staff.

Miss Okell in her report paid tribute to Miss Whitwill and Miss Bell who had recently retired after a lifetime of service to the School, to the creativity, organisation and presentation of the special Jubilee events, to the excellent academic results achieved at O and A level which were a source of pride, and finally to the work of the Form Mistresses who ensured that each member of School felt she could make a contribution to the well-being of the whole.

After the presentation of the prizes and certificates, Dame Mary spoke in such a friendly and informal manner that everyone was aware of the warmth of her personality and was charmed by her soft Irish accent. She assured us that there was in fact 'no magic about being grown up' and suggested that 'what you are now is what you will be later on'. Personal success, she said, was only part of life in which we were so bound up with other people that what was even more important was service for others. In this connection, she spoke highly of the service of the school's three Headmistresses.

This theme of service was later to be taken up by Miss Whitwill when she proposed the vote of thanks which she did in her typically humorous manner without the aid of the amplifying equipment! Dame Mary had, in her opinion, confirmed the belief that when a woman speaks well, she speaks magnificently.

Music, as always on these occasions, made its valuable contribution to the success of the evening. The School Orchestra, conducted by Mr Duckworth, bravely played where the world famous Hallé has cast its spell. The Choir, conducted by Miss Anderton and accompanied by Miss Porritt who had earlier received a prize in acknowledgement of her twenty-one years valuable service to the school, gave pleasure to the vast audience. The first form girls, sitting in tiers behind the platform guests, charmed everyone by their appearance and exemplary behaviour.

After Miss Okell had led her guests from the platform everyone left the Free Trade Hall feeling proud of the school and its traditions, and glad that for an event of such importance in its history, all present members, many Old Girls, parents and friends were able to come together, to share an occasion which was at once impressive, warm and friendly."

And so ACGS heralded the swinging sixties with a celebration of traditions and achievements built up over fifty years, but what was in store for it during the coming years? Contributions from many girls of this era build up a picture of change tempered by moderation.

Helen Berrisford, formerly Leake, remembers:

"I WAS ONE OF THE JUBILEE BABES as we, who started in September 1960, became known. One of my most vivid memories is walking into the hall and seeing the wallpaper – huge gold lions! Every morning we would have Assembly there and would be played in and out by either the school orchestra or a solo pianist. My friend Marjorie and I were chosen in the fifth form to play a duet – *The Skaters Waltz*. Our piano teacher was Mrs Chadwick, a lovely lady, very quiet, who never shouted, and always put us at our ease.

In 1961 the school started employing male teachers! There was Mr Cookson (Latin), Mr Buck (French), Mr Rija (maths) and Mr Jowett (scripture). Mr Buck was our class teacher in the 3rd year – IIID (always Roman numerals). Our classroom was over in Breeze Hill and I hid from him one time as a joke – I squeezed into a cupboard and when I eventually came out he said 'I've heard of a leak in a pipe but never a leak in a cupboard!'

How can I forget Miss Porritt and Miss Anderton – the 'Hinge and Bracket' of their day! I

Sixth Form, 1961
Back row: Anna Hamilton, Margaret Kenna, Irene Preston, Jane Woodford, Susan Cluely, Jennifer Reed; middle row: visitor, Mary Fecitt, Carolyn Adams, Sheila MacDonald, Sheila Surman, Beatrix Wilshaw (behind), Mary Anderson, Monica Roscow; front row: Valerie Colledge, Elizabeth Thompson, Frances Brown, Jean Waller, Olga Talbot, Patricia Walsh

remember borrowing *The Dream of Gerontius* from the music department – record and score – and listening at home with my mother and following the score.

What about Mrs Cooke – the art teacher! She was young and vibrant and wore Mary Quant makeup – quite bohemian in those days.

I look back on my time at Alty Girls with much affection and a great deal of thanks for the values instilled in me and others. May it continue to do so for many more years to come."

Barbara Stockton and Dorothy Beckett, formerly Eaton, were both keen walkers and recall:

"MR COOKSON, together with a fellow form master, teamed up and took a party from their respective forms for walking days out in the Peak District. We went several times and enjoyed some lovely walks."

Dorothy continues:

"EACH CHRISTMAS a large star-shaped lampshade was placed over the light outside Miss Okell's room as part of the decorations for the festive season. When I was in the Lower Sixth it was decided to replace the old one, which was beginning to disintegrate. It fell to our maths group to take on the task. The shade was a stellated icosahedron (i.e. twenty faces, each with a star point) and was made of papyrus. It was an enjoyable challenge, successfully completed under the expert guidance of Miss Holderness. [Editor's note – the original Epiphany star was a gift to School in 1928 from a visiting teacher from Germany.]

Derbyshire
Dorothy Eaton, Jennifer Mason, Helen Reeves, Barbara Breckon

These are just a few of my memories of a school at which I was very happy and to which I owe a great deal."

And now for some sound advice from Elisabeth Johnson, formerly Andrew, who speaks from hard experience, in a piece entitled 'Location, Location, Location':

"IT WAS INEVITABLE, I SUPPOSE. The last person to arrive always gets the worst seat. This was my experience when I arrived as a new girl at the beginning of the fourth year. I found my way up two flights of stairs to Treetops which housed IVA, a class of about thirty-five, billeted up there because it was the largest form room in the school. Only one desk remained. It was right at the front, so far forward that it was on a level with the teaching desk. This was to be my home for the next two years. There were some obvious disadvantages to sitting there as I could

Miss Walkley, Miss Gourlay, Mrs Poller

not whisper subversively, pass notes around or read something other than the text book, as the others who had bagged seats further back could do. On the other hand, I was certainly able to observe teaching styles close up.

My prize for the ultimate in lesson preparation went to the formidable Frances Gourlay who taught us English. Such organisation! She always arrived with a list of points she wanted to go through during the lesson. The list I could see started with 'Good Morning, girls' with which she greeted us and then duly ticked off. But how many of us found true delight in literature from her rigorous lessons? The balanced sentences of Addison and Steele were hardly the talk of the lunch breaks. In the Lower Sixth form she gave us a solid grounding in authors such as Chaucer and Hardy but proclaimed that she 'did not feel compelled to read modern novels,' so we had to wait for the Upper Sixth before we were introduced to the pleasures of D H Lawrence by the much more approachable Mary Titterington.

In my time the school was bursting at the seams. While many lessons were taken in Treetops, for minority subjects we found ourselves in other locations. Rooms were rented at the Congregational Chapel in Bowdon Road. We took A level exams in the hall of the chapel with Miss Colenutt sliding toffees across my desk for encouragement. In another room in the 'Cong' complex – known as the Boat House – we had fourth form Latin lessons reading Caesar's *Gallic Wars* with Winifred Hull. Selecting one's desk for these classes was all-important as she had a policy of going round the room with one girl reading a paragraph and the next translating it. Reading was infinitely preferable to translating. So one had to work out which were the reading desks. To this end we assessed the seating plan from every angle. Mrs Hull, who had a benign twinkle in her eye behind a rather reserved exterior, must have had a shrewd idea of our tactics. She frequently started somewhere in the middle of the class throwing our careful calculations into disarray.

My contact with Miss Okell was at her weekly Prefects' Meetings which she managed very deftly. I thought I had picked the perfect seat for these meetings in an inconspicuous spot on the floor. Unfortunately to no avail. Someone had to take the minutes and, without asking for volunteers or suggesting a rota Miss Okell had decided it was me. There was much surreptitious chortling among my friends.

So during my four years I learned many important things at ACGS. Indeed I have certificates to prove it. But the most profound lesson was the importance of arriving early and getting a good seat."

Memories from Vivien Arnold-Roe, formerly Arnold, include:

"IN OUR EARLY DAYS AT SCHOOL we played in the trees surrounding the tennis courts, claiming a spot for our gang in the twisted tree opposite the lodge. We played steps seeing how many we could leap down at a time in the flights from the hall onto the terrace and then on to the grass tennis court.

I had my first piece of writing, entitled *My Brother's Music*, printed in the school magazine. My school report said 'Vivien works with interest and enthusiasm; she is a happy and helpful member of the form' and was signed by Miss Qualtrough (from the Isle of Man) and Miss Okell.

In second year I remember Josie weeping copiously when the Manchester United players were killed in the plane crash in Munich. We had stopped jumping off the steps. I was learning violin from Clarice Dunnington in a small room upstairs in Treetops and feeling anxious about missing out on lunchtime chats with the others. My school report said: 'Vivien takes an active interest in all form affairs but her enthusiasm must be more controlled.' Signed by Miss Dedman from Wales and soon to be Mrs Williams – excitement!

In third year I moved into the A stream, thanks to Miss Walkley who thought I might make it to university to read English and would therefore need Latin at GCE O level. Pat Cooke organised a fashion parade. Marjorie Hadwin and I made a dress out of some old curtains and a hat out of a pale green plastic lampshade. Pat Cooke drew a little cartoon of us for a Christmas card. New summer dresses – green, yellow or blue check shirt-waisters were designed (hooray).

The only adverb and adjective in our vocabulary was 'dead'. We were 'dead chuffed', 'dead annoyed' and things were 'dead good'.

Years in the Lower and Upper Sixth were the happiest. The study of selected subjects was in more depth. We learned about sub-plots and the foreign policy of Louis XIV. In music with Miss Porritt we came to appreciate sonata form and be able to take down dictation of melodies and harmonies by ear. Linda Ferguson and I played duets for the girls to march out of Assembly. After the more erudite offerings of other players our vamped versions of *The Harry Lime Theme*, *When the Saints Go Marching In* and *Pack up your Troubles* were received with merriment. It was the birth of the sixties and the times were a-changing. I accompanied a promising jazz singer in *I've got a crush on you, sweetie pie*."

Many memories of this era feature Mrs Pat Cooke, who, of anyone on the staff, epitomised the swinging sixties, drawing admiration from her pupils and causing a few raised eyebrows amongst the traditionalists. Pam Bradshaw recalls:

"AGED ELEVEN, having come from a very small primary school, I found the grammar school huge and overwhelming, and spent the first week being very frightened, despite the kindness

Pam Bradshaw, 2006

of my form teacher Miss Colenutt, Miss Porritt, Miss Okell and others. The tide turned for me at the first art lesson. Just before the move to the large airy art rooms at Breeze Hill, art classes were held in the main part of the school, with a cosy coal fire in the winter and the wonderful, stimulating and fun teaching of Pat Cooke – who remained a lifelong friend until her too-early death a few years ago.

Gradually I settled in, and finally gained the respect of the Maths teacher, one of my poor subjects, when it was announced in morning Assembly that, aged twelve, I had had a painting accepted for an exhibition at County Hall, Chester.

My path in life decided, I followed the arts route and spent every free period in the Art Room. In the Lower Sixth, six of us emerged as 'Cookie's Babes' in the art room – Valerie Pownall, Pamela Clarkson, Sarah Curbeson, Andrea Pugh, Claire Moore and myself – and we all applied to and were accepted into Manchester School of Art on the foundation course, a stepping stone for us all on to degree courses around the country and subsequent careers in art and design.

The day I left school aged seventeen, I burned my beret, declared myself an art student and felt liberated. It has only been in later years returning to Altrincham after a varied and glittering life, and meeting up with staff at reunions that I realise how devoted they actually were to their work and to us, and I now realise and appreciate how worthy these women were of our respect and attention – all of them specialists in their field, committed to communicating their knowledge and enthusiasms, and genuinely concerned for the welfare of the girls."

Other recollections from Pam Heaton, formerly Brereton, Angela Yardley (Litchfield), Marilyn Portner (Woolf) and Kay Hall (Martin) include:

"MRS PAT COOKE was the most fun teacher. She lived in Knutsford and girls catching the same train used to walk with her to the station in a bunch of adoring groupies. She was always trendily dressed with particular memories of her wearing full skirts with lots of petticoats, winkle-picker shoes and a boater hat. Others mention her low heeled canvas pumps dyed all sorts of colours to match the outfit of the day which may have included wearing her husband's shirt back to front! Life was never dull!"

Chris Bailey-Green, formerly Disney, recalls some random memories and the ingenuity needed to raise money each year for the Christmas Fair.

"EACH FORM WAS ALLOCATED a day to bring in cakes. My mother did a nice line in chocolate cakes that proved so popular with the staff that they were sold off complete rather than cut into slices.

Another year I went round local decorating shops and obtained out-of-date wallpaper sample books. Our form provided a book-covering service at a small fee and girls could choose their pattern. Decorating glass jars to make useful 'tidy' pots was another initiative. Even in those far-off days, recycling was nothing new.

Another memory was when we made regular visits to old people in local homes. I didn't have any elderly relatives so it was quite an experience."

Christal Barlow-Bates, formerly Christine Barlow, joined the school halfway through the second year. She writes,

Christal Barlow-Bates

"IT WAS PRETTY MUCH like jumping in at the deep end but I was up for it as I had been bored at Cheadle Grammar School, with its new building, vast open areas and young teachers. I was warmly welcomed at Altrincham and introduced to the teacher of every subject by my classmates. Enid Burns and I struck up a close friendship which is still going strong today. Everyone seemed keen on learning and the history of the school and small classrooms brought a sense of purpose and continuity that I loved. In each subject I was given the work of the best students in the class so that I could take it home and catch up. This daunting task served to fire me into study and I worked at it with the fervour of a conforming child. My marks came back for each subject and I was excelling! Total delight and pleasure filled my days. Miss Brown was our form mistress and I adored her. She was totally beautiful and always had lovely clothes, matching skirts and twin sets, gentle hues of purple and green and perfect painted nails. She took us for geography and I remember spending hours on my homework on cumulus clouds, and with a 10/10 from her, I was thrilled.

I hope that sharing my thoughts has helped you to remember the good times and to carry with you as I do the school motto which so very concisely describes my life. Fortiter, Fideliter, Feliciter. Bravely, Faithfully, Cheerfully."

The sign on Christal's garden gate

Carolyn Phillips, formerly Edwards, and Wendy Wakefield (Holden) have enjoyed a trip down memory lane:

"PUPILS WERE ENCOURAGED to look and behave well, both in school and out in the community. Neatly dressed in our navy tunic, tie and blazer with its distinct hexagonal badge, we were instantly recognisable locally. Initially seen in traditional berets or velour hats with a school ribbon around it, we felt really 'with it' when later allowed to choose between a trendy Baker Boy beret and a smart Air Hostess hat, worn at the correct angle!

PE was a favourite part of the curriculum for me. Thanks to the early lessons from Miss Pollitt, I grew to love tennis and I continued to play actively for the next fifty years! I remember how we would even race to get on the courts before school began each morning. Lacrosse was also very popular, and we all used to rush eagerly to the Games Board whenever Miss Pollitt was due to post the team list. Weekly matches took us to distant schools across the North-West, but one highlight was when we competed in an all-England lacrosse tournament in New Malden, Surrey – the only time I have ever been picked for such an event.

School days and years had a certain pattern. Everything seemed to go according to plan and modifications were rare. Fire drills, like performances, were practised to perfection. I recall that Form IVA was up on the third floor, so for fire drill they had to exit via the window, go down the outside ladder and stand on the roof of the Hall! I was never too sure which was more dangerous, that or the fire, but it provided some excitement and quite a spectacle!

On reflection, it was a privilege to attend ACGS in the sixties, and we still feel proud whenever we hear of its continued success. We learned so much, in the fullest sense of the word, including the attitudes and standards we carried forward into adulthood. It was a very special time, and we loved it all."

And for something completely different, in her own inimitable style, Lesley Hale, formerly Bushell, writes:

Fortiter

Feliciter back combed
her hair to obliterate
a regulation pair
of badge and beret.
She was not fideliter.

Wendy Helsby, formerly Lewis, recalls:

"THE BULGE YEAR WAS ALSO in that era called the 'swinging sixties'. We were at the tail end of the teddy boys, big sloppy jumpers, tight ski pants and skiffle, and at the beginning of the Beatles phenomenon. Some hair was back-combed to look as though the owner had had an electric shock whilst others were still in plaits. But school uniform prevailed (almost) and berets were worn (pinned onto the beehive by Kirby grips) by all outside the school gates.

Fund-raising at Christmas, entertainments, concerts such as *Hiawatha* in which every girl had to be involved (my contribution was the sewing of some leather fringe) and trips for sporting or foreign visits punctuated our years. Concerts, rehearsals, sports training, matches and the Union filled our out-of-school hours with the occasional detention thrown in. We learned to work, play and organise. I started the Duke of Edinburgh Award at school and took a group out into the Peak District for an adventure day. No health and safety issues then.

The outside world, although always present, sometimes exploded on to our routine. The Cuban missile crisis clearly showed the danger of nuclear war. The informal meeting of the school community in the Hall at the end of the school week for a final hymn became more significant. The death of President Kennedy was particularly poignant as we had an American Field Service scholar, Beth, in our class at the time. Politics and general elections with the Labour party coming to power and the Lib/Lab alliance were seen in Union sketches. Feminism was still in its infancy, but as the inheritor of an all-female education I feel very privileged. We were able to make our mark in school without reference to our gender. Once in the outside world it was a surprise to me to discover that women did not take charge. Our role models were strong and influential.

The enduring memories of Miss Whitwill's booming voice, 'barbarians, lambies'; Miss Colenutt's white hair; Mrs Delides' glamour; Miss Porritt's total enthusiasm; Miss Whittle's quiet authority; and others who stayed and worked in the school for many years who became a thread of continuity. These are the type of teachers who provide that link for old girls from different eras. Inevitably this will slowly die away for our generation, but I hope that a new link will continue for those to come. For years when possible I attended the London reunion. Ex-pupils from around the south and from many eras met up to reminisce, to listen to the news from school given by people like Miss Okell, Miss Porritt and Mrs Delides, to touch base with the ideals of service and learning which such an education delivers. How many other schools from the north of England could claim such a reunion? Nothing stays the same, nor should it. Change is the essence of vitality and health in any organisation, but continuity of values also provides strength and rootedness.

Miss Whitwill, Mrs Elsie Gregory, Miss Okell, Miss Drought

So for the current students and those who are to come – look at the portraits of the Head Teachers not as rather old-fashioned and fusty individuals but as the bearers of the belief in education for which you are the inheritors. *Carpe diem*."

Janet Jones, formerly Husbands, comments,

"I ENJOYED MY SCHOOL YEARS and thrived on the academic diet, especially history and languages. I didn't realise it then but the habit of learning and a wish to pass on a love of it as well as the values the School tried to promote have been the cornerstones of my own career in education. On the downside: what a logistical nightmare it must have been to organise lunches, sport and additional classes away from the main site! I hated the walk in the rain to the sports fields and still have an aversion to Wednesdays which always seemed to be the day on which this was timetabled!

There was a strong sense of identity for me, a sense of belonging and, from the other side of the fence now, a realisation of how it shaped my life and career."

Two demountable classrooms at Breeze Hill

By the autumn term of 1961 the school had a record number of 811 pupils on the register. Two new classrooms had been built on the Belgrave Road field and equipped for needlework and art–craft lessons but were too remote to be used as form rooms, so both the gym cloakroom and zoology laboratory had to act as 'form bases' with lockers for storage of books. The school was literally bulging at the seams with every available square inch of space in use. There was a desperate need for more accommodation even though no increase in school population was envisaged. By 1963 two demountable classrooms had been erected in Breeze Hill garden and plans were being prepared for a major extension at the main school. In the meantime more space was rented and in January 1964 the church hall of the Dome Chapel was requisitioned for physical education periods. On 14 September 1964 tree-felling and demolition of the music room, biology laboratory and the east cloakroom started in preparation for a new East Wing. Interestingly, excavations revealed two wells but no hidden treasure. Music lessons were transferred to the Congregational Church Hall and Breeze Hill was used as a quiet base for GCE exams. By the spring of 1966 the roof was on the new building which was finally ready

for occupation on 12 September 1966. The new accommodation comprised science laboratories, music rooms, the gym, housecraft rooms, dining hall and kitchens and was officially opened by Lady Bromley-Davenport on 26 October. The sports facilities at Belgrave Road were upgraded with five new all-weather hard courts which could be used for hockey, lacrosse or tennis, and the old dining room was used as changing rooms.

The East Wing seen from Enville Road

On 4 July 1964 the Old Girls' Society celebrated its Golden Jubilee with a buffet supper in the School Hall to which husbands were invited. Special guests included Miss Drought, Mrs Elsie Gregory who was a member of the Society in its first year (see Chapter 1), and Miss Whitwill who proposed a toast to the Old Girls' Society, and after a salutation to 'lambs of all ages and sizes' said a heartfelt thank you to the late Miss Howes Smith, and to Miss Drought and Miss Okell.

Lynne Rose, formerly Greer, writes:

"1964! THE BEATLES, mods and rockers, Jean Shrimpton and my first year at ACGS. Hundreds of girls of all shapes and sizes were streaming up The Downs laughing, chatting and relaxed. My friend Kathy Ormerod and I didn't admit that our excitement was tinged with just a spot of anxiety as

Lynne Greer

Alison Carter as Hiawatha, Jean Murray as Nokomis and (lying down) Veronica Needham as Minnehaha

we walked along, so obviously first-formers in our smart blazers with spanking new badges. I had chosen an air hostess hat which needed a bit of balancing and a leather briefcase whose sharp edge cut into my calves.

A variety of teachers spring to mind. Miss Ashworth taught domestic science. In the first lesson we were shown how to wash up properly before making cocoa and toast with marmalade. I've since grown to like it. Miss Newbrook brought history alive, especially in the Sixth Form. Miss Okell was just perfect as Headmistress. A mature lady with short wavy grey hair and sufficiently superior to keep us all in check but in a kindly way."

1964 was also *Hiawatha* year. For the second time in the School's history *Hiawatha's Wedding Feast* was performed at the Garrick Theatre. An immense amount of work went on behind the scenes by staff, girls, parents and friends: for example working parties of girls made 150 pairs of moccasins in their dinner hours from material supplied by parents. Five evening performances were given starting on 13 July.

Jean Usher, formerly Murray, recalls many musical memories.

"STRANGELY, I CANNOT REMEMBER the first time I met Miss Porritt, the teacher who was to have the greatest influence on my life. I was lucky enough to have been one of the very few girls who had piano lessons with her. Probably my greatest musical memory was a performance of *Hiawatha* which took place in the Garrick Theatre. We helped Mrs Cooke to paint the costumes which were made of some sort of sack-cloth, and since the performances were in the summer we got very hot and sticky in them. I had a small solo part – Nokomis, Hiawatha's grandmother – a role which I shared with another girl, and on alternate nights I sang in the chorus. I can't imagine what the inhabitants of Altrincham must have thought of the hordes of female Native Americans riding down by coach to the theatre in full costume and make-up. The biggest surprise in the performance was the singing of *On, away, awake beloved* which was performed by the new Latin teacher, Mr Cookson, who had a stunning tenor voice. Since he was dressed in costume, which made him indistinguishable from those of us in the chorus, it must have been quite a shock for the audience when he began his solo!

In 1960, I also had a part to play in the Jubilee Speech Day which took place in the Free Trade Hall in Manchester. The orchestra performed an arrangement of Rimsky-Korsakov's *Scheherazade* in which I played the harp part on the piano, as we didn't have a harpist. I was very proud to be able to tell everyone that I had played the piano in the Free Trade Hall."

Jean Usher with one of her grandsons

By 1965 the Sixth Form had increased significantly. In the light of this the function of the prefect system was re-evaluated and after much deliberation was revised. The Head Girl and her two deputies were now supported by a termly-elected committee whose task it was to organise Sixth Form duties and responsibilities, the Lower Sixth taking over the summer term when Upper Sixth girls were absorbed in their examinations. This committee was chaired by the Head Girl.

Jenny Aitchison, formerly Carman, says:

The completed East Wing with dining hall, gym and laboratories

> "CONTRASTING SOME OF THE SCHOOLS I have taught in with ACGS, I realise just how fortunate we were to be able to learn in such a beautiful environment.
>
> Random memories come to mind: the Sick Room clock with its monstrously loud ticks and clunks; the shrubbery behind the school where we used to play at riding horses and making jumps with branches and logs; Room 9, the echoing Congregational Church Hall and 2nd year form room, where we practised our French choral speaking of *Le Corbeau et le Reynard*; lunch in the canteen down the road, where the table prefects served the meal from metal tins, which made my teeth ache when the spoon was scraped across them; Miss Davenport made you eat up all your lumpy mashed potato when she was on duty; sitting on benches on the gallery at Speech Day, the evening John F Kennedy was shot; being invited to lunch at Mrs Wynn-Griffith's house for an S level French class. She showed us how to make radish 'roses' – how sophisticated we felt! These are all small memories, but ones that could not be repeated in the same way in other schools; they make up the rich fabric of my seven years at ACGS, happy years for which I am very grateful."

Lindsey Pilkington remembers:

> "WE STARTED SCHOOL in tunics with sashes and 80 denier stockings complete with suspender belt (the days before tights!). Then came the mini! Morning assembly, girls rolling skirts up at the waistband to create a miniskirt from our longer than knee length school skirt. Miss Holderness made girls with short skirts kneel on stage to check the hem was not more than two inches above the knee. Humiliation! Years later when the midi skirt was fashionable we were again penalised if our skirts were too long!
>
> I remember learning the French alphabet with Miss Colenutt in the form of a French play with the Prince, a Princess and soldiers (U, V, W, X, Y, Z). Even now my Mum (Leila), Auntie Shirley (formerly Jones) and I cannot recite the alphabet without the intonations and emphases of the playlet!"

Wendy Wood, formerly Welsby, recalls with humour many personalities from her era:

> "MRS MCCUTCHEON WAS an enormously tall Canadian physics teacher who used to wear the gaudiest shoes possible and arrive in the smallest sports car imaginable – a Triumph Spitfire convertible. The car would stop, the door would open, out would come the peacock blue stiletto sling backs first, then she would gracefully unfold herself like a butterfly emerging from its cocoon until she reached her full height, towering over the tiny little car below. Miss Daniels, the history teacher, shocked everyone, staff as well as pupils, when she arrived in a TROUSER suit! Never before had a pair of trousers been worn to school, as she was informed from above.

East Wing entrance

Barbara Stockton, Wendy Wood, Susan McEvoy, Janet Aldridge, 2005

The best cookery lesson we had with Miss Ashworth was when we were to make meringues. There were several hand whisks and only one electric whisk. We had a girl in our class who was always the one to get the best of everything and, needless to say, she got the electric whisk. We had to stand our bowls of egg white in a bowl of cold water in the sink before whisking. I don't know whether she got a drop of washing up liquid in her bowl or what, but, whilst the rest of us were busy developing biceps that even Popeye would have been proud of and still making no impression whatsoever on the white liquid, this girl had turned on her whisk and, Hey Presto, she had instant meringue. It filled the bowl. It overflowed, went onto the bench and then the floor and, still, it kept on coming! We called for the teacher's help. Miss Ashworth duly arrived with a mop and bucket and not even the hint of a smile.

I have so many happy memories of my time at Alty Grammar (as it was then known), and they were the best years of my life and definitely the best cheese pie I have ever tasted."

Moira Percival, formerly Flanagan, writes:

"1966 WAS A BRILLIANT YEAR for me as England won the World Cup and I started at ACGS several weeks later. The East Wing was being constructed and I recollect it was opened a month later by Lady Bromley-Davenport. Miss Okell retired in 1967, passing the reins on to Miss Jackson, who always reminded me of the Queen, especially as she was accompanied by her little corgi dog.

My classroom was in the West Wing and Miss Daniels was our form mistress as well as a brilliant inspirational history teacher. Mr Jowett, the scripture teacher, was a Special Constable and one day instead of telling us about the Dead Sea Scrolls he taught us self-defence. Thankfully I have never needed to use the upward knee thrust he taught us.

The swinging sixties was the time that Manchester United were doing brilliantly. I managed to get tickets for the European Cup Final against Benfica at Wembley in May 1968 and was able to have the afternoon off courtesy of Miss Jackson to travel down for that glorious Wednesday night fixture.

I had a great time at ACGS and there was never a dull moment. A wonderfully committed staff opened up my mind to the possibilities that such an excellent education prepared me for."

Another ambitious event took place in December 1966 when three performances of Malcolm Williamson's modern opera *The Happy Prince*, based on a fairy story by Oscar Wilde, were given in St John's Church, Altrincham to mark the occasion of its centenary. The opera, composed for solo voices, two pianos and percussion, had only been produced once before. The School was delighted to receive a telegram of encouragement from the composer. The following year the opera was performed again by the School in a BBC recording studio and broadcast one Sunday morning in July.

Helen Myers-Halling, formerly Myers, recalls her

"HAPPY INTRODUCTION TO LANGUAGES and fond memories of time spent in the choir, the highlights of which were appearing in *Hiawatha* and playing a dark-haired angel in *The Happy Prince*."

Helen Myers-Halling

Jennifer Reed writes with great affection:

"THE SCHOOL RANG WITH MUSIC when I was there. In the early sixties the nerve centre was the old music room, a beautiful long wood-floored room with a row of windows along one side looking onto the grass tennis courts. I can still hear Miss Anderton, hand clasped to her diaphragm, saying 'Feel it here, girls, feel it here,' as she took us through our warm-up exercises, and the distinctly pre-war pronunciation of the word 'piano' with a long 'a'.

As well as choir and orchestra, there were two madrigal groups, junior and senior, and countless small instrumental ensemble groups, trios, quartets and quintets. If anyone wanted to learn an instrument, lessons were provided free by the County. I once totted up the numbers of staff; my conclusion was that we had around forty academic staff, but, including all the part-timers, we had about sixty staff teaching us music in one form or another.

The quality was of such a high standard, too. When I was in the junior madrigal group we won the sight-singing prize at the North West Music Festival, which was a competition open to all ages. We were given a piece of four-part harmony, a single leading note (by Miss Porritt of course) and off we went unaccompanied.

From time to time since leaving School, I have recounted this story to people from other schools, always to be met with amazement, because no-one else had experienced anything like it. I suppose it was part of the accepted training for young ladies, bearing in mind it was not long since the school had changed from being a private one, though I always prefer to think of it as being part of a proper training in the liberal arts that is missing from so many educational establishments now."

So many others have paid tribute to the music department, which was unquestionably a force in its own right, running in parallel with top quality academic teaching. They include: Pamela Smith, Sue Wilson, formerly Williams, Erica Wilks (Jones), Judi Edwards (MacIver), Virginia Castick (Whipp), Ruth Horsley, Kit Clay (Kathleen Finn), Janet Billingsley (Horner), and Christina Vivian (Flashman), who comments on

"MISS PORRITT'S PASSION for her choirs – if other activities tempted, we were to say we had a prior commitment. I recall so much about Miss Porritt with her straight back, her iron grip on classes, her deep respect for Miss Clayton and her loyalty to me. That may sound a strange way round, but she kept in touch with me through the years by Christmas card and letter, even attending my ordination in London in 1983. Miss Clayton was much more relaxed but kept control just as much in a subject where it would be easy not to. I remember her smile, her directing of the local light opera group and the time when she had her radio in the Music Room to listen to the third moon landing."

Christina Flashman

And finally Charlotte Monk, formerly Jane Taylor, adds:

"MY FAVOURITE TEACHERS WERE Miss Kathleen Porritt and Miss Heather Clayton of the music department, for both instilled a love of music in me – Miss Porritt encouraged me to pursue singing and helped to get me into the

County Youth Choir. She was very 'old school' in her ways but she went up in my estimation on returning from a school trip to London with us on the train when she brought out a silver hip flask and took a good swig! Heather Clayton accompanied us on a trip to Bregenz in Austria and she and I stood at the front of the swaying bus harmonising to yodling songs as we travelled along. Both Miss Porritt's and Miss Clayton's efforts with me had a lasting effect and I now run Amorata, a professional theatrical vocal ensemble in Bristol."

Charlotte Monk

1967 was a year of retirements. Miss Anderton had become a legend in her own lifetime – the tributes paid to her from former pupils in this book alone serve to underline the tremendous respect and admiration felt for her throughout five decades of teaching. She was born in 1886 and appointed in 1913 to the school she served so faithfully for fifty-four years.

The following extracts are from tributes in the School Magazine.

"GENERATIONS OF GIRLS could not fail to be impressed by her striking appearance and quiet dignity; the movements of her often large classes controlled by simple gestures with the minimum of speech. Everyone was aware of her musical ability but what was not widely known was an interest she had of an entirely different kind. At their Golden Jubilee dinner the 'Old Girls' presented her with a portable radio, not so that she could listen to good music in her bedroom, but so that she might not need to go downstairs to listen to boxing matches from America in the middle of the night!"

Miss Colenutt was born in 1902 and appointed to the School in 1930, becoming Head of Modern Languages four years later.

"SHE WAS OFTEN TAKEN for a French woman, for her mastery of the language and her insight into all things French were quite exceptional. Moreover, she was a woman of infinite variety, for not only was she a linguist, but she excelled in many other ways. Her acting ability and knowledge of the theatre was renowned, and the School had much to thank her for in her work for dramatic and operatic productions. In addition she was a needlewoman, an artist and a poet; gifts which she never allowed to lie dormant. Her dynamic personality and wit endeared her to everyone and she inspired all who came into contact with her brilliant teaching."

Christine Moore (right) with friend Marita Frank

At this point it seems appropriate to include a personal tribute to Miss Colenutt from Christine Willey, formerly Moore:

"QUAND JE SUIS ARRIVÉE au lycée, je me suis trouvée dans la classe 1A. Notre professeur principal s'appelait Mademoiselle Colenutt et elle était aussi notre professeur de français. Son nom donne l'impression qu'elle devrait avoir les cheveux noirs, mais en fait elle avait les cheveux totalement blancs comme neige, quoiqu'elle n'ait que cinquante ans – je crois, mais je ne sais pas exactement. Elle nous a dit qu'elle avait les cheveux blancs depuis plus de vingt ans. C'était un trait génétique et elle en était très fière. Elle était toujours très bien coiffée. Elle était très gentille et aimable envers cette classe de petites filles. Elle m'a ouverte aux études des langues étrangées. Elle avait beaucoup d'enthousiasme; elle adorait la France et tout ce

The School Orchestra at
Breeze Hill.
Members include Susan Willacy,
Deborah Bryde, Ann Stirling,
Jenny Reed, Hilary McCormac,
Cathy Manning, Virginia
Whipp, Arlene Rose, Christine
Bell, Lesley Shrigley-Jones.

qui est français. Elle nous racontait aussi beaucoup d'histoires de ses souvenires de ses séjours en France et de la vie chez elle quand elle était plus jeune. Elle nous a parlé par exemple de ses frères qui voulaient absolute conduire la voiture familial. Elle n'avait jamais gagné un permis de conduire quoiqu'elle ait su conduire. On ne lui permettait que de sortir la voiture du garage. Je crois qu'il était un sujet de disputes chez Colenutt!

Elle a continué à donner des classes de conversation française longtemps après s'être retirée et elle est morte très vieille il y a quelques années – *requiescat in pace*."

Miss Okell was born in 1907, appointed Headmistress in 1953, and retired after fourteen years.

"DURING THIS TIME she guided the school with great wisdom, strength and kindness. She came to a school with a good reputation and left it with an even better one.

During her headship the school had grown from 570 pupils to over 840, with a corresponding increase in staff. She had to cope with the difficulties of overcrowding and managed to maintain a sense of unity at a time when the school was spread over so many locations, and spent countless hours planning major improvements to Breeze Hill and the building of the new East Wing.

Miss Okell kept alive all the best of the school's traditions as well as introducing new ideas and encouraging the idea of 'service for others'. Like her predecessors she seemed tireless in her dedicated service to the school, and her personal elegance set a striking example to her pupils."

Miss Joan Jackson was appointed Headmistress succeeding Miss Okell. She was born and educated in Manchester, attending the Manchester Central High School for Girls. At the University of Manchester during the second world war she gained an honours degree in geography on an intensive two-year course and a diploma in education. Initially she taught at Winsford Verdin Grammar School then Stockport High School for Girls before becoming Head of the Geography Department at the North Manchester High School and later Deputy Headmistress there. Her first headship was at Cavendish Grammar School for Girls in Buxton.

Lydia Dyer, formerly Kakabadse, joined the School at the same time as Miss Jackson and recalls:

"MY FIRST YEAR COINCIDED with Miss Jackson's first year as Headmistress. I was introduced to lacrosse played at the Dome, and was so relieved when this sport was removed from the curriculum the following year. Catching a fast, hard hitting ball in a pouched racket at head level was not my idea of fun and it certainly didn't tally with Enid Blyton's description of lacrosse games in *Malory Towers*!

My great passion was for music, especially composition, and I loved playing the piano at Assembly, playing the double bass in the school orchestra and various ensemble groups, taking up the viola in the Sixth Form as well as singing in madrigals and the choir. Miss Porritt with her enthusiastic yet no-nonsense approach was a true inspiration. One winter's day I clearly remember her asking us to put our hands up if we were wearing a vest. Only I and two other girls raised our hands. She was clearly unimpressed with the rest of the class.

I took music, German and Latin at A level and I was rather fortunate that both teachers, Miss Yorston and Mr Cookson respectively, were not only great music enthusiasts but also amateur musicians. Miss Yorston was an accomplished guitarist and lute player and Mr Cookson was an amateur opera tenor.

After leaving ACGS I went on to read music (BMus Hons) at the University of London (Royal Holloway College). In my thirties I switched to law, entered the legal profession and balanced composing with working as a commercial solicitor. Looking back,

Miss Okell in a relaxed moment with Miss Rowbotham's dog Toddie, 1959

I would say that ACGS with its impressive school motto – *Fortiter, Fideliter, Feliciter* – instilled in me a deep sense of duty and discipline, which has served me well both in my personal and professional life."

Gill Lowe has bitter-sweet memories of the sixties. She writes:

"WHAT I RECALL MOST is being a teenager in the sixties and the confusion and rebellion that resulted as a consequence of the social change occurring at that time. I remember the feeling of pressure – I had to pass the eleven plus as my sister and brother had done so. My sister was already at School so I also felt I had 'big shoes' to fill.

I was definitely considered as more rebellious than conformist and resented having to wear a uniform, especially the hats. The prefects, the religious assemblies, the élitism that resulted

Miss Joan Jackson

from what form you were placed in, were not in sync with my way of looking at the world. Miss Daniels, who taught history, was a great influence on me, as was Mrs Cooke the art teacher, who believed in my talent.

In retrospect my time at ACGS was influential in that it gave me a good education. I believe I did not take advantage of it at the time, but have since become a successful businesswoman working in Canada and Australia in the field of medical education."

Margaret Rathwell, formerly Hardman, recalls:

"THE YEARS AT ACGS were important ones in my life as I expect the secondary school years are for most of us. We enter as naïve eleven-year-olds and leave at eighteen as young adults. The teachers and Headmistress were slightly to be feared and also like gods to us as models of the adults we were to become. I remember the climate at school being positive, correct and mostly friendly with the right amount of discipline.

Of our teachers my geography teacher Mrs Delides was the biggest influence on me as on other girls. I remember her elegance and grace, her long black hair tied back in a loose bun, and her wisdom: she was a perfect role model for us. She talked to us about life and the world always very honestly. I still remember a lot of her insights and practical advice to us about TV being a waste of time, about not worrying about getting married (a pressing concern for girls of our age), there would always be time for that even if we looked like 'the back end of a bus'. I loved geography; it all seemed so relevant and I went on to study geography at Durham University. When I won the Sixth Form Maths Prize, I was awarded a book token with which I bought an atlas and a book on India, both of which I still have. I didn't know then that I would visit India many times!"

In 1969 the portrait of Miss Okell painted by Harold Riley was completed. The *School Magazine* records:

"IT WAS PRESENTED TO HER at a special ceremony on Founders' Day on behalf of pupils, parents and staff by Carol Goulden who had been Miss Okell's last Head Girl. By eight o'clock everyone was assembled in the Hall. Propped up on an easel on one corner of the platform stood the object of everyone's curiosity veiled in voluminous blue velvet. When it was unveiled there was a short pause while everyone studied the somewhat unconventional representation, and then Miss Okell gave an amusing and fascinating account of how the portrait was painted. She said that it had been a wonderful experience for which she was grateful as it had given her a better understanding of an artist's method of expression. She spoke of her curiosity to see how the portrait was progressing during sittings and also expressed something of the honour when Harold Riley having visited School to see his subject agreed to undertake it! His name was now well known and his fame was increasing. The portrait now hangs in the Hall but Miss Okell was given one of the preliminary sketches for it as a keepsake, as well as a book containing the names, arranged alphabetically, of all who contributed to the fund, each letter being assigned a different flower painted by a pupil of the School."

Miss R G Okell
by Harold Riley

The 1970s

1970	15 January – PTA founded
1970	4 July – 60th anniversary of Founders' Day
1970	July – School Diamond Jubilee celebrations
1971	April – *Noye's Fludde*
1971	July – retirement of the Misses Davenport and Porritt
1972	April – two Deputy Heads, year tutors introduced
1974	30 March – 60th anniversary of Old Girls' Society
1974	1 April – School name change
1975	1 October – work starts on Sixth Form Centre, Devisdale
1977	1 July – Sixth Form Centre opened
1979	August – Miss Rowbotham, School Secretary, retires

CHAPTER 7
THE 1970S

The inaugural meeting of the Parents' Association was held on 15 January 1970. Dr Michael Winstanley, MP for Cheadle, talked about his work in the House of Commons. This was the precursor of a regular programme of meetings and fund-raising activities for the benefit of the School and the girls in particular.

Another decade and another significant anniversary was celebrated, this time the sixtieth year since the School was founded in 1910. On Thursday 2 July the Founders' Day service was held in the afternoon at St Mary's Church, Bowdon. The next day Founders' Day excursions went to London, Chester, York, Stratford-upon-Avon, Blackpool, the Lake District, Malham and Ingleton – to mark the Diamond Jubilee. The following week on Tuesday 7 July, Wednesday 8 July and Sunday 12 July School was open to visitors in afternoons when exhibitions, displays and lessons were in progress. On Saturday 11 July the Old Girls' Society held a Buffet Supper for 240 members and guests. The *Old Girls' News* reports that:

> "MISS JACKSON, Miss Drought, Miss Okell, Mrs Hinchcliffe (Chairman of the Governors), Old Girls, past and present members of staff, husbands of a number of old girls and even some Old Boys, gathered in the Hall. The MC was Mr James Gardiner, an old boy now on the staff of Sheffield University.
>
> After the usual greetings everyone made a determined move to the Dining Room for Supper, following which the toasts were given including the final one to the School by Miss Whitwill. The meeting was timed to end at 10.30pm but half an hour later so many groups of people were still talking hard that the poor Committee was driven to turning off the lights one by one, as a gentle hint!"

ALTRINCHAM COUNTY GRAMMAR SCHOOL FOR GIRLS
DIAMOND JUBILEE 1910-1970

Old Girls' Society Buffet Supper
SATURDAY 11th JULY 1970
AT
THE SCHOOL

Reception 7-30 p.m. for 8-15 p.m.   Cars 10-30 p.m.

Admittance only by this ticket

Admission ticket

Doreen Harrison, who had been at School at the time of Miss Howes Smith, decided to accept the invitation to attend the celebrations and see for herself how things had changed after a gap of over thirty years. She wrote in the *News*:

> "I GOT A GUILTY FEELING for a start when I entered by the front door: surely I should have gone in by the cloakrooms? And when a shortage of ash trays necessitated my flicking ash on

OGS Buffet Supper
Mrs Hinchcliffe, Miss Jackson, Miss Drought,
Miss Whitwill, Miss Okell, Mr Gardiner

OGS Buffet Supper: Miss Okell, Miss Drought, Miss Jackson

the floor, how gleefully I dismissed any sense of guilt. Stubbing out the end on, what to me is the 'new' part of the parquet floor, however, was another matter and I walked round with it in my hand rather than grind it beneath my foot. I was remembering the days when the Hall extension was finished, we were still not allowed to walk on it in shoes until the polishing operation was well under way. Now it is barely possible to discern the difference between the two parts of the floor. Polished to perfection, it has mellowed with the years.

I made my own contribution to the racket which was going on in the corridor en route for the Buffet and thought that we must all be making up for those years of 'no talking in the corridors' and revelling in the thought that not a prefect amongst us could call us to heel.

No ghostly feelings for me as I wandered along corridors where my feet had so often been told not to run. I was back forty years and full of happy memories. True there was a tinge of regret that the murals painted by the sixth formers of the day on the top corridor in the New Wing (a misnomer now indeed) had been sacrificed to the need for redecoration, but with a smile I noted the piano tucked away by the stairs where once stood a table at which we queued for, of all things, hot milk!

Inspection of the new buildings dispelled all preconceived ideas of 'horror and sacrilege'. The sacrifice of the woods has been more than compensated for. How I could have lingered over all the exhibits – and how I wished I was starting School again in September. I thought we had everything in the thirties. I still think we had, but now everything is multiplied and gilt-edged. I am fascinated.

I talked to Miss Whitwill about things far removed from School, but at the back of my mind her voice was saying patiently: 'Doreen, my infant, weren't you listening?' (Of course I was or why should I have donned my kilt and gone to fight in the '45 Rebellion just as she asked me something? That was her trouble – she made history LIVE). I talked to Miss Bell and laughed with her over the 'bloomers' we had to make and which turned out so large as to be suitable only for a circus clown. If only I had known then that she thought they were hideous, too!

Having thus reminisced, regretted, marvelled, approved, enjoyed the delightful Supper and met up with old friends, how had I found HS's 'building'? I found it doing fine. Over the years three architects have made their mark in the style of architecture and the fourth is now leaving hers. Each has had her wishes and ideas carried out by a dedicated team of 'workmen' who made, and are still making, a wonderful variety of 'bricks' from all manner of materials – but always in the same basic mould. Long may they go on being made and as each new one is laid may its owner feel as proud and as privileged as I do to be a 'brick in the building which is not made with hands', for surely this building is what ACGS is really all about – isn't it?"

OGS Buffet Supper
Miss Whitwill proposed the toast to 'The School'.

Diamond Jubilee Buffet Supper: the OGS Committee and helpers
Back row: Edith Percival, Betty Bradshaw, Evelyn Aldhouse, Jean Clark, Jean Whipp, Edith Skene,
Muriel Smith; middle row: Mary Kryzanowska, Lillian Corris, Frances Noden, Claire Allen, Muriel Stainton,
Joan Dew, Sylvia Ashworth; front row: Ella Seed, Joyce Kendrick, Ruth Blakeney-Flynn

The School continued to be outstanding in the music sphere. In April 1971 at St John's Church, Altrincham, four evening performances of an ambitious production of a triple programme of Benjamin Britten works were staged: *Psalm 150*, *Missa Brevis* and *Noye's Fludde*. Over 200 girls and staff were involved and were joined by trumpeters from Sale Boys' Grammar School and many friends of our School who played in the orchestra.

At the end of the summer term in 1971 both Miss Davenport and Miss Porritt retired. Miss Jackson wrote:

"MARJORIE DAVENPORT, born in 1905, was a pupil during Miss Howes Smith's time and appointed to the staff in 1937. She was particularly associated with the junior part of the School, eventually becoming First Year Tutor, and gave the first forms a keen awareness of the school's traditions and the standards they would be expected to maintain. Her firm but kind guidance has been remembered affectionately by countless former pupils, many of whom now have daughters in school.

Kathleen Ingham Porritt was born in 1907 and appointed as music mistress in 1939. When the school grew in size she became Head of the Music Department. An accomplished musician, she inspired her classes with her own deep love of music. Under her direction our choirs and orchestra acquired a well-deserved reputation for excellence in music-making and their performances in festivals, concerts and productions such as *Hiawatha* and *The Happy Prince* gave pleasure to the School and public alike.

Together they gave sixty-six years of service to the School. They saw it grow in size and change and develop: and their enthusiasm and involvement in all aspects of its life could only be matched by their adaptability and their youthful outlook. Many girls will remember with pleasure the sight of Miss Davenport joining in the games at the first form Christmas Party and of Miss Porritt jigging about at the dance to the strains of a local pop group."

May Lindsay, formerly Lennie, recalls:

"THIS WAS THE TIME of feathered hair, above knee socks, platform shoes and skirts shortened by waistbands folded up into several layers. School hats (air hostess type or beret) had just become non-compulsory. Miss Davenport (English teacher and Mistress in charge of First Forms) was renowned for her 'jumpers off' and 'windows open'! A door guard was posted to signal the approach of Miss Holderness (maths teacher and Deputy Headmistress). She is well remembered for her strictly frightening demeanour and temper that left many a girl in floods of tears.

Miss Porritt with Barrie and Heather Clayton (left) and Yvonne Bertin (right) on their last day at School in 1950

Domestic science lessons with Miss Ashworth were tolerated with interest. We made and wore tabards with gingham trimmings and cooked rock buns and bread and butter pudding. Music lessons with Miss Porritt; her wrinkled elegance and enthusiasm – 'Cools my brow and rests my blood – sets my spirit free.' Prior to becoming Deputy Headmistress, Mrs Delides's eloquent geographical monologues necessitated many hours of homework. I was fortunate to have been taught for O and A levels by Mrs Hurd.

Games lessons were my favourite. There was a short trail to the Dome – here, we played netball, hockey and tennis. Lacrosse was abandoned after 1968. Miss Reid – who resembled Virginia Wade – expertly coached tennis. Our greatest success was winning the Lady Harley Cup in 1974, a competition open to all schools in Cheshire. Less pleasurable were the gym lessons when we had to reveal our ghastly navy knickers and pretend to have a shower!

Mrs Driver was a dominant figure in the games department and inspired many a games team to victory. I was the first to dare imitate her in the entertainment of Christmas 1974 – wearing a short mid-blue pleated games skirt and wig and covering my legs with red chalk. I had to run along the balcony – shouting and blowing a whistle. I was not recognised as she had never heard me shout before!

Hockey and tennis matches were played on Saturday mornings against various schools in

Winners of the Lady Harley Cup, July 1974 Back row: Janet Fordham, May Lennie, Suzanne Millard, Lynda Hale, Hilary Cope; front row: Christine Jenkinson, Susan Whitehead, Suzanne Lewtas

the district. I recall one occasion when the coach became jammed under the canal bridge at Dunham on the way to Lymm. The bridge began to leak and we were all evacuated.

We were one of the first not to wear uniform in the sixth form and about the last to wear green jumpers. My time at the school spanned Miss Jackson's reign as Headmistress. I recall her regal trail round the corridor from study to platform with Head Girl and Deputies in tow, to sit on huge carved wooden thrones with those famous lions looking on from behind."

Sarah Flynn, formerly Sheppard, remembers:

"MY FIRST IMPRESSIONS OF THE SCHOOL as an eleven-year-old were that it was massive with so many people. It had a great gym with amazing apparatus, science labs with taps that could be turned round so you could send a jet of water across the room, and a fantastic room with huge windows where we had geography lessons and could watch the different shapes of the clouds floating by. The Hall had a balcony – wow!

Uniform was strict and in my first year hats had to be worn. The choice was the air hostess version favoured by girls but not their parents because it was more expensive than the beret that I had! Skirt length was an important issue policed by Miss Davenport. The other uniform infringement that she didn't like was any deviation from plain white or fawn knee socks. The fashion of white socks with little flowers down the sides was most definitely unacceptable. By the time I got to the Sixth Form we could wear non-uniform clothes but they had to be smart. Trousers were frowned upon!

Miss Clayton taught us music and was instrumental in some brilliant singing lessons. Miss Gowland was passionate about drosophila flies, soil and the botany garden. Mrs Peckett taught us physics and was very encouraging and would no doubt be pleased that I did get my act together at university and came out with a good degree in the end. Learning about the stars around the third year helped turn me on to science. My favourite English teacher was Mrs Clegg because she was just so kind. Miss Holderness was a force to behold and a very good mathematician.

Mrs Driver made PE and games fun, especially hockey, where we could shout to encourage our team-mates. She encouraged me to run the 800 metres in the summer when we were doing athletics. I wasn't very keen but Mrs D would be pleased to know that I have since run half marathons so she was right to spur me on. For a while we had country dancing in the hall as part of PE which most of us really enjoyed.

The Christmas Fairs were great fun with all manner of craft work and homemade goodies. The best sellers one year were posters of Marc Bolan and David Cassidy drawn by one of the girls who was very talented at art.

I was at the school when it was the Diamond Jubilee open day. I was thrilled that my Mum and Auntie Essie came to watch me in a performance in the old gym of schools throughout the ages with authentic costumes from bygone times. The costumes for the school of the future were made out of plastic tablecloths. Unfortunately the tape keeping the pieces of plastic together was not very strong and one poor girl lost her skirt mid-performance but she bravely hitched it back up and carried on keeping to the thespian mantra of 'the show must go on.' The whole day was full of exciting demonstrations and displays in all the different departments for parents, guests and girls to see.

Some of the best things about the school were that you always felt safe and people were generally polite and caring. You could leave things on your peg, and in your desk, and they would still be there the next week. Some lessons were boring but mostly I felt inspired to learn. I made brilliant friends, a few of whom I still keep in touch with and see from time to time."

Julie Cardoza, formerly Booth, recalls:

"WHEN I LOOK BACK ON IT I realise my school years were when there was a period of change at the school. When I started, the school was very much a traditional girls' grammar school with its lovely old-fashioned atmosphere with schoolmistresses rather than teachers.

I remember going with my parents during the summer to Henry Barrie school outfitters in Manchester with my list of required school uniform. It is a really clear memory and I know I felt a mixture of excitement and trepidation about starting at Altrincham County Grammar School for Girls. My navy knife-edged pleated skirt was about six inches below my knees and my green science overall came down to my ankles. This was nothing to do with school uniform regulations, it's just that my mum said they were expensive and I would have to grow into them! I don't think I ever did grow into the science overall. What I do remember about science is having to pay for the scores of test tubes I broke on a weekly basis, endless experiments involving Bunsen burners which never worked and one brave and daring soul climbing out of a first floor window in the middle of a science lesson to see if the teacher noticed! Funnily enough I don't recall learning very much about science. My school report for chemistry for my third year says 'Julie would do better if she were less silly in class.' I wish they had written 'Julie would do better if she had a slightly shorter science overall.'

By fourth year, however, the seventies had well and truly arrived. My school shoes were now six-inch heels with platform soles, my skirt was rolled up as much as possible over the knee socks that were in fashion. I loved to sit in the conservatory of the downstairs art room at Breeze Hill reading my *Jackie* magazine. We didn't like Room 9 in the church at all though. Older girls had told us that it was used at the weekend for storing coffins before funerals and for some reason we believed them.

By the time I went into Lower Sixth in 1974 the decision had been made that sixth-formers didn't have to wear uniform. There didn't seem to be many rules about what we wore. I remember I used to wear a purple maxi coat and a Manchester City scarf.

I like the fact that in the forty years since I started there, the School has changed with the times but the essence of it is still the same. There are still the ultra-clever girls, the ultra-sporty girls, the not-so-sporty-at-all girls who would do anything to get out of a PE lesson, the fashion followers, the rebels.

Bravely I stood before Miss Jackson and her corgi when I was in trouble for swinging on trees. Faithfully I learnt and recited French verbs for Miss Huddart. Cheerfully I attended Mrs Driver's netball practices at Dome in the hope of making the team. I hope there will be Alty Girls being brave, faithful and cheerful for the next hundred years. Good Luck!"

By April 1972 there were 940 girls on the roll, which entitled the School to two Deputy Head-mistresses. Miss Holderness was joined by Mrs Delides, who had been Head of Geography since 1956. Increased numbers and social changes both demand continual modification of one sort

Form 5A1, 1972–73

Upper Sixth,
1974–75

or another. No one person can keep a close eye on the individual needs of nearly a thousand young people; hence the development of a system of year tutors. These members of staff are charged with the pastoral care of all the girls in one whole year group. They interview parents and watch over each girl's progress. A year tutor is also a form tutor within the year group for which she is responsible, and often she moves up with her group at the beginning of a new school year and so continues to be year tutor to the same set of girls. In this way she comes to know them very well and they are helped to feel at home in a large community.

The system of morning assemblies also needed modification so that all girls could attend an Assembly in the Hall at least once a week. It had been a long time since the school was small enough to meet as a whole, but in the summer, when sixth-formers had finished their exams and left, it was still possible for the remainder to congregate in the Hall for the last few weeks of term.

On 28 September 1972 Miss Anderton died. Miss Porritt wrote in the *Old Girls' News*:

"ANDY, HOW ELSE CAN I write of her? This is how we knew her, spoke of her and thought of her. When I was appointed to the School on 20 March 1939, I first met Andy. She was living then, temporarily, at a farm on the Hough at Wilmslow, and it was at that farm and on that evening that we made each other's acquaintance. There will be others who recall her years of music making before this date, those who will remember that she had a singing career of national standing ahead of her. A breakdown in health brought an untimely end to this happy prospect. The concert platform and the operatic stage were deprived of a consummate artist, but instead, her brilliance was to be expressed in another direction – hundreds of young people were to have the privilege of benefiting from her artistry.

In 1953 she no longer lived at her bungalow at Alderley Edge; she had moved some little time before this to Grange over Sands, and it was there that she suffered a severe illness. Although she travelled each week to School, she was away from the surroundings she knew so well and from everyone and everything concerned with her life. Her removal to Grange just did not work out and the illness caused six months' absence from School. As she recovered I suggested that she come back to Cheshire, share my home, and return to School, and all of this she did. To be back at School brought joy into her life again, for she was among her old friends and she was able once more to make music. Perhaps, some of our most ambitious music making was undertaken during those years between her return in September 1953 to her retirement in 1967.

At her funeral there was a joyousness through music, and I felt so proud to be with the ten senior choir girls and with Heather Clayton in command. They sang *Brother James's Air* with great beauty and they led us all in the singing of the hymn *Blest are the pure in heart*. And so, although she had gone from us the memory of her and of her great artistry will live on, and in what better way could I finish than to quote the words of an 'old girl' in her letter to me: 'May she rest in peace and her soul soar into eternity.' "

Tina Serb – daughter of Inger Serb (see Chapter 4) and niece of Patricia Bottrill (Chapter 5) – is proud of the family tradition at School.

"I WAS THE THIRD MEMBER of my family to go to ACGS. I have very happy memories of my time there. By this time the school was quite large – around a thousand pupils – and Miss Jackson was Headmistress with Miss Holderness and Mrs Delides as Deputy Heads.

The 1970s included the three day week and power cuts and I remember walking to school in the dark and having to do my homework by candlelight when the power suddenly went off.

Tina Serb, Patricia Bottrill, Inger Serb

My first form was 1.10 – our form room was a small room hidden at the back of the Bowdon Congregational Church. It must have been the most distant classroom in the school and was often so cold in winter (I recorded temperatures of 8°C and 10°C in a diary!) that we had to have lessons huddled by a radiator in the Hall instead.

During our first year the Sixth Form ran lunchtime clubs. I really enjoyed an origami club held in Breeze Hill and was very much in awe of the sixth-formers in their navy uniforms (we wore green jumpers with the school colours around the V neck).

I was taught history by Miss Davenport, singing by Miss Porritt who had taught both my mother and aunt, biology by Miss Gowland and geography by Mrs Delides, both of whom had taught my aunt. Christmas was always a special time – I loved in particular singing carols in Latin. Our small carol books, which were covered in wallpaper for protection, were unpacked and returned to us each Christmas term. There was always tremendous excitement about the Christmas Fair and the build-up which included wonderfully silly contests at lunchtime in the Hall for both girls and staff. We also had the first Christmas Fair to be held in the evening when parents were able to attend.

A great memory for me was being part of the orchestra for the production of *Noye's Fludde* by Benjamin Britten performed at St John's Church, Altrincham. Miss Clayton was in charge of the music, Mr Cookson (Latin teacher and a wonderful singer) played Noah and Mr Telford (geography) played the voice of God.

School trips included a great day out in the Lake District where we crossed Lake Windermere on a boat from Ambleside to Bowness and visited Grasmere and Wordsworth's Dove Cottage. In the Sixth Form we had an ambitious trip to Llandudno which started by train to Liverpool, then a crossing by boat to Llandudno Pier, and ended with us having the freedom to explore the Great Orme and the attractions of the town and beach, and then back home by train.

My favourite subjects were history, geography, English and Latin, and I went on to study history at King's College, London, where I met my partner David. My subsequent career has been in broadcasting. My own daughter Sophie is now ten and we are currently trying to choose a secondary school for her in the South East. I hope her future school will turn out to be as happy and successful a school as ACGS and that she will one day also have very special memories of her schooldays."

On 6 January 1973 Miss Drought died at the age of 83. Ella Seed knew her well and wrote a poignant tribute in the *Old Girls' News* of 1973. Some extracts follow:

"A STILL, SELF-CONTAINED FIGURE standing near one of the pillars in the empty school hall – that was my first impression of Miss Drought. The year was 1933. Later, I often saw her stand on the platform in the same aloof way, especially on the last day of term, waiting for things to settle themselves. It was almost as if that first glimpse had foreshadowed much of the next twenty years. Inevitably, a Headmistress is set at some distance from the community she serves and leads, and DMD's natural reserve of both mind and manner tended to emphasise this distance. But those who could break through – perhaps a better word would be thaw – this reserve, found a gentle, easy, delightful companion, with a quick tongue and an impish relish for very bad puns.

I find it difficult to think of DMD as a Victorian, though her manner could be chilly and very formal if she were feeling unsure of herself or ill at ease. I think this coldness was an instinctive defence against possible disapproval to which she was unusually sensitive. On the other hand, such inner sensitiveness was a help when she had to deal with nervous or troubled children and staff, as she was able to approach their problems through her own feelings, and yet provide that quiet experienced atmosphere and truthful independent assessment which went a long way towards finding a solution.

If in some things she was a Victorian it did not show on the surface. She had a good working knowledge of modern slang and idiom which she used sparingly but surprisingly, and with effect; she ordered her affairs that she might travel light – 'too many possessions can become a millstone round one's neck'; she enjoyed having a few shillings on the Grand National, usually backing the winner, and on one occasion happily scandalising Miss Howes Smith by stating that she was going with friends to Aintree to watch the race. But the world into which DMD had been born in 1890 had very different standards. Her fundamental convictions and guiding principles of conduct came from the older, deeper level.

Thoroughness in all she attempted, constant hard work whether the work were congenial or not, an eye that missed little, a clear mind, independence of judgement – 'I tell the truth with my little hatchet'; these were the tools of a professionalism which put her duties first and herself second.

Since her death I have heard many words of affection and regret spoken of her, but one sentence written before her death comes oftenest to mind. DMD's housekeeper, Miss Patrick, was with her from the time she was at Farnham until the Autumn of 1970 when they were both so crippled with arthritis that their home at Rudgwick could no longer be kept on. DMD made her home with her nephew and his family near Oxford, while Miss Patrick went to an old people's home in Horsham. She died in the late summer of 1972 and in the last letter I had from her, wrote: 'No one will ever know what it cost me to leave my beloved Miss Drought.' Some of us, now that DMD is gone, are slowly learning that cost."

Fiona Key, formerly Harrison writes:

"I WAS IN 2A3 from the second year onwards and our form spent many fun times between lessons – making up silly songs, imitating teachers, even exploring the cellar in the old gym. Fondest memories include those of Mrs Driver's dance group and of music concerts produced by Miss Clayton and Mrs Sumbler.

Mrs Driver formed the Dance Group after we started second year and we continued with it until we entered Sixth Form when we suddenly became rather self-conscious prancing around in black leotards! We gave a performance in the School Hall for teachers, parents and

*The Dance Group in the School Hall,
1973–74*

friends each year using a theatre-in-the-round staging. We performed many stories from the big (*Jonah and the Whale, Oliver, West Side Story*) to the small (*January Sales, Lorelei*). Mrs Driver introduced us to so much classical music during these years including Mussorgsky's *Pictures at an Exhibition*, Prokofiev's *Romeo and Juliet* and Tchaikovsky's *1812 Overture*. Whenever I hear these pieces of music now I am transported right back to Dance Group and whenever my friends and I meet up this topic always crops up in conversation! Mrs Driver truly inspired us.

Making music was also very important to me – Mrs Sumbler gave me private singing lessons throughout school, enabling me to take my Grade 8 Singing in Lower Sixth. The music department was very active, with orchestra and choirs giving concerts at Easter and Christmas. My most magical memories are of our performance of Britten's *Ceremony of Carols* at Hale United Reformed Church in late November 1975 and our performances of Purcell's *Dido and Aeneas* in March 1977 in the School Hall. I sang the part of Dido... and I still have the music and can remember it all! I am still singing and the choir I sing with now performed the Britten last Christmas... very poignant. My love of singing and classical music was well and truly nurtured at AGGS.

*Fiona Key as Dido and
Tina Nobbs as Aeneas*

Six of us within Dance Group made a special bond and we are friends still, meeting as often as we can. In 2008 we organised our thirty-year reunion which included a tour of the school and it was delightful to meet up with Miss Clayton, Mrs Sumbler and Mrs (now Lady!) Driver and a warm and fabulous evening was enjoyed by all."

The Old Girls' Society celebrated sixty years of its existence by holding a buffet supper at School on Saturday 30 March 1974 which was attended by 250 Old Girls (some with their husbands) and past and present members of staff.

Miss Jackson launched the evening with a welcome for all, then handed over to Marjorie Bennion (MC for the occasion) who proposed the loyal toast. Miss Zena Walkley, former Deputy Head until she left in 1966, proposed a toast to the Old Girls' Society to which reply was made by Margaret Christie (formerly Hacking) who left School in 1948.

A toast to the School was proposed by Miss Kathleen Colenutt, Former House Mistress of Delamere House and Head of the French Department for many years until her retirement in 1967. C Marjorie Smith, who left School in 1927, replied:

"WHEN I WAS ASKED to reply to Miss Colenutt, I was assured that I need only be on my feet for a very short time. Later, Miss Colenutt herself sent me an outline of what she was planning to say, and having read this I realise that it was so comprehensive that my task was, indeed, a very small one.

I suppose I could claim to be better qualified to speak of the very early days of the School, when, although purpose-built, it retained much of the atmosphere of a gracious private house, and when the garden still preserved parts of the original Bowdon Lodge.

Some of you will recall that funny little round summerhouse at the far end of the front lawn. Although I believe it had no door at all it was always a point of honour for the small fry of 1915 to make entrance or exit by the window, and pairs of long black woollen-stockinged legs were to be seen wriggling over the sill in an 'in' or 'out' direction.

Also there were those semi-derelict greenhouses down in the far corner beyond the pear trees, that intrigued us so much. We were assured by those 'in the know' that there was an underground tunnel that ran all the way from them to Bowdon Church. One young man – I believe he was called Hughie – told us, with the greatest secrecy, that he had crawled along it himself.

| ALTRINCHAM COUNTY GRAMMAR SCHOOL FOR GIRLS |
| OLD GIRLS' SOCIETY |
| DIAMOND JUBILEE 1914-1974 |
| *BUFFET SUPPER* |
| SATURDAY 30th MARCH 1974 |
| AT |
| THE SCHOOL |
| Reception 7-30 p.m. for 8-15 p.m. |
| Cars 10-30 p.m.   *Admittance only by this ticket* |

Admission ticket

But these details would only be small decorations to the very adequate picture that Miss Colenutt had delighted us with. And how grateful we are to her for recalling for us, so vividly, the history of this place that is so much part of us all.

In a gathering of this kind, the contrast between then and now is always present, and there is a temptation for us oldies to think that our ways were the best. But this School has always been forward looking, moving with the times. How reassuring it is to be reminded how the wisdom of Headmistresses and staff have guided it, with reason, dignity and success through educational whims and fashions so that the School's essential qualities of scholarship and service have been maintained, and are as lively today as Miss Howes Smith's dreams of them in 1910.

We are here as part of something we love and honour, we are here because each of us has contributed towards its making. Today it is not the done thing to be emotional about one's place of education unless one's feelings are the kind that erupt in strikes and sit-ins, but I am sure that many of us tonight are full of gratitude that our educational 'lot fell in a fair ground even in a goodly heritage' (Psalm 16).

Several old girls have written to me lately to say 'I shall try to get along on March 30th because I shan't be about for the next big do.' These sentiments conjure up for me a delightful picture of the present Old Girls' Committee lolling at ease on heavenly clouds, watching their successors in 2010 coping with centenary celebrations.

None of them has said 'and it won't have anything to do with me' for none of us can really disassociate ourselves with the School's future (I hope my shade, anyway, will be lurking behind one of those pillars, having a good gawp at the goings on!).

There is such unity here that all that has been done is being done and will be done fuses and knits together to make this whole that we call 'Our School', and I am sure, tonight, that we are particularly grateful to those who, sixty years ago, brought our special department into being – the Old Girls' Society.

Thank you, Miss Colenutt, for reminding us so clearly of 'this, our heritage' – and thank you, everyone, whose efforts have culminated in such a happy occasion as this evening is proving to be."

After all the formalities had been completed, everyone adjourned to the Dining Room to partake of a most delightful supper, the effect of this being to loosen tongues, and the rest of the evening passed in happy conversation, the renewing of acquaintances and exchange of memories. The time allotted did not seem nearly long enough and even some time after Jean Whipp had given a decisive rendering of the National Anthem, Miss Porritt was at the piano and a choir of more than a hundred burst into *Land of our Birth* which they sang right

Breeze Hill

through without a falter. It was a touching and a fitting conclusion to, perhaps, the Old Girls' most successful celebration.

To mark its Diamond Jubilee the Old Girls' Society published an excellent book entitled *A Short History of Altrincham County Grammar School for Girls, 1910 to 1974* by Myra Kendrick, herself an 'Old Girl'.

Clare Vogt, formerly Higenbottam, recalls

"WALKING UP THE STEPS of Breeze Hill in my bottle-green socks, new navy wool blazer, pleated navy skirt, green jumper and navy and green striped tie. It was my first day at Altrincham Grammar School for Girls and the start of a privileged education in a school steeped with tradition which I didn't appreciate then but do now. Miss Johnson, a music teacher, was our form mistress. She had grey hair and a gravelly voice which she explained was due to an operation which had ruined her previously good singing voice. Her motherly approach was perfect for us newcomers and we quickly settled into the Art Room on the ground floor of Breeze Hill which Miss Johnson explained was our temporary form room whilst awaiting a new mobile classroom. I loved Breeze Hill and the fact that it had originally been someone's home. I used to imagine what the rooms would have looked like and my favourite ones were at the top of the house where the maids would have slept. I spent many an hour daydreaming about the previous inhabitants and watching the many squirrels running around the garden. Once the new classroom arrived we indulged in stomping to Gary Glitter songs on its shiny but thankfully durable floor. Not the ladylike pupils that we should have been!

Although mainly taught in Breeze Hill we went over to the main school for lessons in the new science block and also attended assemblies taken by the Headmistress Miss Jackson, who always wore a black gown, as did many of the other senior teachers. Miss Jackson was always perfectly coiffured but remained remote and untouchable. In all the time I was there I don't think she ever spoke personally to me. I do remember her addressing us all in Assembly one day and stating that we must not fraternise (I remember the word to this day, as I wasn't sure of its meaning at the time) with the workmen who were painting the West Wing.

After two years we moved to the main school for good and at about the same time our uniform changed. I think that we may have had some say in what we wanted and the consensus was to opt for an all-navy uniform of sweater and skirt. We were allowed to wear any navy jumper or skirt, so looking back we were a hotchpotch of styles and a generally untidy bunch, particularly as some skirts became very short and some girls wore make-up and huge platform shoes.

Some of the memorable teachers from this time included Miss Gowland, the biology teacher, Miss Holderness, the Deputy Head, who had to care for her elderly mother, and Mr

The magnificent golden lions in the Hall

Bully, the Latin teacher with a wholly inappropriate name, as a more diffident and polite man would be hard to find. My favourite subject at school was English, inspired by my one and only English teacher there, Mrs Copeland. She was another lovely, motherly figure who I felt understood me as she had a daughter of the same age. She was never censorious (even when I forgot my exercise book three times in a row) and always encouraging. Although I had to leave school after O levels for family reasons, I took an English A level shortly afterwards, and many, many years later I am now nearing the end of an English degree, thanks to the love of the subject which Mrs Copeland nurtured in me.

I look back on my time at AGGS with fond remembrance: the carefree days spent playing tennis at the Dome and chattering on the deliberately long leisurely walk down to Bowdon. There we played athletics and hockey and went long distance 'running' which consisted of a sprint off the field in sight of the teachers to a stroll around the River Bollin where we were left unsupervised, and then a quick run back to an impatiently waiting Mrs Driver with stopwatch in her hand. As you can imagine, our times were always very poor.

I feel lucky to have traversed the narrow school corridors of the main building with its glazed tiled walls, gazed at the magnificent lions on the wallpaper in the hall whilst hanging wistfully over the balcony, and spent lunch hours hurtling down the slope to the back lawn where many a confidence was shared and lasting friendships forged. I felt blessed and proud to have been part of that ivy-clad institution where girls were taught to have confidence in their abilities and make real careers."

The School sign on Cavendish Road

On 1 April 1974 there was another significant moment in the School's history, when with the boundary changes of that date it passed from the care of founding Cheshire County Education Authority to the Metropolitan Borough of Trafford, with another change of name to Altrincham Grammar School for Girls, and an unknown future.

Miss Jackson wrote to the *Old Girls' News*:

"IN SEPTEMBER 1975, we had 1013 pupils on the roll with 200 in the Sixth Form. Quite a record! Needless to say that we are working in very cramped conditions and desperate for the need of more accommodation. We have lessons in the Hall on many occasions – sometimes two different lessons if it happens to be wet and the hall is needed for games – and I have been teaching General Studies to some forty Sixth Form girls in my room. It was good news, therefore, that work had begun on our new Sixth Form Centre on the Devisdale on 1st October. This will add to our problems in some ways – yet another site at some distance from the main school – but it will provide accommodation for 115 Sixth Form students and will give them a large common room and a library. We shall look forward to its completion in about two years' time."

Now, fast forward to 1 July 1977 when Miss Jackson's letter to the *Old Girls' News* reads:

"UNDER LOWERING SKIES and heavy rain we moved girls, books and some furniture to the new buildings which are near the Green Walk end of the Devisdale.

The Sixth Form girls are naturally delighted with their new surroundings, even though there are 217 of them based in the building designed for 115. There is no science or domestic

The Sixth Form Centre on the Devisdale

science, however, so these lessons take place in the main school buildings. The spacious library and the common room are very much appreciated, as are the snack lunches which are served. The centre was planned to provide an environment suitable for young adults and the atmosphere is relaxed and informal.

The overall numbers on the roll have now grown to 1054 but with the major part of the Sixth Form on the new site, we are a little bit less congested than formerly and no longer have to use the old classrooms of the Bowdon Downs Congregational Church."

Miss Newbrook, formerly Head of the History Department, was in charge of the centre from the beginning, and her outstanding skill in organisation, and her pastoral care for the girls and the needs of their careers, shaped its development. Her special interest in social and community work led her to encourage such interests in the sixth-formers and to arrange experience for them in this sphere. There was some regret about the segregation of seniors from the rest of the school. This was countered by two practices: Sixth Form girls helping once a week with registration in junior forms and also running lunch-hour hobby clubs for juniors. Some of the Sixth Form duties were devolved upon fifth-formers, giving them valuable experience as well as increased status in the main school.

Jeanette Marsden, formerly Gray, recalls that

" 'YOU'LL BE A LITTLE FISH in a big pond...' were words spoken to me as I left my primary school, where presumably I'd been a big fish in a little pond. I stood bewildered in my over-large new blazer in a classroom full of strange faces. Everything in those first few weeks seemed to present fearful challenges. Where did we go to buy dinner-tickets; was the netball court really this far away; how would I ever remember my timetable?

After what seemed only a very short time, I was a slightly bigger fish in a smaller pond, with a group of friends and the confidence to find my way. My form 1.4 was for the first two years based at Breeze Hill, moving into the topmost room of the house for the second year. This was a very small room with sloping ceilings, and my desk seemed to have the least headroom of all; luckily I was never tall and, once sitting, found the space sufficient. Moving from room to room perplexed me somewhat in the early days; negotiating the journey from one room to another and getting there in time was always a challenge!

In the third year, I chose to take Latin rather than German. I thoroughly enjoyed my year of Latin tuition, especially those lessons where a bit of careful questioning would result in Mrs Webster forgetting completely about our vocabulary homework and instead take the full lesson to describe just how the Romans obtained the purple dye used for their state robes and togas! She was fascinating to listen to, with a wealth of knowledge and wonderfully entertaining. I always had, and still have, a keen interest in Roman history (and indeed all things Italian!).

Our Latin group had the opportunity to visit Rome at Easter. I jumped at the chance and persuaded my best friend that it was something she too should do. We travelled by train, the journey taking the best part of two days. We were accompanied by Mr Bully (Latin), Mrs Brock (history) and Mrs Peckett (physics). Lovely Mrs Peckett, whose enthusiasm for her subject and patience (with me!) enabled me to gain my physics O level – I shall always be grateful. Our trip naturally included the ruins of ancient Rome, the catacombs, the Spanish Steps and the Trevi Fountain where we eagerly threw in our lira coins in the hope of returning. All that is except my friend who, after having her bag stolen on the first day, never wished to see Rome again.

French was taught by Miss Huddart. I remember well, standing outside the room, waiting to go in for our forty-minute lesson with butterflies in my stomach. I spent the whole period in fear and dread, terrified she would ask me

The Sixth Form Centre library

something. Unfortunately, my expression probably said it all and she would turn to me with 'you look rather perplexed…' and begin to question me. I had to answer in perfect French (of course) and only then would she move on to someone else. The penny eventually dropped – if I concentrated in class and learned to conjugate French verbs then I could answer correctly with confidence, and get the minimum of her attention.

Life in the Sixth Form was mainly spent in the recently opened Sixth Form Centre. A good deal of time was spent in the Common Room where we had the privilege of making hot drinks in the small kitchen. Many a free period was spent drinking copious mugs of coffee!

Biology had always been my best and most enjoyed subject. Our A level tutor was Mrs Lee – a brilliant teacher who one moment was warning us of the perils of 'grotty boys' and the horror of ending up with 'grotty children' and the next, was on her hands and knees, pulling a toy train with carriages round the floor to demonstrate the molecular structure of DNA!

I also took art A level and became one of Mrs Heaton's 'chicks'. Most weekends were spent painting or drawing still-life compositions such as a trout and various vegetables, with a knife and a decorative plate. This would be set up on the table at home where they stayed from Friday evening until late on a Sunday – or as long as my family would tolerate the smell of fish. One of Mrs Heaton's stock phrases when assessing a piece of work was 'Like the curate's egg, chick; good in parts!' The A level art syllabus included art history; I can still remember Mrs Heaton's descriptions of various works, most vivid being the *The Marriage of Arnolfini* by Jan Van Eyck, the dish of oranges, the mirror in the background and the little dog all having significance. The Greek orders, Doric, Ionic and Corinthian, were constantly referred to and have been surprisingly useful to me in various situations, from crosswords and quizzes to architectural features seen on our holidays to Greece and Italy. I left AGGS in 1981 – once more a little fish in a very big pond!"

Miss Jackson wrote in the 1979 *Old Girls' News*:

"WE HAD RELATIVELY FEW staff changes in the summer but the retirement of Miss Rowbotham in August marked the end of an era. Miss Rowbotham has been school Secretary for thirty-one years. She was appointed by Miss Drought and served under the succeeding Headmistresses. She was intensely loyal to the School, proud of its successes and anxious to preserve its positions. We remember, among other things, her enjoyment in its musical achievements and her interest and help in the various types of community service undertaken by the girls. She was a keen supporter of the Old Girls' Society and I know that she hopes to maintain her link through the Coffee Mornings at the YWCA."

*Miss Nancy Rowbotham,
taken just prior to her
90th birthday in 2009*

Miss Nancy Rowbotham has sent her memories from the office.

"ON A WARM AFTERNOON during the summer holidays in 1979 I was working quietly and quite alone in my little office near to the front door when I did something I had never done before – I had finished all my tasks and had nothing left over for tomorrow. There wouldn't *be* a tomorrow, as I was about to retire. For my final half hour at the school I sat on a bench under a tree on the front lawn and allowed my thoughts to wander back to my earlier days.

During a large part of World War II I had been in the Fire Service driving almost everything except fire engines and when, in 1948, I became School Secretary (the only one) it was oh, so different. Miss Drought realised this and was most kind and patient as I battled to regain my shorthand and typing, so happily discarded in recent years. After a while, though, I learnt that absolute accuracy was essential at all times and any careless mistakes I made brought our Headmistress to the office door, red in the face and chest and beads rising and falling as her voice boomed 'Have I, busy as I am, to check everything you dooooo?' (The tone rising half an octave on the final word.) On one occasion I somehow managed to type the word DEFINATELY ... and in came those beads again. This time the words ended with 'FINITE, child, FINITE.' After I had scraped myself off the floor I realised that this was most helpful – and even now I never write that word without a chuckle.

Soon I discovered that Miss Drought also had a great sense of humour and a very kind heart. Having at one time decided to resign, I then stayed for thirty-one years and I kept in touch with her almost to the end of her life. I still have a note from her thanking me for two letters I had written to her 'and not a spelling mistake between them!'

My years were punctuated by a number of regular milestones. Each new term I had to balance all seven of our school accounts and then type out the Headmistress's Report for the Governors' Meeting. July brought Founders' Day with a service I always enjoyed, plus the interest of meeting the special guest speaker. The autumn term brought several weeks of midnight oil before Speech Day (the programme alone took ages to prepare) but what a special sight it was to see all the girls file into the Hall from all the entrances and, in silence, find their seats. Again, another VIP guest for me to meet.

The Christmas Fair I never saw as I was frantically busy counting the money – mostly small coins – and taking it in heavy bags to the bank, who promised to accept it after hours. One of my greatest joys was the Service of Nine Lessons and Carols based on the one from Cambridge.

My two greatest interests have always been natural history and music, so imagine how I enjoyed hearing the School Choir and the School Orchestra – and solo items, too – when they rehearsed in the Hall outside my door. I have fond memories of many performances, with high standards achieved after much hard work – *Hiawatha* (what a week that was!) and then *The Happy Prince* and *Noye's Fludde*.

Thinking again back to earlier times, I remember when Miss Drought retired and was replaced by Miss Okell, who seemed to follow her so naturally and cared equally about the School. She, too, had a great sense of humour and had two secret weapons where I was concerned – her kindness and her charm, which meant if, as I prepared to go home, she found a letter which 'really ought to catch tonight's post' I naturally removed the cover from my typewriter, unlocked my desk and did my best.

I was always most deeply grateful to both these Headmistresses for one very special reason.

When my mother suddenly died I was allowed to bring my little black Scottish terrier to School – firstly Barrie and later he was followed by Toddie.

Yes, mine was a far from easy post but an interesting one, and meeting so many visitors was quite special. One of them occasionally called unexpectedly and, if I should be out of the office when she arrived, I knew who was within, for on the table outside my door – summer or winter – was a pale mauve neatly folded umbrella. It belonged to Miss Howes Smith.

Two of my most treasured possessions were presented to me when I retired… thank you all so much. From the Girls a super writing-case and from members of the Staff a picnic case, both of which have been used lovingly and often. I was so grateful to have them – and still am.

For quite a time I was a liaison officer between the Old Girls' Society and the School and, at my final committee meeting, I was surprised and delighted when the Chairman (the late Marjorie Bennion) suddenly presented me on behalf of the members of the committee with a most generous book token. What happened next, though, shattered me completely and I shall never cease to be most deeply grateful. Marjorie informed me that I had been made an Honorary Life Member of the Old Girls' Society. This was something very special indeed and I still feel humbly proud and greatly honoured.

I made many good friends during those thirty-one years and I do appreciate a number of both former members of Staff and Old Girls who still keep in touch with me and, too, for the ones who attend the OG Coffee Club Christmas Lunch and send me a Christmas card signed by so many, after the feast.

I shall always remember with deep affection the place I permanently called ACGS and which Miss Drought, from the bottom of her heart, always referred to as 'Our Dear School'."

The 1980s

1980	19 December – Miss Jackson retires
1981	6 January – Mrs Delides appointed Headmistress
1981	21 March – netball team U-14 National Schools Champions
1981	1 June – Mr Welsh appointed Deputy Head
1981	May – Trafford MBC announces proposals for change
1984	15–19 October – HMI inspection
1985	16 March – netball team U-18 National Schools Champions
1985	19–22 March – *HMS Pinafore* performed
1985	July – Miss Gowland retires
1987	September – Mrs Kerr appointed Deputy Head
1987	September – Education Act (No 2) 1986 comes into force
1987	10–11 December – *Cinderella* performed
1988	2–7 January – hockey team victorious in Barcelona
1988	15–18 March – *The Mikado* performed
1988	29 July – Education Reform Act
1989	August – Government decision on the future of the School

CHAPTER 8
THE 1980S

On 19 December 1980 at the final Assembly held in the afternoon, presentations were made by the School to Miss Jackson to mark her retirement. The Parents' Association presented a portrait of her to the School.

The Chairman of the Governors, Mrs Jean Gill, paid this tribute in the *School Magazine* of 1981:

Miss Joan Jackson

> "SHE CAME HERE from Cavendish Grammar School for Girls, Buxton, to be Head of a school twice the size – 839 girls in 1967 and by 1975, the numbers had risen to over 1000 and have remained at this level ever since. Despite this increase Miss Jackson maintained high standards and results during her time at the School. She can, and should, feel justly proud of her endeavours and dedication to this end.
>
> Another important happening during Miss Jackson's years at the School was the opening of the Sixth Form Centre which officially came into use in September 1977. After years of planning under Cheshire this 'miracle' sprang into being on the Devisdale and now supports more than twice the number of girls for which it was built.
>
> Miss Jackson's particular subject was geography and in recent years she taught government, economics and commerce to small O level groups. With her knowledge of photography she helped to run a Photographic Society in the School.
>
> Pippin, her corgi dog, was a well known character in the School and many girls, both past and present, still remember her. Miss Jackson now enjoys the company of Pippin's successor, an Alsatian.
>
> I would like to thank her on behalf of everyone connected with the School for giving thirteen years of tireless service. We all wish her very many happy years of retirement to enjoy, especially, the countryside and her garden, both of which mean so much to her."

Miss Joan Jackson recalled in 2006:

> "WHEN I WAS ASKED to write about my memories of Altrincham Girls Grammar School for the centenary book, I realised that after thirteen years as Headmistress and 25 years of retirement my earliest impressions still remain most vivid.
>
> I came to Altrincham in 1967, having previously been Headmistress of a much smaller girls' grammar school in Buxton. ACGS had more than twice the number of pupils on roll, but this was no problem as my last post as a full time teacher and Deputy Headmistress had been in a large establishment. One of the greatest differences, however, lay in the large number of sites which were in use. The new East Wing, opened the previous year, was wonderful, as was the

Miss Jackson with Tara

very impressive Hall – the first part of the building seen by parents and visitors; – but then….!! There were the two classrooms tucked away in the adjacent church buildings in Bowdon Road, the house and pre-fab classrooms at Breeze Hill, the Dome classrooms and netball/tennis courts and the playing fields which were twenty minutes' walk away.

Buildings apart, my first impressions were of a very welcoming, friendly school with a strong sense of community and pride in its traditions. I had met Miss Okell previously on a few occasions at meetings of the Headmistresses' Association and I had worked for a short time, many years earlier, with Mrs Delides (then Miss Brown). I also received an early visit from the officers of the Old Girls' Society, Miss Joyce Kendrick and Miss Ella Seed, anxious to welcome me into their midst. I was delighted later to meet Miss Drought when she came to the Society's Diamond Jubilee celebrations in 1974 – a very memorable occasion indeed.

I knew, of course, of the school's fine academic achievements and soon became aware of its other important strengths, in art, music and physical education. I heard a great deal about the music department's production of *The Happy Prince* but I have my own happy memories of school concerts which included performances from the choirs, orchestra and individual instrumentalists under the direction of Miss Clayton and Miss Porritt. Later, there was to be a memorable performance of *Noye's Fludde* in St John's Church.

The work in Mrs Heaton's art department was often on view in the East Wing entrance hall and in the dining room corridor, and a special display on an Open Day, held in the early 1970s, was greatly admired by visiting parents and governors. Several senior pupils went on to achieve successes in the National Exhibition of Children's Art and one or two gifted girls went on to gain admission to The Slade.

In physical education the school teams seemed to go from strength to strength but many girls enjoyed their personal successes in our sports days. Modern dance was one of the activities I enjoyed watching and another was to see our trampoline team working on their routine in the gymnasium (indeed, dare I mention that Miss Holderness and I both 'had a go' on the trampoline one evening under the watchful eye of Miss Jones and to the applause of the girls… we didn't try again – once was enough!).

Other memories spring to mind: a first form enjoying a very active history lesson, in enacting the battle of Hastings on the front lawn (paper helmets and wooden swords much in evidence); a very memorable occasion, when having gone out briefly during the lunch hour, I drove back to find the whole school assembled on the front lawn and a fire engine outside the front door. Some rather boisterous girls had 'accidentally' set off the fire alarm and Miss Rowbotham, who had served in the fire service at one time, had dialled 999. (At least it proved that our fire drill procedures were effective!)

The School Hall, as I soon discovered, was generally a hub of activity. As the numbers of pupils increased it became impossible to fit them all into one morning Assembly so rotas had to be arranged, involving also the dining room and the large music room. The Hall was also used as an extra classroom for television lessons, music rehearsals, dance practice and wet lunch hours! There were times when I blessed the thick walls of an old building.

Founders' Day was new to me and came as a pleasant surprise: the Governors' lunch in the music room; the walk to Bowdon Church (thank goodness when it was a fine day!) where some of our girls who were bellringers showed their skills and roused the neighbourhood; and the service itself which for some older pupils was a kind of farewell to the school.

Pre-Christmas activities were always memorable. The Christmas Fair in aid of charity was great fun amid much noise and eating and drinking. Then there was the Sixth Form entertainment and finally the Carol Service before the school dispersed. I also remember the Old Girls' Society Christmas lunches held, at one time, in the YWCA.

The interest in helping others seen in the Christmas Fair fund-raising was of course very evident in other spheres. There were weekly collections for charities chosen by the girls. Senior pupils helped at youth clubs for the handicapped. One year the Sixth Form held a Christmas party for deprived children. In the early seventies, when sponsored walks were popular, staff organised such an event one Saturday and I well remember one very junior girl who, having completed the fourteen-mile course, proceeded to turn a series of somersaults on the lawn!

These are but a few of my memories but I also remember with affection, and gratitude for their help and support, all my teaching colleagues and members of the clerical ancillary and domestic staff."

Miss Jackson's successor in January 1981 and the School's fifth Headmistress was Mrs Doris Delides, who had been appointed second mistress in 1972 and first Deputy Headmistress in 1974. She had joined the staff as Head of the Geography Department in 1956 so came to her new appointment with an already deep knowledge of the School and a strong attachment to it. Like her predecessor she was a graduate in geography of Manchester University. She had the distinction of being the first member of the teaching staff in the School's seventy years to become its Headmistress.

The Deputy Heads were Mrs M Webster and from June 1981 Mr David Welsh. Born in Staines, Middlesex, he was educated at Hampton School and

Mrs Doris Delides

Durham University, where he read modern languages before qualifying as a teacher at Leicester University. After three years in Zambia he returned to England in 1972 and secured a post as a senior teacher at Sale Grammar School for Girls with special responsibilities for Sixth Form students.

Pamela Emery, formerly Hirst, writes:

"MEMORIES OF SCHOOL begin with my first and second years at Breeze Hill with Miss Cheetham and Miss Huddart as my form tutors respectively in classroom numbers 14 and 22. We attended netball and tennis at the Dome playing fields along with art classes with Mrs Heaton.

Third year took me across to the West Wing at main school and then on into classrooms in Treetops and Room G. Then it was on to the newly built Sixth Form centre which omitted the needs of us science students. Hence, two years of trudging back and forth to main school labs ensued.

I was appointed one of the three Senior Students in 1981 and held that post throughout my Upper Sixth year, with Clare Pendlebury and Jane Watkins. Our Sixth Form play was based on the story of *Alice in Wonderland*. I played Alice and Clare was the Queen of Hearts aka Lady Driver (PE).

I remember an April Fool's Day prank involving a 'one pound note' attached to a length of fine fishing line dangled from the balcony above the staff room. The note rested on the parquet floor waiting for an unsuspecting member of staff. Many will remember Miss Tate (chemistry), always good for a laugh; she painstakingly and arthritically bent down to retrieve the note, only to find it whisked away before her very eyes! All pupils in the Hall exploded with laughter along with Miss Tate. The teacher I admired the most was Miss Walker (biology)."

Pamela Hirst, Head Girl, 1982

Mrs Driver wrote in the *School Magazine* for 1981:

"THE HIGHLIGHT OF THE NETBALL YEAR was when the Third Year A team won the English Schools Championships in Essex on Saturday 21 March. This they did in convincing style winning all their matches, the only team out of a total of 56 competing teams not to lose a point all day. The girls concerned deserved their success. They had worked extremely hard during the preceding months and were by far the fittest and most skilful team there."

Plans for the re-organisation of Trafford Education Authority's secondary schools had been mooted for several years, firstly because of a national drive towards a comprehensive instead of selective system and also a need to cut escalating costs. The numbers in primary schools were already declining so amalgamation and even closure of some secondary schools was considered. During May 1981, first staff then parents of the Altrincham Boys and Girls Grammar Schools met Trafford education officers to discuss the future of the two schools. Mrs Delides explained in the *Old Girls' News* of that year:

"DETAILED KNOWLEDGE OF THE SCHOOL, its population and its traditions has been a decided advantage in a year of increasing constraints, cutbacks and unsettling discussions about our future. The widespread national problems of falling rolls in schools are affecting Trafford and although we ourselves are not yet feeling the effects the School is involved in the Local Authority's current attempt to find solutions."

Many parents and staff were satisfied with the two schools as they were, believing that falling numbers would mean achieving adequate space for pupils and their activities: an end to serious overcrowding. The Old Girls' Society was dismayed at the prospect of traditions lost: the School was over seventy years old and its excellences past and present were deeply appreciated. Parents and past pupils campaigned vigorously to 'save our school.'

Margaret Davies, formerly Rowland, remembers:

Margaret Davies, Graduation, University of Worcester, 2007

"MY FIRST AND SECOND YEARS were spent in Breeze Hill. Our form was located in the top of the house in Room 12 and Mrs

Larlham was our form tutor. The school was enormous to us, all fresh-faced and new, and getting lost was easy. In our second year we moved downstairs to Room 11. Our tutor now was Mrs Sumbler who had a great musical talent and sang and danced beautifully. She also directed the choir. Now finding our feet at the school, confidence grew and characters and friendships developed.

Third year found us across the road in Main School where the West Wing was our home. Mrs Emmott took over the reins as form tutor. She taught French to the top sets. Tackling all three sciences was great. I loved biology and chemistry. Physics was not my strong point and only now in my forties can I really appreciate it and apply it to my hobby of SCUBA diving. Mrs Lee was our biology teacher – a lovely lady of a calm nature, who taught me from first year to fifth year, and there was never a dull moment.

Margaret Davies in her favourite environment!

Miss Tate was an excellent chemistry teacher who made the lessons extremely interesting. Not shy with her measures to demonstrate an experiment, she tended to use an extra spatula-full to get a better effect. I remember the day she exploded the water bath with a lump of sodium.

Fourth year was a time to choose the subjects for O level. Our form tutor was none other than the fabulous Mrs (Lady) Driver. A formidable sportswoman, she led us through our fourth year and also taught us PE. Hockey was my favourite part of the physical education lessons. French was with Miss Huddart and I thought her method of teaching was excellent.

Fifth year equals O levels. We were under the care of Mrs Anstice, Head of Maths at the time. Of that year I remember mostly my group of friends from the form and I do still have contact with a couple of them.

It is almost thirty years since I left the Grammar School but have resounding memories and the impression it made on me is immense. I sing hymns that transfer back to Assembly and I find myself standing up when my son's Head Teacher walks in to address the parents. I visited Altrincham with my family two years ago to show the boys my school. We went to Taylor and Cross so I could replace my school scarf which had disintegrated.

We have been very fortunate and privileged to attend such a fantastic educational establishment. I still use the school motto in my daily life 'FORTITER, FIDELITER, FELICITER' – Bravely, Faithfully, Cheerfully."

Mrs Delides informed the Old Girls in their 1985 *News*:

"IN OCTOBER WE HAD a one-week visit by a team of Her Majesty's Inspectorate. They agreed with our frequently expressed concern at the lack of internal decoration in the main school for well over twenty years, but they concluded that 'this is a very good school' and 'the quality of teaching and learning is impressive' – very satisfying comments in the seventy-fifth year of the School's life."

Rachael Bollom, formerly Steeples, remembers with great pride and affection:

"MY LOVE OF NETBALL started to grow at primary school and then took off with the help and guidance of Lady Sheila Driver and my great team-mates. It's not many people who can say their team of seven players stayed the same from the first year right through to the end of the Sixth Form.

Under 18 All England Netball Champions, 1985
Standing: Sarah Mooney (reserve), Caroline Quigley, Carolyn Evans, Rebecca Reid (reserve);
sitting: Lisa Gross, Rachael Steeples, Deborah Kershaw, Alicia Pivaro, Paula Thompson

So what do I remember? My first memory was playing as a first-year for the second-year C team with my best friend Carolyn Evans. It was at Sale Grammar School on a very frosty cold Saturday morning. Not all went well. Carolyn fell over and banged her head so I had to go on… as goal shooter… 'But I can't shoot,' I tried to tell them! I did get one goal!

What else? How about playing netball at Dome at lunchtime in our school uniform in the pouring rain. The fitness training in the gym to ensure we could last throughout the tournaments without tiring. Playing in the dining room after school because of the dark winter nights. Feeling jealous of our friends who had Saturday jobs while we dedicated ourselves every Saturday to netball matches. Our blue tartan skirts setting us apart from all other teams. Later on we even managed to persuade one of our team, Caroline Quigley, not to leave after the fifth year but to stay on in the Sixth Form so we could remain together. I loved every bit of it.

We owe our success to Lady Sheila Driver and her dedication to our team. I thank her from the bottom of my heart and have many fond memories of our school netball. She needn't have given her free time to drive us to matches in the evenings in order for us to get to play against better opposition… ladies.

What did we achieve?

Under 14 All England Netball **Champions** 1981
Under 16 All England Netball Runners Up 1983
Under 18 All England Netball Runners Up 1984 (a year early)
Under 18 All England Netball **Champions** 1985
Under 18 Barclays Bank Netball Club **Winners** 1985 – what memories."

The music department's major production of 1985 was Gilbert and Sullivan's operetta *HMS Pinafore* performed in the School Hall for four nights in March. The production team was Miss Clayton and Mrs Greensmith with the help of Martin Bussey, a professional musician, conductor and producer active in the area, with a special interest in Gilbert and Sullivan. The following is an amusing account from the *School Magazine* written by Amanda Rosenfield, a senior student at that time:

"PREPARATIONS FOR THE MAIDEN VOYAGE of the *HMS Pinafore* began as early as September 1984, even though the scheduled departure was not until March 1985. The crew was carefully hand-picked by the First Sea Lord Bussey, whilst Petty Officers Clayton and Greensmith vetted the passengers to ensure that none would succumb to the dreaded sea-sickness.

Having thus gathered together a total of 42 who were ready, willing and able to sail in her, the *HMS Pinafore* underwent a process of refurbishing carried out by that reputable firm of shipbuilders, Slinger and Newhall Ltd. The crew and passengers, meanwhile, were put through a rigorous training programme until they found their sea legs.

The passengers – all fashionable ladies – decided that new outfits were in order for this voyage, and so they knocked upon the door of that well known boutique 'Chez Madame Heaton' and, thanks to the dressmaking and millinery skills of Mesdamoiselles Barrat, Mills and Kelly, were more than adequately supplied with exquisite fineries. With the crew similarly kitted out, much of the preparation was now complete.

Everyone was put through their final paces under the watchful eye of the omnipresent Sea Lord Bussey, and with the guidance and encouragement of First Mates Kershaw, Barlow and Horlock, and an orchestra was provided for the purpose of giving the ship a smooth send-off and an equally smooth voyage. March 19 1985 marked sailing date. At 7.30pm the ladies embarked, the sailors manned the rigging and, to the swish of long skirts and bell bottoms, it was anchors away!

The journey was short but profitable and immensely enjoyable since adventure proved to be the key note. The ship withstood the high seas, the crew were unfailingly energetic and boisterous – with only one or two falling prey to scurvy – and the ladies giggled and squealed with delight when riding along on the crest of a wave.

It was a sad moment when, on 22 March 1985 the *HMS Pinafore* sailed into port. Although all those who had sailed in her were given a hearty welcome by the landlubbers, there were a few tears sparkling in the eyes of both sailor and lady alike.

The sea is now calm and the ship motionless – but, messmates, let's give three cheers to a life on the ocean wave!"

At the end of the summer term Miss Barbara Gowland retired after thirty-nine years of loyal and totally dedicated years of service to the School. She came in 1946 as assistant biology mistress, becoming in 1948 joint head of the science department with Miss Nan Bowen, in succession to Miss Alice Chorley. When Miss Bowen left, Miss Gowland was appointed sole head of the Science Department. She was responsible as well for audio-visual and other technical equipment, and for many years ran the wild flower competition. She was something

A scene from HMS Pinafore, *1985*

of an educational pioneer, having a strong belief in her pupils learning through experience rather than precept long before this became official policy.

Catherine Heys, formerly Baldwin, remembers especially:

Miss Gowland seated second from the right at the 2002 Class of '51 Reunion

"MRS LITTING WAS my favourite French teacher. I always regret not taking French 'A' level. Mrs McCartney was the typing teacher and Room A was the typing room at the top of the old school building. A thankless task trying to teach thirty girls to do memos on Olympus typewriters. The noise was unbearable! Always having to sit in alphabetical order was annoying.

Mrs Kershaw was the one teacher who made history come to life. She was inspiring! Genuine, kind, and a fabulous teacher. Sadly she died soon after retiring. Miss Ashworth was very talented at sewing. 'Elsie' the mannequin used to 'stare' at our lessons: it was quite unnerving. My friend Caroline and I were constantly in trouble for wiping flour on our skirts, forgetting our aprons, being unable to use the electric sewing machines and having cakes that always sank in the middle. I still have a fear of the treadle sewing machine.

Mrs Delides was an 'iron lady', a strong leader who knew many of the girls. Mr Welsh was Deputy Head, famous for his gold tie, and was a fabulous German teacher who made the lessons enjoyable and memorable. Mrs Wickstead taught German as well, a quiet and gently spoken lady but we all listened and learned. I met her on a course recently and she had hardly changed in thirty years!"

Susan Attwell says:

"I DIDN'T PARTICULARLY ENJOY SCHOOL but neither was it unbearable! I remember the school then as being extremely old-fashioned and outdated, my first day walking up The Downs proudly clutching my new schoolbag to enter what to me then at aged eleven was a huge assembly hall with polished floor and the senior girls at sixteen years old seeming soooooooo grown up! My biology teacher, Miss Stelfox, had previously taught my mum at Sale Grammar School. I survived for five years and left with a modest collection of O Levels. I would dearly love to see the school again; however I now live in Tenerife, but as my parents still live in Altrincham I am never far away from it."

In 1986 and 1988, two important education acts were passed by Parliament as part of a drive to raise standards of education in general, and to encourage both parents and society to become more involved in the running of local schools. The composition of governing bodies was changed to include two serving teachers from the school, four parents, and five co-opted members representing the local business and professional world, along with four governors appointed by the local education authority. A major change in function of the newly formed body was to take responsibility for finance. The governors also assumed responsibility for ensuring that what was taught in school corresponded in subject and content with the requirements of the National Curriculum.

Changes in the examination system affected the pupils themselves more directly when the two fifth year options of O levels (later GCE) and CSE were replaced by the General Certificate of Secondary Education which retained some features of each of the older examinations. There was less emphasis on preparing for two-and-a-half-hour written papers, as a two-year period of course work, assessed by the teaching staff, gained importance in most subjects.

Public examination results in 1989 showed the candidates' grades at GCSE level to be well above the national average and at A level the pass rate was over ninety percent, reflecting the quality of staff and pupils alike.

At the end of the summer term in 1987 Mrs Webster, Deputy Head, resigned after twelve years. She had contributed much to the School's organisation through her gift for expert timetabling. She was also experienced in dramatic production and co-operated with Miss Clayton in producing Purcell's *Dido and Aeneas* with the senior choir. She moved to the Midlands where she later became headmistress of an independent school in Leamington Spa. She was replaced by Mrs Kerr, who had been Head of the Geography Department since 1981.

Bronwen Davies recalls being inspired and fascinated by Latin America.

"WHEN I WAS AT SCHOOL my geography teacher was Mrs Kerr. Her lessons were always interesting so I chose geography at both O and A level. I remember the A level syllabus as being different from other schools – half the course related to the European Union (then the EEC) and the other half was Latin America. Mrs Kerr's enthusiasm for that area, and the slides she brought in to show us of her visit, fascinated me about the countries and their cultures.

Some years later, in 1999, I had the opportunity to spend a month in Peru which literally changed my life. I was dissatisfied with things in England and this gave me the impetus to do something about it. I took a Teaching English as a Foreign Language Course, applied for a job in Mexico and spent four of the following five years living and teaching there.

So an enormous thank you to Mrs Kerr for starting my love affair with Latin America (I have visited many other Central and South American countries on holiday too)."

During the winter of 1987–88 two music department productions were undertaken. First, on 10 and 11 December Years I to III performed Peter Maxwell Davies's version of *Cinderella*, and from 15 to 18 March the Gilbert and Sullivan operetta *The Mikado*, produced again by Miss Clayton, Mrs Greensmith and Martin Bussey. Girls taking part in the lively, professional performance were from the fourth year upward and the orchestra was augmented by some keen instrumentalists from the Boys' School. Costumes, make-

The Mikado, *1988*

up and scenery were again undertaken by Mrs Heaton and her Sixth Form art groups.

Heidi Smith, formerly Kennedy, writes:

"I AM IN THE MIDDLE of three sisters (the Kennedy girls) and between us we served well over a decade of time at AGGS. However, it was anything but a sentence for us – we all have many happy memories of our school days.

It was a strange combination of feelings to be both nervous and excited following in my sister's footsteps and wearing my AGGS blazer to school that first day starting in form 1.3 over at Breeze Hill. Of course, by second year, I soon realised it was the most 'uncool' piece of kit

Form V3, 1990
Heidi Kennedy (front row extreme right) with her classmates

to be seen in as we were all desperate to move across the road to be part of the main school as third years and leave Breeze Hill behind for the youngsters!

There really are too many stories and wonderful teachers to mention every single one but being particularly into sciences – Mrs Wood's chemistry lessons deserve a mention, as do Miss Tate's – I think ten was the maximum number of test tube holders we managed to attach to the bottom of her lab coat at any one time without her knowledge! Mrs Lord somehow made physics fun – bringing Dennis her cat into nearly all the equations and experiments – not literally of course! I remember Mrs Marchbank and Mr Finch being equally enthusiastic teaching us French… and how Miss Walker put up with us in biology lessons I will never know!

We were put through our paces in PE by Lady Driver, Mrs Kellett and Mrs Ellis down at Dome – the walk down there always seemed like an eternity. I was also inspired into dance by Miss Pullen and a group of us continued this with her once she left AGGS, culminating in a performance at the Wythenshawe Forum Theatre in 1988 which I shall never forget.

I took part in many musical performances, playing flute in the Orchestra or singing in the choir in that beautiful School Hall. Imagine our excitement as a group of teenage girls when the decision was made to join forces with the Boys' Grammar School to rehearse and carry out those performances. It took strong and dedicated teachers to keep our concentration levels on the music score! The highlight of this was when, in the Lower Sixth Form, we carried out an evening of *Songs from the Shows* which included dancing as well as singing. The only slight disappointment was when I was partnered with a teacher from the Boys' School for the love songs, as opposed to a hot-blooded male from the Upper Sixth!

I feel very privileged to have spent my school years at AGGS. We had no computers then – just simple black and green boards to chalk on and a small library on the gallery above the main hall – but what made it so great was the expertise of the teaching staff, led by our Headmistress Mrs Delides and Deputy Head Mr Welsh, and some wonderful friends whom I shall never forget."

The first hockey eleven in 1987 deserves special mention for its skill and commitment, both individual and team, resulting in victories at every level up to the finals of the National Hockey Championship in which they were runners-up. The team's supreme achievement was winning the fortieth anniversary International Tournament in Barcelona the following January. These results could not have been achieved without the dedication of the team trainers, Mrs Ellis and Mrs Kellett. Support from the girls' parents, and also the Bowdon Hockey Club, with whom the School shared pitches, were a great help. For the Barcelona tournament almost £5,000 was raised by parents and girls to cover the team's considerable expenses.

On 27 April 1988, a few weeks before her ninety-sixth birthday, Miss Mary Whitwill died in a Somerset nursing home not far from her family home at Sandford near Bristol. She was the youngest member of a large family, children of a Bristol shipper. Some extracts from her obituary written by Myra Kendrick (herself an Old Girl) in the *Old Girls' News* recall:

"MISS WHITWILL JOINED THE STAFF of the then Altrincham County High School for Girls as history mistress in 1916, when the School was only six years old, and worked under the first three Headmistresses. In 1959 she retired after forty-two years' service on the staff, as Senior History Mistress, Housemistress of De Massey House, and finally as Deputy Headmistress.

Such a long span of service has helped to give a sense of continuity and stability to the School and has formed a link between one generation of schoolgirls and another. To succeeding generations her history lessons were unforgettable and delightful experiences, not tasks; her sense of humour and of drama ensured that. Her striking appearance, as well as her high standards and her kindness, are all memorable. As the years passed, her pupils became her 'lambies'. Small wonder she was much loved and trusted."

At the end of the summer term of 1989 Miss Mary Titterington retired after thirty-six years on the staff. Herself a former pupil and Deputy Head Girl of the School, she was appointed in 1953 to teach English and French and in September 1961 became Head of the English Department in succession to Miss Zena Walkley. Hers was a happy department through her consideration towards its members. She was fond of young people and had her pupils' appreciation and respect. A special interest of hers was the *School Magazine* to which she gave much hard work, modernising its contents and introducing amusing black and white pen sketches. For a number of years she was also responsible for organising continental holidays for small parties of senior girls.

Since May 1981 the future of the School had been in doubt with proposals and counter-proposals debated with all the interested parties in the intervening years. Against this backdrop of turmoil and uncertainty, it is absolutely remarkable that the quality of teaching was of such a high and consistent standard that academic results continued to improve year on year, and sport, music, art and service to others outside the school environment continued to attain the top awards in each sphere of activity. In December 1989 there seemed to be a glimmer of light at the end of the tunnel when Mrs Delides said in her annual letter to the *Old Girls' Society News*:

"FOR SOME TIME there has been considerable debate at local and national level about the possible merger of this School with the Boys' Grammar School on their site or in a new purpose-built school on the Devisdale. However, one of the first decisions of the new Secretary of State for Education, Mr John McGregor, early in August 1989 was to keep the two schools separate: we still await the final decision of Trafford Borough Council. In the meantime we keep a comfortable size of 727 pupils, including 199 in the Sixth Form."

The hockey 1st XI, victors at Barcelona, 1988

The 1990s

1990	November – final decision on School's future
1991	April – Education Authority introduces change of year names
1991	July – Mrs Delides retires
1991	September – Mr Welsh appointed Headmaster, and Mrs Speakman Deputy Head
1991	Fairlie and grounds acquired
1992	Major building and refurbishment programme started
1993	September – new sports facilities on the Devisdale
1994	July – the Misses Clayton and Newbrook retire
1994	14 October – Fairlie opened
1995	School inspection
1997	April – grant maintained status achieved
1998	More buildings improvements
1998	December – Mr Welsh retires
1999	January – Mrs Ross-Wawrzynski appointed Headmistress
1999	April – foundation school status achieved

CHAPTER 9
THE 1990S

In August 1990 Lady Driver retired after twenty-one years on the staff. She was appointed in 1969 as Mrs Sheila Driver; her title resulted from her husband's knighthood some years later. Under her leadership the School's teams thrived, netball being specially dear to her. She writes of her time at School,

Sheila Driver with Don McCormac (author's husband), 2008

"I WAS VERY FORTUNATE to be Head of the PE Department from 1969 to 1990. During those years there wasn't one day I woke up and thought; 'Oh, God'; it was always 'Oh, Good.'

I was, and always will be proud of our girls. Teaching in such an excellent school became a big part of my life. I used to tell prospective parents – if you want a complete education for your daughter, then AGGS is the school for you. Effort, commitment, and standards are high in academic study, art, music and sport.

My career at the school began in the summer when Ann Jones won Wimbledon, and ended when I was fifty and we were celebrating in a very suitably decorated gym with my cake in the shape of a netball court, and the score was 5–0!

Like the song, our girls and our school are *SIMPLY THE BEST*."

After a decade of great uncertainty for the future of the School, Mrs Delides wrote with great relief in the *Old Girls' News*:

"AT ITS MEETING IN LATE NOVEMBER 1990, Trafford Borough Council finally accepted the decision made in August 1989 by the then Secretary of State for Education, Mr John McGregor, to retain the School as a separate single-sex grammar school. Political change, either local or national, could overturn that decision, of course, but, for now, we have a welcome measure of stability for the first time for many years, together with the promise of future expenditure on very necessary structural maintenance and redecoration. It will always be a matter of deep personal regret that there has not been funding available to establish a rolling programme of general upkeep, and I am grateful for the efforts of small working parties of parents and staff who have painted some of the shabbiest rooms and corridors."

In the academic year 1990–91 the Education Authority changed the system of numbering school years. Year 1 became the first year of primary school and year 7 the first year of secondary school. The former Upper Sixth became year 13.

In July 1991 Mrs Delides retired after thirty-five years at the School. She was first appointed as a teacher of geography in September 1956, and subsequently became Head of the Geography Department, Deputy Headmistress and then Headmistress, a position which she held for over ten years. The following tribute to her in the *School Magazine* of 1991–92, reads:

Mrs Doris Delides

"Mrs Delides was much admired throughout her successful career, leading the School through a period of great uncertainty about its future. She ensured that the School maintained the highest possible standards, and we shall always be much in her debt.

Concern for the girls was always her highest priority. She had an open door to those with problems or seeking advice, knew each pupil by name and often their families as well. She followed every girl's academic progress with great interest, taking pleasure in the commendations they were awarded and in their achievements at all levels. She was especially fond of the artwork in her room, which was much admired by visitors, and she supported concerts, dance and drama productions and sports events with great pride.

Girls applying for courses in Higher Education or for employment could rest assured that references on them would be supportive, well-worded and perceptive, capturing the essence of each individual. If sixth-formers narrowly missed required grades for university entrance, sound advice and practical help often opened the way to their securing suitable places.

Mrs Delides believed firmly in education providing as broad an experience as possible, and her Assemblies often offered an open door to literary, thought-provoking or reflective themes. Staff were encouraged to accompany pupils to lectures, conferences and open days, and Mrs Delides took great interest in the girls' activities out of School.

The reputation of the School was something Mrs Delides always prized. At times she thought to enhance it in practical ways with secateurs or paintbrush, but more often she focused her attention on academic achievement, behaviour and the maintaining of the best traditions. She had the future of the School at heart, and, when she left, it gave her real satisfaction to see it looking ahead positively with plans for growth and development."

Mrs Delides's memories of her time at School, particularly when she steered a difficult course through stormy waters, make very interesting reading:

"At the end of February 1956, quite out of the blue, I had a letter from the Headmistress, Miss Okell, of Altrincham Grammar School for Girls inviting me to attend for interview for the post of Head of Geography Department. I had not heard of the school, had never even been to Altrincham and was still only in my second year of teaching, but both my then Headmistress, and my Head of Department, Miss Joan Jackson, suggested that it might be a good idea to go to the interview 'just for the experience'. Late in March, therefore, I duly made my way across Manchester, pausing only to buy a new hat (considered essential in those long-gone days), and caught the train to Altrincham.

Walking up The Downs on a clear blue day, when the gardens were bright with spring flowers and a magnolia tree was in full blossom, trepidations about a possible ordeal lying ahead disappeared and my first sight of the Main School, so very different from the box-like architecture of the new schools that were being built at that time, was intriguing. I will never forget the sudden impact of walking through the front door into the beautifully proportioned hall with its polished parquet floor, bowls of spring flowers on tables, a scattering of interesting antique furniture and unusual objects and the sound of a Chopin piece being played by a clearly talented senior pupil who was having a piano lesson with, as I later discovered, Miss Porritt. When the bell rang, smiling members of staff and girls moving busily between lessons, quietly chatting and laughing together, reinforced the sense of a very happy community.

I was delighted to be offered the post and the special combination of happiness, laughter and music has always remained vividly in my mind.

I started in September 1956, vaguely intending to stay for about seven years that was generally recommended at that time, thus seeing an 11–18 years group through O levels (now GCSE) and A levels. As was so often the case with women teachers, however, marriage intervened and the seven years stretched to thirty-five! They were happy and fulfilling years, which fell into three distinct periods as my role changed from Head of Department until 1972, Deputy Head to 1981 and Headmistress to 1991. These changes certainly provided me with plenty of interviews 'for experience'.

It was quickly apparent that beyond the lovely hall were many serious problems. Numbers of pupils had increased over the years but the available space had not: the School was literally bursting at the seams, with teaching on split sites which were often in very poor condition. Many Old Girls will remember peeling paint, crumbling plaster, roof leaks, the mad dashes from one site to another (often the heavens seemed to open just as the lesson bell rang), out-of-date text books and equipment. The trouble, of course, was lack of money to provide for better maintenance and additional building. The fundamental reason for the failure to spend money on us was that we were constantly under threat of closure first by the controlling Cheshire Education Committee which was establishing co-educational comprehensive schools throughout Cheshire and later, after the political reorganisation of 1974, by Trafford Borough Council, which was committed to reducing the number of its secondary schools.

From 1980 onwards the threats to our future gathered momentum. Plans to replace us included every kind of educational establishment imaginable: these were proposed, rejected and often proposed again with dizzying rapidity, and surfacing at intervals, almost like a little chorus, was the notion of turning the Main School into a retirement home! Sometimes the situation became unpleasantly strained, but it always seemed to be worth a fight to retain our school which, after all, was continuing to serve the area so very well. Education officers and advisors were invariably helpful in their suggestions on matters relating to the curriculum but the main pressures were relentless. There were times when it was almost impossible to keep a sense of perspective and to make sure that all the uncertainties about the future did not damage the underlying aims to maintain the continuing work and well-being of pupils and staff, together with all the excellent educational qualities for which we have long been known.

In addition to local worries, we were also coping like all other state schools in the 1980s with a seemingly unending flow of initiatives, directives and bureaucracy from the Government. The traditional school motto, so often repeated in prefect investitures – Bravely, Faithfully, Cheerfully – certainly seemed particularly appropriate throughout that troubled period.

Pleasant memories far outweigh the unpleasant, however, and there is an abundance of those. We were always grateful, as the years went by, when any help was forthcoming, especially when extra accommodation was provided – even if it was only in the form of pre-fabricated classrooms. Far more significant acquisitions, however, included Breeze Hill

*Miss Brown (later Mrs Delides),
Miss Titterington, Pat Allbones
Lake Como, Italy, 1956*

(complete with dry rot!), the new East Wing with its varied teaching (and dining) areas, and the Sixth Form Centre on the Devisdale. Cosmetic improvements were also welcomed and I remember the prolonged discussions about choosing a very expensive new wallpaper, with a controversial pattern of gold lions, for the Hall, together with dramatic red and gold silk curtains to set it off! One of my own special moments came when finally, finally, there were enough atlases for everyone to have a copy. There were only twenty-four when I arrived…

A wide range of extra-curricular activities always played a major part in supporting the traditional academic curriculum, and talented, committed members of staff were unfailingly generous in giving their time and efforts to appreciative students. At the end of my first year I accompanied Miss Titterington (herself an Old Girl) to Italy on one of her regular, well-organised trips abroad. The name of a tall, lively member of the group was Pat Allbones who now, as Pat McCormac, is currently directing her energy, enthusiasm and loyalty to the school to masterminding the compilation of this centenary book.

I have fond memories too of the many residential geography field trips for A level pupils, later ably organised by Mrs Litherland (another Old Girl and former Head Girl in Miss Howes Smith's day). One unforgettable incident involved blood-curdling screams in the middle of the night from a girl who suddenly discovered an unknown man fast asleep in the bathtub. He turned out to be the son of the hotel proprietor, dispossessed of his own room and his yells were quite as loud as the girl's.

Walls were covered in changing displays of excellent varied art work from all age groups, and the Headmistress's room often resembled an impressive modern art gallery. The physical education department constantly encouraged enthusiastic, highly successful teamwork in all its specialisms, including modern dance. The music department, led by Miss Porritt and, later, Miss Heather Clayton (yet another Old Girl) regularly presented wonderful concerts and musical productions which entailed hours of rehearsals after school. Visits to theatres, scientific establishments, and universities were increasingly frequent in order to offer wider experiences for the students.

There are also many affectionate memories of activities and events largely organised by the girls themselves, like the traditional Christmas Fair, in order to raise money for charity or simply for entertainment. The annual pantomime, written and acted by the Upper Sixth for the rest of the school, brought great fun and enjoyment to the end of the Christmas term, in rehearsals as well as in the actual performances. Who could forget the Sunday afternoon rehearsal when a makeshift stage suddenly parted and the Prince Charming of the year delivering an impassioned romantic speech, abruptly disappeared into the gap?

The Parents' Association was committed to raising money to swell school funds, and help with functions like the Summer Fair, Fashion Shows and Plant Sales generated friendship as well as appreciation of the results! I remember the triumph – as late as 1983, which seems unbelievable now – of the gift of our very first computer!

Links with our Old Girls were always valued and the demise of the long-established

London Tea Party, held annually in October, was inevitable but sad. The warm interest and constant support of the governing body was always welcomed and it is gratifying that so many retain their keen interest in the school's activities until the present day.

So many memories come flooding back of all the dedicated members of the teaching, clerical, ancillary and domestic staff who could never be thanked enough for their invaluable and unfailing contributions to the life of the school and all its pupils. Their work and friendship will never be forgotten.

In 1991 the school's future seemed, at last, to be relatively stable. Fairlie, the large house next to Breeze Hill, was acquired and would eventually provide extra much-needed teaching space. A new era was beginning and it seemed to me to be the right time to make way for a successor: to my delight this turned out to be David Welsh who had been an effective Deputy Head.

Mr David Welsh

It has been a remarkable achievement, especially in view of all the pressures from so many directions, for the School to reach its centenary in such an excellent state of health. I wish it every success in all the years to come."

Mrs Delides was succeeded by Mr David Welsh: a landmark in the School's history for a Headmaster to be appointed. However, Mr Welsh had already made his mark on the School as a modern language teacher and Deputy Head. He had been on the staff for ten years and was known and trusted. Mrs Speakman was appointed Deputy Head.

Stacy Samuels, formerly Houston, recalls,

"THE TEACHERS AROUND THAT TIME were Mrs Carrington, my favourite English teacher, who always had a good way of making you understand something different. Mrs Arber (maths) was another. Ms Bell was another maths teacher, who was quite new at the time, and I think she took the higher ability maths lessons. There was a PE teacher called Mrs Finch who was always very jolly and loved hockey; she married our excellent French teacher, Mr Finch. I always liked him as he was quite strict and I found that you could concentrate in his lessons. In fact I remember getting told to put my hand down and give other people a chance because I liked French so much. Mrs Taufiq was our German teacher; she was so lovely, always willing to help.

I think that my happiest memories from AGGS were competing in the Talent contest where I used to get up on stage and sing and dance in front of the whole school. It was a real buzz and so much fun."

During 1991 the acquisition of Fairlie and its grounds was finalised. Originally built by Lord Stamford as part of a development to attract wealthy families to the area, access to the property was gained from Catherine Road which lies at the junction of Cavendish Road and The Firs. Just such a family was that of Frank Crossley and his wife Emily, the first occupants, in 1874. Frank and his brother William had moved from Northern Ireland in the mid-1860s and set up business in Manchester making machinery for producing India rubber and flax. Whilst struggling to keep their business going they acquired the patents of the Otto gas engine in 1867. Their foresight recognised the potential of a small engine that could replace steam where low horse-power engines were required. Frank improved the original designs and the resultant Crossley engine made the name famous throughout the world and generated untold wealth for both men for years to come.

Frank and his wife, both with deep religious convictions, entertained prominent philanthropists at Fairlie, where many schemes for the social and religious regeneration of Manchester were formulated, and money was given away as quickly as it came in. General Booth of the Salvation Army and his wife were frequent visitors. The damage done to people by alcohol caused Frank to become a teetotaller and he prohibited sales of his company's engine to brewers. In 1890, Fairlie was sold and the

Fairlie prior to 1991

Crossleys moved to Ancoats, one of the worst slum areas of Manchester, where they had acquired an old music-hall, known as The Star. They had it demolished and in its place built and ran a mission hall, named Star Hall, with meeting rooms, bath-rooms and coffee-rooms for the benefit of the local population. Frank and Emily lived and worked amongst the poor until his death in 1897; Emily then lived for a while in Hale before moving to Switzerland where she died. Given the early history of the occupants of this house, it is fitting that Fairlie was now to be used by a school with service to others so high on its agenda.

By 1992 an extensive buildings and refurbishment programme was underway. The West Wing had a new heating system and preliminary work had commenced on the Devisdale to provide two all weather hockey pitches, one grass pitch, six netball and tennis courts, an athletics track and changing facilities. A technology block was being planned for Fairlie with several other new classrooms.

On 4 December 1992 Miss Porritt died aged 85. An extract from Miss Clayton's obituary to her in the *Old Girls' Society News* read:

> "IN RETIREMENT, which was as full and productive as her working life, Miss Porritt was able to indulge her many interests – entertaining, travelling and 'discovering'. She continued her piano playing, mostly with friends at home, and regularly attended orchestral and chamber concerts, as well as local musical events in which Old Girls were taking part. She maintained her contact with School, attending its events regularly, particularly looking forward to the annual London reunion and to the meetings of the Coffee Club. She became absorbed in her work with the adults whom she taught during her long association with the Reading and Writing Scheme and spent many hours helping with charitable pursuits, especially at her church and at St Anne's Hospice."

The new sports facilities on the Devisdale were opened in 1993 with the first event being an international hockey match between England and Scotland schoolgirls. Sports results reflected talent at the highest levels, and congratulations were due to the first eleven hockey team becoming All England Champions.

In 1993 Miss Okell suffered a serious accident in her garden on the day of the great December storm. She died peacefully in hospital aged eighty-six. The following extract from the obituary in the *Old Girls' Society News* written by Miss Walkley said:

> "MISS OKELL HAD HAD a wonderfully fulfilled life. The home and garden she created with a friend in North Wales gave her great happiness. Coming to Glan Conwy on retirement in 1967,

The Sixth Form Centre and all-weather sports facilities

she found old friends, made new ones, persevered with the Welsh language, and enjoyed the beautiful scenery of Snowdonia. Miss Okell threw herself into this new life with characteristic energy, revealing talents for cooking, dressmaking and simple crafts and frequently holding office in the local WI branch. She resumed a lifelong interest in the Guide movement, and did voluntary service working in a WWF gift shop and, in spring, protecting the wild daffodils. Both church and village communities depended on her to do many useful jobs over the years. Then there were wonderful adventures: journeys in almost all the continents of the world.

Nevertheless, her interest in the School and in the girls for whom she had worked with such dedication never faltered. To the very end of her life, some of the most important dates in her crowded diary were School events – concerts and ceremonies – or Old Girls' gatherings in Altrincham or London."

On 30 July 1994 Miss Colenutt died aged 92. An extract from the obituary in the *Old Girls' Society News* by I M Lucas records:

"MISS COLENUTT HAD a great interest in the theatre. She played minor parts at the Garrick in both amateur and professional productions and latterly was a solid supporter of the Club Theatre. Miss Colenutt maintained her interest in the School and its affairs as well as being a founder member of the Old Girls' Coffee Club. Her last great enjoyment was to accept Mr Welsh's kind invitation to say a few words to the School on her 90th birthday – that really did make her day!"

1994 saw the retirement of Miss Carol Newbrook, Head of the Sixth Form Centre and Miss Heather Clayton, Head of Music, with 63 years of service between them.

Mrs Anne Dixon wrote in the *School Magazine* of 1993–94,

"MY MEMORIES OF MISS CLAYTON go back like many of yours to the first music lessons in my new Grammar School. Miss Clayton taught me at Sale Girls' until I left to go to music college. It is, however, other memories that I treasure: the concerts we gave: the day trip to Chester music festival where

A presentation at School to Miss Colenutt on her 90th birthday

Miss Clayton took the choir 'just for fun' and we won three cups! I remember the box of chocolates she gave us on the coach home.

Her energy infected all the music activities. We loved orchestra rehearsals: choir practices started before she arrived, such was her enthusiasm.

Miss Heather Clayton

Soon after I left Sale, Miss Clayton moved on to Manchester High School and finally to Altrincham, where she has remained. Over the years she has produced performances of *Hiawatha*, Gilbert and Sullivan operettas and many varied concerts, all of an amazingly high standard.

One of her pupils, a contemporary of mine, is now an opera singer at Covent Garden. There are few families in Trafford who do not know someone who has been taught by Miss Clayton and will not say 'it is the end of an era' as she goes. She leaves behind her a wonderful music tradition and many girls and staff who are determined to keep the standard high. We wish her well in her retirement."

Miss Newbrook, the longest serving member of staff at that time with thirty-six years service, was interviewed by Susie Gibson and Helen Martin for the *School Magazine* before she retired.

Why did you decide to become a teacher?

I don't know! It was probably because there were few other career possibilities at the time. Young ladies either went into nursing or teaching. There was no range of opportunities and no career conventions like we have today – I didn't know about many other careers.

When did you become Head of the Sixth Form Centre?

When the centre opened, although I was head of the Sixth Form when it was based over at main School as well.

What was your favourite subject at school apart from history?

Sport, especially hockey and tennis.

What was your least favourite subject at school?

The sciences. I'm disappointed that I didn't do better at science now because I enjoy gardening. If I was a student now I would concentrate on science and then go into a job involving horticulture.

Which historic figure do you most admire and why?

Possibly Gladstone, the great statesman of the nineteenth century, because he had enormous energy, principles, perseverance and never let problems get him down.

Miss Carol Newbrook
Lady Captain at the Golf Club, 2000

Have you had any embarrassing moment at AGGS?

Probably my most embarrassing moment was when the outgoing Upper Sixth arranged for a man dressed as Superman to come into the last Assembly with a message. It was totally unexpected.

What have been the highlights of your career?

I don't think I have any personal highlights. The highlight is seeing other people's successes. It is particularly pleasing when a less-gifted student, who has to work extremely hard, gets good results.

Have you any future ambitions?

To play more golf, and get another hole in one. Believe it or not, I did get a hole in one a few years ago in a competition.

Thank you, Miss Newbrook – and here's to the next thirty-six years, and another hole in one!"

On 14 October 1994, Mrs Delides was invited officially to open the Fairlie block – an apt choice as the development of the land in this way was her idea. An article by Wendy Withington in the *Old Girls' News* describes the building and facilities:

The original entrance to Fairlie on Catherine Road

"IF IT IS A FIVE STAR education you are looking for then Fairlie is where you will find it. It is impressive from the outside as it has been cleverly and sensitively designed so that it is difficult to tell where the old house ends and the extension begins. Yellow brick, arched windows to the ground floor, black and gold entrance gates all help to give it a traditional appearance, whilst acting as a cloak to a thoroughly modern interior which is even air conditioned.

The ground floor is home to three maths rooms, two technology rooms, a dark room, lift (for authorised use only), and various cloakroom facilities, all containing the latest in everything. The first floor has yet another maths room and technology room, two information technology rooms with about forty computers between them and an art room and further cloakroom facilities. A partly glazed roof provides just the right environment for a second floor conservatory. A very lasting impression was made upon me by Fairlie."

Laura Hollis recalls with gratitude the teachers who inspired her:

"AFTER SIXTH FORM, I went on to university to study linguistics and Hispanic studies and took part in a Spanish play in my final year, all thanks to the teachers and my experience at AGGS.

I loved the old building, the old house and mobile classrooms at Breeze Hill, and just towards the end of my time there, the newly acquired Fairlie building with artificial lighting that would give me a headache during double maths with Mr Brown! We also witnessed the change from having to walk a fair way to the old sports facilities before the brand new Devisdale was built.

Many of the teachers had an impact on me. Thanks to Mrs Speakman I now analyse every political speech that I hear and can't read an advert in a magazine without circling all the linguistic features that are used to sell! She also gave me an obsession for books and I remember afternoons translating *Macbeth* – I still can't resist seeing that play every time that it is on at the theatre. She had such a wonderful manner with us, and now that I am a teacher I recognise all the techniques that she used to help us, way before they were

Fairlie, rear elevation

made 'trendy' and given specific names such as 'AFL' (Assessment for Learning).

My language teachers were also a huge influence on me. From Mrs Arnold who taught me French right through the school, to Mrs Carter and Miss Huddart with her oh-so-peculiar way of teaching but somehow it worked and now I can spot traces of her temper in me when I am in the classroom teaching Spanish! I just don't have the strawberry jumper to go with it. And probably the most influential of all who had made me thoroughly obsessed with the subject, the very glamorous Mrs Napier. She used to tell us fabulous stories of when she lived in Spain; she was disgusted with us – 'oh girls!' – when we admitted that we didn't know who the suffragettes were in English, never mind Spanish: and she made us learn a poem from Lazarillo de Tornes and I can still recite it off by heart! When I got to university I was better at the subjunctive than some of my lecturers, and now in the classroom my students tease me for my obsession, but I love the Spanish language and everything grammatical about it because of her.

We were given many fantastic opportunities for trips at AGGS. I had a great time on the French trip to the Loire and still have the scrapbook that Mr Finch asked us to prepare when we got back. The geography trips were always good, but in particular the residential course at Cranedale with Mrs Higgins, and with the male instructors and an actual bar that we were allowed to go in!

Mrs Stuart was also wonderful and is the reason that I am obsessed with *Pygmalion*. We put the play on 'in the round' during Sixth Form, and had a brilliant time. I was Mrs Pearce, the housekeeper, and I remember the day when a few of us missed a lesson so that Mrs Stuart could drive us to a costume shop to pick out our clothing for the play. She also used to arrange theatre tickets to the Royal Exchange on Monday nights which encouraged my passion for the theatre."

Pygmalion *handbill*

In October 1995 Mr Welsh reported in the *Old Girls' News* that the School underwent a full HMI visit earlier in the year.

"WITH 14 INSPECTORS and a total of 49 inspector days spent in School we felt thoroughly and rigorously inspected. Every time we opened a door or turned a corner we encountered a notetaking, questioning but always courteous presence. The final verdict ('this is an outstanding School') reflected enormous credit on a 'committed and highly competent' staff and 'well-motivated, confident, articulate and friendly pupils'. Old Girls would have been proud to see their modern counterparts upholding the standards and values of the school in this way."

Leane Muckle says,

"MY MEMORIES ARE EXTREMELY FOND as I thoroughly enjoyed my time at school. I wouldn't describe myself as a 'geek' but throughout my time I wanted to do my best and the teachers made that possible for me and constantly encouraged academic success.

The Headmaster at the time was Mr Welsh and although he appeared to be very quiet and content out of the limelight he ran the school very well. Under his management I always felt you knew where the line of discipline was and fortunately for me I don't recall crossing it!

One teacher who really stood out from the others was Miss Huddart. She took my French class and demanded 110% from everyone at all times and in her words wouldn't let us stop writing until we had writer's cramp! Mrs Higgins was another teacher who meant a lot to me. She was my geography teacher in my early years at the school but when I got to Year 11 she was the Head of Year. I went through some bad family times in my last year of school relating to my parents' divorce and subsequent decisions over where to continue my life. I decided I wanted to move to Kent to be with my dad but Mrs Higgins encouraged me to wait until I had completed my GCSEs, for which I am eternally grateful. Had it not been for her I doubt I would have achieved such good results.

There were so many other teachers that really made my time there special; Mrs Mears (religious studies), Miss Thistleton (geography), Mrs Sumner (geography), Mrs Berry (art), Miss Mawdesley (English), Mrs Arnold (French), and Miss Lucy (chemistry)."

Amy Warburton says:

"I DON'T THINK that I properly appreciated what many of the teachers at the School did for me until I left and went into teaching myself. Particularly, I would like to highlight the educational talents of Mrs Winter, whom I was fortunate to have for the last four years of my education. This marvellous woman taught, supported and inspired me throughout my lessons and time which I was able to spend with her.

Also Miss Walker, who although she was only ever my class teacher gave me the most enjoyable years of my education in my bid to make her smile. When first meeting this formidable teacher my class were told, 'I don't smile, I don't laugh and I certainly don't joke.' Well, that was a challenge if ever I had heard one. This lady had an arid sense of humour but after months of trying and failing I finally managed to get a smile out of her and the rest is history, as they say. I formed a strong relationship with her even though most of it was based on sarcastic banter and she really helped me to see my potential as something more than a face in the sea that bobbed along doing nothing remarkable.

I started at AGGS in 1997 as a nervous but fairly confident girl. I left knowing that I had made friendships for life not only with my fellow pupils but also with some of the staff who took me under their wing.

I was told in no uncertain terms in choosing my GCSEs that it would be unwise of me to follow my desire to do the separate sciences. I was a strong-willed and stubborn young thing and was determined to prove wrong the teachers who seemed so willing to doubt me. Thankfully I was allowed to continue and thank goodness I did. I found myself being taught by some of the best scientific minds that AGGS had to offer, Mrs Winter, Mr Newall, Dr Pickering and Mrs Boothman to name but a few. It is thanks to these teachers and the school that my love for science evolved. I went on to gain high GCSE and A level grades in all the sciences and as my specialism in primary education I am taking science in the hope that I can inspire children in the same way as I was.

Finally, I find myself reading through this and noticing that I have not mentioned very much about the School itself. Well yes, it is grand, impressive and a caring, secure environment to be taught in, but it is the teachers that shape our education and affect the attitudes which we have regarding our place of learning."

"Simply the Best"
Altrincham Girls' Grammar School's U16 Netball Squad are the
ALL ENGLAND NETBALL NATIONAL SCHOOLS' U16 CHAMPIONS

Helen Gray (capt.), Olivia Flanagan*, Loren Taylor*, Laura Banks*,
Tina Thirlwell, Jill Stephens, Marietta Smith*, Beckie Smith,
Sarah Jones, Katrina de Massey, Sarah Eardley.
*scouted by England selectors

From the School Magazine, *1997–98*

Arts Festival programme

In April 1997, under the provisions of the 1988 Education Reform Act and following a parental ballot, the School opted out of the control of the local education authority to become grant maintained. This change of status meant more responsibility and autonomy in respect of the budget, buildings and staff. Following the introduction of the School Standards and Framework Act 1998, in April 1999 the School achieved foundation school status, funded by central government via the local education authority, and with greater freedom for the governing body to run the school.

As Mr Welsh approached retirement in December 1998 he reviewed the achievements of all spheres of activity during the year in his annual letter to the *Old Girls' Society News*.

"PUBLIC EXAMINATION RESULTS were again really excellent. At advanced level every girl achieved the matriculation requirement for university entrance and the average number of subjects passed was four. Well over half of all results were grade A or B. At GCSE 60% of all results were A* or A and 99% of the girls achieved the government's benchmark of 5+ subjects at grades A* to C. The girls and the staff who taught them deserve our warmest congratulations.

Highlights of the year must include winning the All England National Schools Netball Championships in Ipswich. This is the fourth time in six years that a school team has been the best in England at netball or hockey. Our second Gala Concert at the Royal Northern College of Music was a resounding success, we made our first compact disc recording and it was a thrill for a Year 7 choir to sing on national television on four Sunday mornings.

Other notable events included an excellent performance of *Twelfth Night* by sixth-formers and our seventh successive Arts Festival. We celebrated a National RE Festival in a number of ways, including an 'Any Questions' evening at which major world faiths were represented. There are currently 60 different types of extra-curricular activity on offer to the girls, including in the Sixth Form Young Enterprise and Understanding Industry which prepare them for the world of work. Community service and charity fund raising are high on our list of priorities. This year £6,537 was raised for good causes.

A major focus of the year has been improvements to school buildings. We worked very hard to generate new money and obtained almost £400,000 through bidding successfully for grants. We added £300,000 of our own funds and have completely redesigned and refurbished Breeze Hill. It is now a pleasure to use. Work is taking place to provide a new laboratory (our tenth) and a new food technology room. There have been major improvements to staff room accommodation, the Sixth Form Centre and we have now installed a kiln to introduce ceramics to the art syllabus. This will be my last letter as Headmaster as I am retiring and Mrs Ross will take over in January."

Mr David Welsh recalls for the centenary book:

"I joined the staff in June 1981 shortly after Mrs Delides had become Headmistress and it did not take long for me to be impressed by the

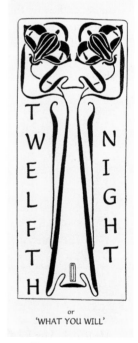

Programme cover

distinctive ethos of the school. Academic excellence mattered greatly of course, and public examination results reflected this, but education was interpreted in the broad sense with extra-curricular activities and awareness of the needs of others also being very highly valued.

Another very impressive feature throughout my time at the school was the commitment and excellence of the staff, both teaching and non-teaching, for which generations of girls had every reason to be grateful. I was always conscious of how invaluable the friendly support of colleagues was.

In my early years I taught mostly German but sometimes other subjects to plug gaps in the timetable and I particularly enjoyed the foreign language trips to Brittany and the Rhine Valley. Volleyball and public speaking were amongst the other extra-curricular activities I was involved in and some readers may remember

Mr David Welsh

participating in local competitions and in the Model United Nations Assemblies which were held annually in Manchester. Community service was undertaken on a regular basis by members of the Sixth Form. They also organised parties for local children in the summer (supported on one occasion by the footballer Bryan Robson) and Christmas parties for the elderly from local residential homes. Fund raising for charity provided much enjoyment as well as help for worthwhile causes. In addition to the regular Friday collections for charities chosen by the girls themselves there was an annual Christmas fair at which vast quantities of food and drink were always consumed, purely in order to swell the total raised, of course.

There were also regular talent shows. On one occasion, never to be repeated, the two Deputy Headmistresses, Mrs Kerr and Mrs Speakman, and I performed Frank Sinatra's *My Way* which was notable more for its novelty value than any artistic merit but it was all in a good cause. On another occasion fund raising for a particular charity had been so successful that some girls and staff were invited to a reception at St James's Palace where we met Prince Charles.

There were many notable sporting achievements including the winning of National Championships in both netball and hockey. The music was superb with young performers carefully nurtured by the dedicated music staff. Concerts were invariably sold out quickly and how many

Mr Welsh, Mrs Kerr and Mrs Speakman perform My Way

schools could boast of two orchestras? The dance performances were rightly very popular and I can remember many first class drama productions including *Daisy Pulls it Off* in which a few of the staff were able to take part. Seldom were visitors shown round the school without their admiring the artwork.

The Parent Teachers Association contributed significantly to the success of the school not just with fund raising but also with putting on events such as the annual Fashion Show which gave girls a chance to star as models.

The committed Governing Body not only worked hard to ensure the school's successful running and development but also generously supported the many performances and other events by their attendance.

In my later years it was perhaps the buildings which were in danger of becoming a major preoccupation. The acquisition of Fairlie, the renovation of Breeze Hill, the laying of first class all-weather hockey pitches on the Devisdale and sundry additions and renovations in Main School and the Sixth Form Centre combined to offer more and much improved accommodation. Even the Lodge House was completely renovated and let to provide greater security and a regular income.

Girls and staff coped admirably with the upheaval caused by all the work but it was important in the late 1990s to keep reminding ourselves where our real priorities lay. At times the battle for funding, the ubiquitous presence of builders and the nocturnal visits to deal with recalcitrant alarms stretched the patience but never more so than in the middle of one Christmas night when a malfunctioning fire alarm not only kept local residents awake but also tested my ingenuity to the uttermost as I tried to persuade it to stop. Had there been a large hammer readily to hand at that moment…

It is impossible to do justice to the contribution of staff and girls during my time at the school and there are many more instances I could give. It was a privilege to be involved and I pass on warm congratulations on the School achieving its centenary and every good wish for continued success and fulfilment in the future."

Mrs Dana Ross-Wawrzynski was appointed Headmistress on 1 January 1999. Born and educated in Scotland, she gained a BSc Hons from Glasgow University and an MSc from Strathclyde University specialising in biochemistry and applied microbiology. Whilst an

undergraduate she met and married Jack Wawrzynski, a young Polish architect teaching at the Glasgow School of Art. She gave up her postgraduate studies and moved to England when her husband was offered a post at Manchester University in Urban Design. At this time there was a shortage of science teachers and Mrs Ross-Wawrzynski fell into teaching 'by accident'. She taught microbiology at the Manchester Metropolitan University and at All Saints Further Education College before moving on to the Central High School for Boys and later to an all girls school – Loreto, Manchester, which then became a Sixth Form College.

Within seven years of becoming a teacher Mrs Ross-Wawrzynski was appointed Deputy Head of Abraham Moss High School. During her sixth year there she was delighted to find that she was expecting twins. Adam and James were born

Mrs Ross-Wawrzynski

on 22 August 1989. She then took up her second deputy headship at All Hallows, Macclesfield whilst her children completed their primary education.

Mrs Ross-Wawrzynski has two great passions in her life, her family and her work in education. She is proud of her sons and her husband's achievements and she is equally delighted when the schools she is working for are successful establishments for both pupils and staff. She enjoys travelling, especially if she can visit some interesting schools around the world, and likes to relax with a good book (usually on education), enjoys topical discussion on television programmes in the late evening and is an avid Radio Four fan.

In March 1999, fifty students and teachers went on the history trip of a lifetime to Russia. Some extracts from Natalie Rampling's account in the *School Magazine* follow.

"MOSCOW WAS A BEAUTIFUL CITY that was dotted with the golden domes of many Cathedrals and churches. That first morning we had a tour which included views of the prestigious University and many other significant buildings like Stalin's Wedding Cakes. We also visited a monastery, the Kremlin and its Armoury, Red Square, the Russian Opera and the Bolshoi Ballet. The Cosmonaut Museum was interesting where we learnt about the Russian Space programme.

The attractive city of St Petersburg was severely damaged and bore the scars of the siege when over one million Russians actually died of starvation during this period of the Second World War. We visited the famous Hermitage Museum, the Peter and Paul Fortress and its Cathedral, Peter the Great's Log Cabin and St Isaac's Cathedral. The final day we saw the place of Rasputin's downfall in the Yusupov Palace including the very room where he was poisoned and shot and the private theatre where we sat in the actual seats that Tsar Nicholas and his family had once occupied.

After a long journey we arrived back at school having enjoyed a great trip that was an experience we'll never forget; but we were ready for something more familiar – our own beds. Our thanks to the history department for taking us on this fantastic trip."

Intrepid AGGS travellers on board the battleship Aurora, *now a museum in St Petersburg. A shot from this ship in October 1917 heralded the start of the Russian Revolution.*

The 2000s	
2000	10 April – Millennium Concert, Bridgewater Hall, Manchester
2000	October – Ofsted inspection
2001	Summer – World Challenge, Brazil
2002	Language College status achieved
2002	New block opened Fairlie/Breeze Hill, and new Library
2003	West Wing refurbished
2003	28 April – visit of His Royal Highness, Prince Charles
2003	Twinned with Zephania School, Durban
2004	Visit to Huaxia Girls' Academy, Beijing
2004	July – Hockey tour, Singapore and Australia
2005	October – Ofsted inspection
2006	East Wing redevelopment completed
2007	Specialist Training School status achieved
2007	October – Northern India study tour
2009	October – study tour to Rome

Chapter 10
The 2000s

The new millennium and the ninetieth birthday of the school were marked by a Gala Concert at the Bridgewater Hall in Manchester on 10 April, with just under 600 girls including members of staff and friends of the School taking part in the first and second orchestras, wind band, junior and senior choirs or in the year group pieces.

Programme for the Gala Concert

The evening's performance introduced by television presenter and former School Governor, Gordon Burns, included a Beatles medley by the year 8 and 9 pupils, a festive fanfare involving all the instrumentalists and a mixture of Disney classics by the year 7 girls. *Song for a May Morning*, a piece specially commissioned for the occasion from Stuart Scott, a local composer, was premiered at the concert. One of the highlights of the programme was Beethoven's *Piano Concerto No 3*, in which the first orchestra, leader Natalie Boardman (year 13), conductor John Beilby (Head of Music), accompanied former pupil, Penelope Roskell, now an accomplished pianist who has played solo throughout the UK.

In October an Ofsted inspection took place and Mrs Ross-Wawrzynski included some extracts from the ensuing report in her letter to the Old Girls' Society later that year:

> " 'THE HIGH QUALITY OF TEACHING and learning stems in all instances from excellent subject knowledge and high expectations on the part of the teacher, excellent attitudes on the part of the learner and a real love of the subject on the part of both. There is a genuine partnership between teacher and learner in almost all classrooms,' and 'the standards consistently attained by pupils at the end of Key Stages 3 and 4 and in A-level, place the school in the top 5% of schools in the country.' Other comments included 'Care of the pupils at the school is excellent,' and 'Throughout the time pupils spend at the school there is an emphasis on developing them as independent learners and capable and confident young women. This reaches fruition in the Sixth Form where students are able, confident and articulate and present themselves as civic-minded young women able and willing to play a key role in society'. Also 'The school is characterised by very good personal relationships – there is an overwhelming sense of a well-mannered, well-ordered and caring community.' "

When such reports are published in the newspapers and at other times when league tables of schools examination results appear, many Old Girls instinctively turn to these pages to seek out the position and achievements of the School and share a feeling of great pride to see that 'their School' is doing so well. This is reflected in the comments in previous chapters of this book and none more so than when several generations of some families have attended the School through all stages of its development and expansion. Just such a family is that of Anne

Priestner, formerly Mercer, who writes with great joy of the time that she and her family were and are still there.

"FOUR GENERATIONS OF OUR FAMILY have attended School. My mother, Marie Louisa Mercer, formerly Kaye, attended the County High School from 1916 to 1920 in the days of Miss Howes Smith. She was taught by, amongst others, Miss Bell (Cookery) and Miss Whitwill (History). These wonderful teachers also taught my sister and me during the war years. One of mother's school friends was Marjorie Davenport. By the time I attended the High School Miss Davenport was teaching in the Junior Department as were Miss Atkinson and Miss Langley. Later, when the Junior Department was disbanded, she became an excellent English teacher.

My sister, Barbara Mayer, formerly Mercer, entered the Junior Department in 1938, and I joined her in September 1939, a few days after the war broke out. I was just seven years old and the youngest girl in the School, which brought a number of pleasant little duties during the year. I remember that it was quite a shock to discover that I was just an ordinary little girl like everyone else after my 'year of glory'! The new Education Act brought many changes and my year was the first to sit the eleven plus.

Barbara and I both left after completing our Higher School Certificate and have very happy memories of the time we were there and of the staff. Miss Newton, Mrs Dore, Miss Porritt, Miss Anderton, and Miss Muir, just to name a few. Miss Drought was a firm but kind and approachable Headmistress and I look back with gratitude on the dedication and the high ideals and enthusiasm which were imparted to us. Highlights were the end of year concerts, plays and entertainments and the Christmas Fair with lots of games, goodies and face creams concocted in the School Laboratory! My daughter, Wendy Meniru, formerly Priestner, came home from a Quaker School in York to enter the Sixth Form in 1976. The first year was spent in quite cramped conditions only to be followed by the excitement of moving into the new Sixth Form Centre on the Devisdale – heady days!

My granddaughter, Lucy Priestner, is the latest of our family to attend AGGS and she has been as happy and enthused by the School as the rest of us. Lucy hopes to study medicine and started her final year in the Sixth Form in September 2009. It has been a joy to be able to attend some of the concerts which Lucy has taken part in and to see so much progress and so much to be proud of in our dear old School."

Likewise, the current achievements of the School are always a topic for discussion at Old Girls' Reunions whether they are large groups that meet regularly or small gatherings of friends since schooldays. Erica Fitzpatrick, formerly Rawlinson, recalls many happy afternoons spent at the London Reunions of the Old Girls' Society,

"FOR MANY YEARS, the first Saturday in October has been the signal for many women, from all over the country, to set off for the Annual London Reunion of the Altrincham County

Old Girls' Society London Reunion at Lauderdale House, 1999
Mrs Williams, ?, ?, Mary Perry, Mrs Delides, Erica Fitzpatrick

Friends from the Class of '66 meet in Kensington, 2009
Liz Loxton (Lee), Gill Zeke (Crook), Leila Zollinger,
Judi Edwards (MacIver), Alison Boukhobza (Sleight),
Karen Fletcher (Waddell), Jan Fyfe (Hollidge)

Grammar School Old Girls' Society. Members came from the length and breadth of England (Newcastle, Somerset, Gloucestershire and East Sussex) as well as from the London area. My first meeting was at the beginning of my university career in 1965 and on this occasion we met in the 'Pride of Cockaigne' coffee bar next to Dillons University Bookshop. In later years the meetings were held in various venues from the YWCA near Tottenham Court Road, and for the last years, at Lauderdale House in Highgate. This very beautiful and superior meeting place was thanks to one of the chief London Reunion members, Elizabeth Nelson, who worked there for many years. I missed several meetings in the 1970s as I was abroad in Thailand and then Australia, but returned when I married and was again living in London. The last meeting was in 2000. By then our numbers had declined as we all grew older, and we had lost our key figures of Miss Porritt and Miss Okell. They had been amazingly faithful in their journeys from Cheshire and North Wales and kept the group together. They both knew and remembered so many of their former pupils and were exceptional in their commitment and interest. We were really privileged to know them and to have their friendship. It was also lovely to have Mrs Delides to join us after her retirement. For years, the hard work of organising the meetings was co-ordinated by Flossie Williams (who had been Miss Florence Saunders at School teaching history in the 1950s). She too is sadly now no longer with us but we remember her with gratitude. My role was to provide enough coffee mugs!

The association with School and the basis of 'Fortiter, Fideliter, Feliciter' gave an otherwise disparate group a tremendous strength in our shared experiences. It maintained and developed friendships between Old Girls who had not necessarily known each other at school, and the annual meetings gave us chance to renew our ties. News of ACGS and its development and successes was always high on the agenda. It was always a great afternoon to share news and ideas with others in the confidence and sympathy of this shared background. Initially it was just a tea party, but at Lauderdale House, it expanded into a meeting for lunch first and then continued into the afternoon."

Early in the decade School was introduced to 'World Challenge Expeditions', an organisation that develops a wide range of leadership and personal skills, provides community service opportunities and off the beaten track exploration. Many months prior to the departure of the first expedition, fundraising started and training was organised for the ten successful applicants and the two members of staff, Miss Boyse and Miss Richardson. Charlotte Green (year 12) wrote of her experiences in *The Insider*:

"I WAS NOT SURE what I expected when I signed up for the expedition to Brazil in the summer of 2001. I remember sitting in Assembly listening to Louise Berry from World Challenge talking to us about the organisation and what was involved. From that moment there was no question whether I was going to take part or what my parents would say and how would I raise the money: I had made up my mind, I was determined to go to Brazil, and I did.

The expedition was divided into different stages. It began in Rio which was mostly sightseeing, before moving on to the Pantanal, a vast wetland near the border of Bolivia. Here we mainly went on day treks which usually consisted of us wading through swamps complete with caymans, piranhas and snakes. The next stage was a visit to the Iguaçu Falls. The highlight here was a white water boat trip underneath the Falls and we all got completely drenched.

I found the most enjoyable part of the expedition was the community phase, where we helped in an inner-city crèche for six days in Florianopolis, a city on the east coast of Brazil. The crèche looked after over 480 children aged up to seven years. It had very limited resources and relied mainly on donations and the tremendous work and endless enthusiasm of the few teachers and volunteers. Our work mainly consisted of interaction with the children and painting an alphabet train on the nursery wall which was thoroughly appreciated and loved by the children. Our time here was made even more humbling by the daily bus run which we all took part in. Every day a fleet of minibuses would collect the children from the shantytowns and bring them to the crèche. We had the opportunity to see at first hand what poverty these people lived in and yet how happy they were with their lives. This part of the expedition taught us many things.

I went to Brazil with high expectations and these were far, far exceeded. Not only do I have so many wonderful memories, I have learnt so many new things. I am more confident and assertive; I believe in myself more and, much to my parents' disbelief I survived a month away from home in an alien environment and had the time of my life."

Photo records of the South American trips in the School Hall

Following this pioneering trip to South America, other groups have followed their example with expeditions organised at two year intervals to visit Ecuador in 2003, Costa Rica in 2005, Venezuela in 2007 and Peru in 2009.

Once the School achieved Foundation status in 1999 and with Ofsted reports continuing to emphasise that high academic standards were consistently being achieved, it was possible to introduce a range of significant new initiatives when funding had been secured.

On the accommodation front a £1 million scheme came to fruition in 2002 with the opening of a new building linking Breeze Hill and Fairlie to replace the old demountable classrooms. Seven new English classrooms, two mathematics rooms, a technology room and a drama studio were provided. Great care was taken to ensure the new block was aesthetically pleasing and blended in with its surroundings. Work then started on the provision of a new library (where the original gymnasium had been) which was ready for use later the same year. Afterwards the West Wing was refurbished and later a new stairwell and lift installed between main school and the West Wing to enable wheelchair access to all classrooms in these areas. In 2006 the £2.4 million East Wing development was completed and provided a new entrance and reception area for visitors, three new state of the art science laboratories, a new

Fairlie new block, main entrance, 2002

staff room and dining area, kitchen and dining room improvements as well as provision of a number of much needed offices and a lift to the science classrooms.

In 2002 the bid to the Department for Education and Skills for Language College status was successful. The aim of Language Colleges is to raise standards of achievement and the quality of teaching and learning in modern foreign languages for all learners with extra funding provided from the private sector and government. The Colleges are expected to develop a visible character that is understood by the girls, parents and the community and to develop partnerships with schools abroad.

Implementation of the scheme has brought an exciting new dimension to the ethos of the School, enhancing pupils' educational experience and opening up a whole range of extra opportunities. In year 7, pupils take either French or German and all will continue with this language up to GCSE, which is taken in year 10 (a year earlier than other subjects). In addition, all pupils take up the study of a second modern language in year 8 (either French or Spanish).

Girls and staff can also take advantage of the many extra-curricular classes on offer at lunch time or after school which can include Italian, Japanese, Chinese and Arabic. School visits abroad and work experience exchanges are organised on a regular basis. There are thriving international partnerships with schools in France, Germany, Turkey, China and South Africa.

Evening classes in a range of languages are offered to the wider community, and many parents take advantage of these opportunities to learn a new language or brush up their linguistic knowledge. The School also supports the Trafford Primary modern foreign language programme, helping local Primary teachers to deliver language lessons.

On 28 April 2003 His Royal Highness The Prince of Wales was invited to the School officially to open the New Library, dedicated to his late grandmother, the Language College and Fairlie Build. During his two-hour visit he met staff and pupils,

Queen Elizabeth the Queen Mother Library, 2002

The Governors,
Headmistress, Staff and
Pupils invite you to the

**Official Opening of the New Library,
Language College and Fairlie Build**
by
HIS ROYAL HIGHNESS The Prince of Wales
on Monday 28 April 2003 from 11am
to be followed by a buffet lunch

Invitation to the royal visit

Prince Charles meets pupils in the new library

*Prince Charles with Mrs Dana
Ross-Wawrzynski*

sat in on a maths class using a high-tech interactive teaching board, French and computer skills classes and watched a workshop of Shakespeare's *A Midsummer Night's Dream* in the new £100,000 drama studio. "Prince Charles was very nice and very interested in what the girls were doing. I was a little apprehensive beforehand but we all felt at ease when we met him," said Mrs Stuart, Head of Drama. Prince Charles also officially opened the new £250,000 Queen Elizabeth the Queen Mother Library. The Prince, who has a special interest in architecture, was impressed with the renovation. "I did very much want to say how pleased I was to see what you have done with the old gym. I am sure my grandmother would have been very pleased to see it and to have known you have named it after her," Prince Charles told 300 pupils, staff and dignitaries in the School Hall. Afterwards The Prince chatted with staff and pupils and said, "One of the things that fascinated me was to hear that the first head teacher was the governess-cum-history teacher to the Princess Royal,

my Aunt Mary." He also unveiled a plaque commemorating his visit. Mrs Ross-Wawrzynski said of the Prince, "He was a very charming man who had obviously done a lot of homework because he knew the School very well. He made one feel relaxed and it was very comfortable showing him the School."

By 2003 firm links through the Afritwin Organisation had been forged with South Africa and School was twinned with Zephania Secondary School in a rural community 100 miles

Prince Charles with Lynda Abrahams, librarian

north of Durban. Part of the commitment to this school was to help provide them with computer facilities. Initial fundraising activities by the girls was sufficient to send a consignment of twenty computers to the school in Durban and some money to purchase a printer, paper and ink to complement the computers was given to the Headmaster, Mr Sipho Khanyile when he visited School in November that same year. Before leaving he was also presented with a laptop computer for his use as Headmaster and to enable him to email AGGS. Previously he had to travel several miles to a teacher centre to use the only facility in the area.

Zephania School, 2004

This link was developed further when the following year fourteen pupils and three staff went to South Africa. After a visit to the Bushlands Safari Park to see some big game the party headed for Zephania. Nicki Baldwin, year 11, takes up the story (which was published in the *Old Girls' Society Autumn Newsletter*):

"WHEN WE ARRIVED at our partner school, we were taken aback by the incredible welcome they gave us. For some of us it was very emotional. It was nothing we had seen before, they were so pleased to see us, running over and hugging us all. The school had barely anything; the

toilets were basically a hole in the ground, but the atmosphere in the school was always positive. We could tell that each and every pupil really enjoyed being there even though for some it was a two hour walk to and from school every day. They were so pleased that we had visited them that we spent our free time listening to their beautiful singing, which was really overwhelming.

There was a strong relationship between the teachers and the pupils and they always seemed to keep the balance between fun and education. The lessons were engaging and everyone was enthusiastic even though they only had basic equipment such as pens and paper.

While we were there we presented them with calculators, geometry sets, dictionaries and other useful things. This small gesture made such a difference to their learning and made us realise how much more we can do to help. We have already as a school raised money and provided equipment to set up a computer room. This helped their education and also enabled them get more sponsorship from large companies in South

Ties with Zephania remain strong and fundraising remains a priority

Africa. We will try through our school charity committee to continue to raise more money for this very deserving cause."

In November 2003 during a two week visit to Beijing, Shanghai and Hong Kong Mrs Ross-Wawrzynski, Mr Osborne (Director of ICT) and Mrs Lord (Head of Science) visited

Huaxia Academy orchestra on stage at Zhongshan Park Concert Hall, Beijing, 2004

schools in each city and had very productive high level business meetings regarding the development of the 'China Project'. This entails training Chinese teachers to teach their subject in English to pupils in China.

A pilot for this project commenced with the arrival of three teachers from Huaxia Academy, who joined School for four months during the spring and summer terms of 2004. Under the guidance of their mentors at AGGS and Manchester University, they were trained to teach their own subject in English. This was the first of similar such visits.

The following year thirty-five pupils and nine staff travelled to China for the opportunity of a lifetime! They were the privileged guests of Huaxia Girls' Academy, Beijing, who hosted the ten-day visit. This report of the trip by Miss Lloyd-Jones, Head of Music, appeared in *The Insider* for 2004–2005.

"THE MAJOR HIGHLIGHT of the trip was a concert in Beijing's largest and most prestigious concert hall, Zhongshan Park. Both schools presented their own programmes of instrumental pieces and songs, and several groups of Huaxia pupils and their teachers performed traditional dancing.

The school choirs then combined to sing three songs, including a folk-song *Jasmine* in Chinese, which brought rapturous applause from the audience. Miss Lloyd-Jones had also composed a song specially for the two schools called *Spirit of Friendship* which symbolised the growing relationship between AGGS and Huaxia.

The group embarked upon a comprehensive tour of the sights in and around Beijing, including a trip to walk on part of the Great Wall of China. They visited Tian'anmen Square, numerous temples and the Forbidden City, and experienced the worst thunderstorm and flooding in living memory! They were also taken on several excursions to interesting factories and workshops, seeing silk being produced, and jade being carved. One evening, the group was treated to a spectacle of acrobatics and kung fu

AGGS in the Forbidden City, Beijing, 2004

174

by performers aged as young as six years. The life, vitality and colour couldn't be missed.

Probably the most lasting memory was of the warmth and friendship shown by the pupils and staff of Huaxia. The experience of visiting China was one that would remain a treasured memory for years to come."

Mrs Stuart and Mrs Dodds remained in China for a further three weeks teaching English to Huaxia pupils.

Also in July 2004 a hockey tour was arranged to Singapore and Australia led by Mrs Judith Finch. The following is an extract from Mrs Finch's report that appeared in the *Old Girls' Society Autumn Newsletter*:

Mrs Thomson, Mrs Finch, Mrs Heaton and the Sydney Opera House

"TWO MATCHES WERE PLAYED in Singapore; the U15s lost 4–0 to a Singapore Development Squad and the U18s beat Singapore Cricket Club 8–2. Some notable places visited included Chinatown, Sentosa Island, the National Orchid Gardens and the shops! The next stop was in Melbourne where the U15s lost 1–0 and the U18s lost 4–2 against a local club. The girls were billeted with families from the Methodist Ladies College for two nights, with the staff staying in a local motel. The girls spent time during the day helping to teach year 6 girls. The facilities included a Centre of Excellence for Gymnastics. (Two years later girls from the Methodist Ladies College visited England and were hosted by AGGS families. Many friendships were forged over the three nights of their stay. The schools played each other at hockey – won by AGGS and netball – won by MLC.)

In Canberra the girls were billeted with their hosts from Daramalan College for three nights. A full programme of activities included a visit to the Australian Institute of Sport and a day in the school sampling Australian lessons before two matches which the U15s won 3–0 and the U18s won 2–1. The next visit to Sydney took in the sights which included a walk along the Harbour Bridge, a view of the Opera House, the surfers at Bondi Beach, Taronga Zoo, and a trip up the ATP Tower, as well as playing some hockey! Matches were played against Wenona School on the practice pitch at the Homebush Olympic Stadium when the U15s lost 1–0 and U18s won 3–1. The next day the final matches were played on THE Olympic pitch against Ascham School when the U15s won 3–0 and U18s drew 1–1.

The final stop was at Cairns when it was time to relax as all the matches had been played. Two excursions were undertaken, the first to Kuranda Village and the Rain Forest where there was a Pamigirri Aboriginal performance, and on the Dreamtime walk the skills of boomerang throwing were imparted. After a visit to the Koala and Wildlife Park the return was made by Skyrail Cableway which afforded breathtaking views across the forest. The final excursion was made to the Great Barrier Reef where everyone snorkelled and saw fish of amazing colours, turtle and colourful coral. An experience not to be forgotten. The next day the party was homeward bound after a trip of a lifetime."

In 2004 there was a change to the School's admission procedure and the first entrance examination took place in January with over 500 pupils sitting the test. In October 2005 another Ofsted inspection was done. The following is an extract from the report which awarded the school the highest category of 'outstanding':

"INSPECTORS AGREE WITH the leadership team that Altrincham Girls' Grammar is an outstanding school. Pupils make excellent progress. Pass rates in public examinations are very high and improve year on year. Teaching is very effective and the school quite rightly prides itself on its reputation as a learning community. Pupils' personal development and the care and support provided for them are outstanding. Similarly, pupils' behaviour and attitudes to learning are excellent and they feel safe and happy. The formal curriculum is augmented by a wide range of enrichment activities and an increasing variety of links with schools in the local

The entrance to the new visitors' reception area, 2006

area and abroad. Language College status supports the raising of standards in all subjects and both primary and secondary schools nearby benefit from the expertise of Altrincham staff. Pupils and staff are very proud of the school and it is held in the highest esteem by parents. The leadership of the school is outstanding. It is managed efficiently and provides excellent value for money. It is a thinking school, one in which performance is always under review, evaluation is accurate and in which the capacity for improvement is a hallmark."

In 2007 the School added another specialism to its portfolio becoming a Training School, as a result of its 'outstanding' Ofsted reports and official designation as a 'high-performing school'. This allows the School to focus on improving the girls' educational experience through enhanced training of the whole workforce, supporting research and innovation and teacher training. It also enables the School to work in a creative way with other schools locally to bring about system-wide improvement.

In October 2007, after two years in the planning, a group of thirty students and four staff, Mrs Reynolds, Mrs Stuart, Mrs Ensor and Mrs Ross-Wawrzynski, set off for Northern India. The organiser, Mrs Reynolds, wrote in *The Insider* for 2008:

"THE IDEA WAS TO SEE as much of the Indian culture as we could manage in ten days. In eight days we stayed in five hotels, visiting Delhi, Jaipur, Agra and Varanasi. We had a fabulous time, welcomed everywhere by splendid hosts and guides. In Delhi we saw the old city from the seats of our hired rickshaws and visited the great mosque the Jama Masjid, as well as Gandhi's memorial and the new city. A long drive by air-conditioned coach took us to Jaipur where we visited the fort by elephant ride and went to visit a workers' textile cooperative, where fair trade

Reception area, 2006

was the message. We were honoured to be invited to the Maharaja's palace to witness the blessing of his animals and marvelled at the technical and scientific know-how of the mediaeval observatory. The next day we visited the Food and Craft Institute, where we learned how to make real Indian curry.

Another long drive took us to Agra, site of the incomparable Taj Mahal; architecture of ineffable beauty designed as a monument to love. We visited Fatehpur Sikri, site of a fort abandoned

Mrs Reynolds, Mrs Ross-Wawrzynski,
Mrs Stuart and Mrs Ensor at the
Taj Mahal, 2007

after only a few years when the river diverted, but again we saw the fantastic artistic and architectural skills of the Mughal Empire.

We travelled on the overnight train to Varanasi, the most famous pilgrimage spot in Northern India. It wasn't quite the Orient Express but we managed! In Varanasi the spiritual atmosphere was palpable as we mingled with the crowds at the Dussehra festival; this involved a human chain of 31 people, absolutely necessary to keep everyone safe in spite of our matching hats. We had a night sail on the River Ganges to view the cremation ghats and returned next morning to experience the sunrise and the early morning use of the river for bathing, worship, laundry and more cremations. We bought diva lamps to float on the river as prayers for our loved ones and took rickshaws back through the throngs of people to our waiting taxis.

Next day, we visited the School of Dance and Culture at Varanasi University and the students showed us how to perform classical Indian dance; we then went to the galleries of art and sculpture and visited temples of the Hindu, Jain and Buddhist faiths. It was a fantastic experience, made all the better by our students, who were praised wherever we went for their interest and courtesy. It was a rich cultural experience that brought us face to face with both the best and the worst of India. None of us will forget the abject poverty we saw, the desperate begging by children for pencils and note books and the hawkers eager to sell us their wares. But nor will we forget the vibrant colours, the welcoming smiles and the wonder of the architects' visions at each magnificent building we visited. We came home with jewellery, wood carvings, saris, silk pashminas and memories to last a lifetime. Oh yes – and a mouth-watering recipe for chicken curry!"

AGGS at the Food and Craft Institute, Jaipur, 2007

The Staff and Teacher Complement, 2009

On 12 October 2007 Miss Joan Jackson died aged 85. An extract from an obituary in the *Old Girls' Society Newsletter* of 2008 recalls:

"MISS JACKSON ALWAYS BELIEVED in maintaining outside interests, and although the exacting demands of her work life left little time for hobbies she greatly enjoyed caravanning, walking (especially in the Lake District), gardening and photography. Retirement allowed her to expand these interests, and painting, mainly in watercolours, became a passion. She was Chairman of the Grosvenor Art Society in Chester from 1990 to 1996 and continued as Membership Secretary, frequently exhibiting her own paintings with considerable success. A remarkably wide range of activities included wood carving, bird watching, geology, natural history, cooking, DIY, learning Japanese, becoming computer literate and she attended many courses to increase her knowledge and skills."

At half term in October 2009, Mrs Reynolds, Mrs Stuart, Ms Taylor, Mrs Read and Miss Stokwisz accompanied forty-one students from Years 9 to 12 on a very successful cross-curricular study tour to Rome. Mrs Reynolds recounts the highlights of the trip:

"THIS JOURNEY INVOLVED visiting religious and historical monuments from the time of the Roman Empire, like the Roman Forum, the fantastic Pantheon with its grand unsupported dome, and the Circus Maximus, then a visit to the Vatican, the Pope's residence and home to marvellous artworks, including Raphael and Michelangelo's Sistine Chapel. We also thrilled to the sculptures and paintings in the Capitoline Museums, seeing the famous bronzes depicting the boy with a thorn in his foot, the 'She-Wolf' nursing Romulus and Remus, and the philosopher-emperor Marcus Aurelius.

We walked miles and miles through cobbled streets and courtyards, including the oldest Jewish ghetto area in Italy, seeing the real Rome at first hand; also beautiful apartment blocks in terracotta colours, decorated with roof and balcony gardens.

We travelled about mainly by metro and public bus – getting 46 of us on to one bus and into one metro carriage was quite a feat, and somewhat stress-inducing for

AGGS in Rome, 2009

the teachers, but our fantastic guide, Sergio Salazzo, managed it with panache.

We tasted wonderful Italian ice cream and at the 'Scuola' of Italian Cookery we learned how to make true Italian pizza dough, stretching and moulding it and then eating our own creations! We wandered through the Piazza Navona and enjoyed lunch at one of its many roadside tavernas, shopped in its delightful shops and admired the famous fountains of Bernini.

A highlight of the trip was our visit to the Villa D'Este, which boasts hundreds of highly technological fountains, powered by a water system designed in the 17th century. Later, we visited the Spanish Steps,

AGGS at the Italian Cookery School, 2009

where the house of Keats and Shelley can be found, and ventured into the smart city shops, such as Armani and Gucci. The visit to the Trevi fountain was our last stop; tradition says that if you throw coins into the fountain over your shoulder, you are sure to return to Rome again – Arrivederci Roma!"

During her time in education Mrs Ross-Wawrzynski has completed her National professional qualification in Headship, her International Leadership Learning Programme, is a member of the Institute of Directors and is a National Leader in Education, and she has been commissioned by the Department for Children, Schools and Families to contribute towards the next White Paper in Education. For the period of September 2009 to August 2010 she is also the Executive Headteacher of Plant Hill Arts College in Manchester, overseeing and preparing the school in becoming the Manchester Co-op Academy. Mrs Ross-Wawrzynski is hoping to lead AGGS into becoming one of only eighty schools in England to be designated as a Teaching School.

With over 1,250 highly motivated pupils at the School, and more than ninety exceptional and enthusiastic teachers, it is no wonder that accolades abound in all departments. They are too numerous to mention individually; however the following examples serve to convey the range of interest, activity and the degree of excellence achieved. The Arts Council of England has awarded an Arts Mark in the silver category for excellence in Drama, Art, Dance, and Music. Art and Design awards have been presented by the Good Schools guide. The School is recognised as an International School by the British Council and is a partner in the

Excellence in Drama
Year 13 students in a scene from Polly Teale's Brontë *in the drama studio, 2006*

Excellence in Art
An exhibition of floral art by Year 12 and 13 A level students, inspired by the work of the
Pre-Raphaelites and the textile artist Alice Kettle.
Wire and tissue flowers were made by Year 7 girls.
A display in the foyer at Fairlie, 2009

Comenius European citizenship programme. In one year thirteen pupils gained entry to Oxbridge colleges, seven at Cambridge and six at Oxford. Pupils have acquitted themselves with distinction in the UK Youth Parliament, in the UK International Mathematical Challenge and the Lionheart Challenge. School teams regularly excel in Trafford Schools Championships in netball, hockey, tennis, badminton, rounders, and athletics, with many individual players going on to play in representative teams and national squads. The School received the Eco-Schools silver award and the National Healthy School Award for 2009. Additionally, the selected illustrations of foreign travel opportunities to South Africa, South America, Singapore and Australia, China, India and Rome earlier in this chapter show how the Language College ethos is providing a springboard for developing leadership skills and self confidence, for understanding and accepting different cultures seen at first hand and for showing compassion and a desire to help others less fortunate than oneself.

From small beginnings a hundred years ago, a vision for the future has driven the School forward through each generation, building on the best traditions of the past to emerge as a vibrant and exciting place to learn and prepare for adult life in the twenty first century – but never forgetting the way forward is – 'Bravely, Faithfully, Cheerfully'.

CONGRATULATIONS, AGGS!

This wooden plaque, which hangs in the Hall, was a leaving present to the School from Miss Atwool.
She was the original Second Mistress, appointed in 1911, who left in 1917 to become Headmistress
of Whyteleafe County School in Surrey.

The Centenary Garden

2008	June – first thoughts
2008	August – concept
2008	September – School centenary expectations
2008	November – professional design
2009	January – presentation to Mrs Ross-Wawrzynski; sub-committee formation
2009	February – expansion of concept
2009	February/March – consultation process
2009	March – presentation to parents
2009	April – 'Name a Brick' campaign is launched
2009	May – suppliers; foster carers; competition; blog and Facebook
2009	June – brick applications keep rolling in; planting scheme
2009	July – Old Girls' Newsletter; breaking ground
2009	August – construction commences
2009	September – initial planting; new help
2009	October – installation of the sphere; Halloween planting
2009	November – brick order processing; planting; pathways
2009/10	December to February – benches; lions; hedges; named bricks arrive... along with frost, ice, snow and rain!
2010	March – in use

EPILOGUE
THE CENTENARY GARDEN

by Sally Haywood

The Old Girls' Society invited me to complete this wonderful, illuminating book by giving an account of the centenary garden from concept to completion. It is a privilege to be Chair of the Parent Teachers Association at such a point in the School's history and an even greater one to have been so involved with the development and provision of this very special garden. At such a progressive School it seems fitting that the final section of this commemorative book should be about a new and significant resource designed to benefit pupils of all ages, yet one that has strong symbolic links with the past.

Sally Haywood
Chair, AGGS PTA

I have tried to show in the following pages how the seed of an idea germinated, was nurtured and came to fruition over a period of twenty one months. This would not have happened without the foresight, imagination and dedication of the organising committee and volunteers who in the best traditions of the School gave freely of their time and energy. The PTA is looking forward to seeing the garden burst into life in the coming months and years for the enjoyment of all current pupils, staff and future generations.

THE CENTENARY GARDEN

In June 2008 the PTA began to consider how it should commemorate the forthcoming School centenary. Reflecting on the substantial sums of money raised during that academic year to enhance facilities for the pupils, the committee realised it was not going to be an easy task to match or exceed the total raised. First thoughts were to develop a project to reflect and celebrate the past that would add value to the daily school life of current and future pupils. It would have to be something special and long lasting that would stand the test of time – but what?

During my summer holiday that year, one idea in particular seemed to keep popping into my mind: the creation of a garden. Although the PTA had previously funded the construction of two gazebos at the front of School to provide more leisure time seating, feedback from the girls suggested that there still seemed to be a need for more outdoor amenities. If a garden was constructed, it could be designed to offer relaxation space with a seated area also suitable for use as a classroom, thereby adding a completely new dimension to the School facilities.

As the front garden area was frequently used by staff and pupils it seemed logical to consider developing an area of the back lawn. My daughter confirmed that many girls liked to sit out on the grass during the summer term, but it was not always possible because the turf was too wet.

An obvious and relevant design based upon the distinctive hexagonal school badge came to mind so I committed a few rough sketches to paper with details of the kind of central feature that could be used and some ideas of how such a garden could be funded.

At the PTA AGM on 23 September it was noted that the Headmistress, Mrs Ross-Wawrzynski, was hoping for two major activities and a Royal visit during the centenary year. This made me wonder whether a garden would be an appropriate and viable proposal. As for a Royal visit, well, that further raised the stakes! There was no doubt that whatever the PTA decided to do it would have to be unique and of a very high standard.

The idea was put to the PTA committee meeting in October which had the Marmite effect (some loved it, some were against it). Despite not receiving universal approval, in the absence of any other ideas, it was agreed the project should be progressed further and reported on at a later date.

After gathering brochures for materials, features and samples, advice was sought from the Sale based garden designer and exhibitor at the Tatton RHS Flower Show, Rory McVean, of Firewall Landscape Consultants Ltd. We were already aware of some of his work with a local primary school. The key ideas and features were outlined which included a bronze sundial as a central focal point and the setting of stonework into the garden incorporating the school motto. The creation of an area where named bricks could be placed would enable parents, families, current and former pupils, staff and Governors the opportunity to be personally identified with the project and the historic centenary. This particular feature was also identified as one of the possible fund raising activities which could also be extended to involve the local business community.

Measurements and photographs of the proposed site were taken. The practicalities of constructing a garden measuring approximately twenty metres in width and which would effectively utilise most of the open grassed space were discussed. John Edwards, the Buildings and Estates Manager, gave advice on technical issues such as drains and electric cabling that lay underneath the lawn. Apart from a centrally located manhole there was nothing that would prevent the space from being used. Rory McVean was then instructed to provide an outline drawing so that the scheme could be presented to the PTA and the Headmistress. The laminated design he produced perfectly captured our initial ideas and a meeting with Mrs Ross-Wawrzynski was arranged for January 2009.

The proposed site for the garden

Presenting the concept in a way which would enable the scheme to be adequately portrayed was a daunting task. Being unaware of any ideas the Headmistress or Governing Body might already have in mind made me feel very nervous. I needn't have worried though as Mrs Ross-Wawrzynski instantly embraced the idea and gave the thumbs up to its suitability for a centenary celebration.

With the estimated cost of the scheme at just over £50,000 the Governing Body had to be approached

The garden sub-committee and Richard's wife Imogen: Jenny Jeffree, Imogen Sawyer, Varsha Makwana, Sally Haywood, Lisa Reid, Richard Sawyer, Reith Baines

for approval and funding to underwrite a percentage of the costs, if needed. The balance of funds would be underwritten by the PTA or raised by donations. Once the Headmistress and Governing Body confirmed their support for the project, the PTA committee appointed a sub-committee charged with bringing the project to fruition and with a remit to report back regularly.

The five-strong team of Reith Baines, Sally Haywood, Jenny Jeffree, Lisa Reid and Richard Sawyer met and set to work straight away. They were joined at a later stage by Varsha Makwana. Additional ideas came along thick and fast with everyone agreeing that the features of the garden should allude to as many elements of the School badge as possible, such as:

Acorns – holly oak specimen trees – *Quercus ilex*

Altrincham Lion – stone lions standing guard at the entrances

Cheshire corn sheaves – etchings to appear on some of the oak benches

Lamp of Learning – the armillary sphere incorporating a functioning sundial, representing ancient educational tools.

As the shape and motto of the badge was the prime inspiration for the design layout, analogies were drawn to show an association with School departments thereby involving the whole community in the project and establishing a very definite purpose as an educational facility. In addition, since the badge contains eleven images it was appropriate to locate eleven five feet, three-seater oak benches bearing symbolic etchings within the garden space. This number would accommodate a full class and one member of staff.

The links to different departments include:

Art & Design/Technology – the use of design skills, and the inclusion of a wide variety of planting with different form and textures, providing potential for use throughout the seasons, as subject material for budding artists.

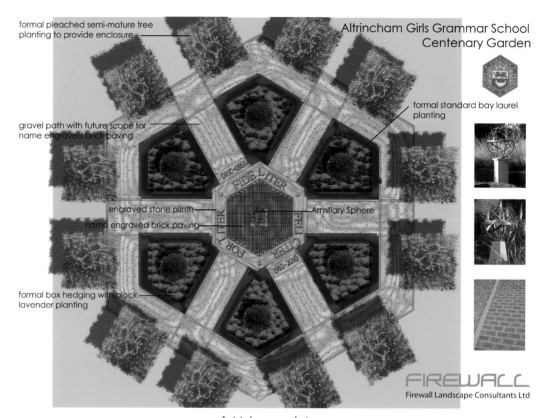

Initial concept design

English – two phrases from English literature etched on benches.

Food Technology – culinary herbs, artichokes and crab apples which can be harvested for use by this department.

Geography – the plants used have origins from all around the world, and the inscription to our twin school in Zephania, South Africa on the armillary sphere links AGGS with the wider world. Stone and granite is studied in geography lessons.

History – the whole garden is a celebration of the first one hundred years of the school itself! The names of all seven Head Teachers are engraved on the sundial, and named bricks provide an insight into school life throughout many generations.

Languages – two phrases, one in French etched on a bench and the Latin version of the School motto inlaid in the stonework. The names on bricks show that girls attending have roots from many different cultures and languages around the world.

Mathematics – the equation of time graph is a link to the mathematics involved in calculating time. The graph allows the dial time to be read and the actual time calculated accordingly. The overall symmetry and shape of the garden design reflects an obvious element of mathematics.

Music – a line from a well known hymn etched on a bench.

Religious Studies – wide and diverse backgrounds and cultures are celebrated at AGGS. The garden should provide a spiritual and relaxing place for all girls to meet friends and to enhance their social experience of school life.

Science – the armillary sphere and sundial are useful teaching tools. Ptolemy used the design to illustrate his theoretical model of a universe that revolved around the earth. Plant division, cultivation and growth can be studied by examining the plants in the garden.

Sport – a subtle link can be found etched on one of the benches.

In February, plans and ideas were displayed in the School Hall and pupils were invited to comment upon the proposed use of space before the project commenced. Initial feedback from form tutors indicated concerns that seating and play space would be lost. The senior management team considered these issues and reported back to the PTA. However, as the usable play space in the front of School would be unaffected, and fears raised by older girls allayed by the inclusion of benches in the new garden, the planning process went ahead. Nevertheless the sub-committee took these concerns on board and agreed to leave a section of grassed area on the back lawn for the girls to use as they wished.

By the end of March, the plans were all set, the timescale agreed and School approval given to the main elements of the design. A Presentation Evening was held at School for parents on 30 March when they were able to discuss issues with sub-committee members and the professionals involved, including David Harber, the designer of the armillary sphere.

The Headmistress asked for the garden to be completed by the end of the term in December so that it could be used by girls throughout the centenary year. The team accepted the challenge with relish.

Fundraising began in April. A leaflet and letter promoting the 'Name a Brick' campaign was posted to all parents, including those whose daughters would be joining Year 7 in September, and to our immense delight, applications started to come in by return.

Pupils and parents were encouraged to volunteer for some of the work to help reduce professional labour costs and to be able to identify with the creation of such an historic project.

Another way to involve families and to make savings was to buy smaller plants at the beginning of the year and grow them on. Lane End Nursery in Lymm had offered assistance with this, and had already potted up 550 box plants needed for growing on but only had room to accommodate just over half of them. An appeal for help went out, in the weekly School *Bulletin,* entitled 'Foster Parents for Plants Wanted!'. The response ensured that the remaining 250 box plants found temporary homes in Wilmslow, Bramhall, Bowdon, Sale, Stretford, Altrincham and Hale.

On 8 May a competition was launched for pupils to come up with a phrase of no more than twelve words which they felt best reflected life at AGGS today. The winning entry would be engraved on the feature sundial. Entries were permitted from whole year groups, forms, friendship groups or individuals and were judged by the PTA committee and senior management team. This was a challenging task, as entries were impressive and delightful, but there was a clear winner: 'We work together, play together, but shine as individuals,' written and submitted by Sophie Diss, Annie Elliott and Zoraiz Zubair.

During May much research was undertaken by the team. Environmentally it was considered important to buy materials and plants from local suppliers, without

The delightful words of the winning entry on the armillary sphere

compromising on quality or value. Stonemasons Mather & Ellis Ltd in Trafford Park had been contacted by Firewall's Rory McVean and initial consultations had taken place. Samples of stone were brought to School and Mrs Ross-Wawrzynksi chose Peak Moor sandstone to form the outline of the School badge. Verde Benico granite was selected for the motto lettering to be supplied to the stonemasons by Phil Miskelly of Manchester Marble.

After an earlier visit by Jon Langford from David Harber Ltd of Oxfordshire to assess the suitability of the site for a sundial, the company was commissioned to make the bronze feature. Decisions about the unique wording to be engraved were taken and permission obtained to include the names of all seven Head Teachers since 1910; the competition winners inscription; Founders' Day date, 4 July 1910; the longitude and latitude of the School to set its location; the School's Latin motto; and last but not least, a distance reference to the AGGS twin-school Zephania High School in Maphumulo, South Africa. David Harber Ltd also agreed to supply an equation of time graph on a plaque fixed to the sandstone plinth on which the sphere would be set.

Online communication was considered vital, so the team created a blog which was regularly updated with information and photographs showing construction progress and videos on care and maintenance of fostered plants. A page on Facebook was added so that the progress of the garden could be followed, and the centenary page on the School web site was also kept updated.

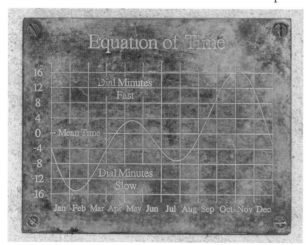

Equation of time graph

By June, the 'Name a Brick' campaign was definitely going well with a steady stream of approximately thirty orders per week being processed by Lisa Reid, our brick sales coordinator who also hosted many of our sub-committee meetings. The date for an official breaking-ground day was set as 24 July. Imogen Sawyer from Lane End Nursery worked extremely hard to link suitable plants to the overall design elements and

19th. September

I am submitting the enclosed form and cheque for a brick in memory of Dorothy Boardman, who sadly died last year. Dorothy was at school from 1943-1950 and I was there from 1941-1951. We were friends for 65 years. She was a very loyal supporter of the Old Girls Society.

Jennifer Roberts

Orders from Old Girls have been received from all over the UK and around the world

to provide interest throughout all seasons, whilst ensuring that its best flourish would not be during the months of July and August when the girls and staff were not at school. New topsoil and soil improver was introduced to combat high alkalinity and increase the planting range. Imogen supplied lists of plants with details of origin as well as form, scent and colour for consideration. Trips were made to trade nurseries to assess suitability, and after much discussion species and varieties were selected.

In July, the Old Girls' Society generously offered to include information about the Garden Project and the 'Name a Brick' campaign in their annual *Newsletter*. We were delighted to find that the response generated almost 20% of all orders. Additionally several Old Girls sent notes and emails expressing how much they liked the idea and hoped it would be a great success.

On 16 July the *Messenger* newspaper ran a feature on the garden following the ceremonial cutting of the first piece of turf by Mrs Ross-Wawrzynski assisted by the winners of the inscription competition. The Headmistress even donned her wellingtons especially for the occasion!

Access to the garden site by contractors was from Bowdon Road and across the staff car park which was due to be resurfaced in mid-August. In order to avoid damage to the newly laid surface, a detailed two-week programme of work was drawn up and construction teams, equipment and deliveries booked to start work on 24 July. It was essential that this phase of

the operation ran like clockwork to ensure that the scheduled work was completed and all the heavy equipment moved off site before work started on the car park.

All went according to plan and on 24 July Rory McVean, Richard Sawyer and I met. Richard manoeuvred the digger into place on the grass and suggested, that as Chair, I should hop in and start cutting away the turf. Never being one to miss such an opportunity, I didn't need asking twice! What a fantastic moment! The excitement that had built up over the previous few months culminated in the exhilaration of actually starting the job. There was no turning back.

Cutting the first sod!
Competition winners Sophie Diss, Zoraiz Zubair and Annie Elliott with Mrs Ross-Wawrzynski

Richard undertook the majority of all the earth moving and soil exchanging over these first two weeks and laid 120 tonnes of crushed hardcore to form the initial foundations of the badge shape. Firewall's construction team headed by Will Lane, then helped us with the key task of ensuring the footings and groundwork were accurately laid. Preparing the badge shape and pathways properly was crucial. Members of our team worked alongside Will laying the grey clay sett blocks demarcating the edgings of the outer hexagonal pathways. Responsibility for the work was then

The digger made a big mess!

handed back to us with an option of recalling the construction team if necessary.

By this time, we realised that in order to complete the edgings of the planting bays and radial pathways, we would need the stonework in place to match the levels. This would need to be done during September to enable us to undertake planting in the October half-term holiday. This presented a significant challenge to Mather and Ellis Ltd who had originally

Ground works and design shaping

been booked to do this work at the end of October. Their representative, Ian Madeley, was very accommodating and agreed to install the stone and granite work to meet the revised timescale. At last the vision we had all had in our minds was slowly but surely taking shape. There was now little we could do until half term, with the exception that Reith Baines completed the laying of the sett blocks to define the edgings.

When the term opened in September there was a mixed reception from the school community. We heard rumblings via our daughters that girls thought it was a total mess, didn't like it and couldn't believe how we had 'trashed' their grass. Staff, on the other hand, thought the stonework was magnificent. To some extent we had anticipated the girls' reaction and in order to help them visualise what

the garden would eventually look like, all four holly oak trees were put into place and one of the bays planted with a crab apple tree in the centre, box hedging around the perimeter, a selection of shrubs and perennials and dressed with bark chippings to give it a finished look. Thus, the garden took on a completely new dimension. Our daughters reported that comments were improving and some of the girls were now starting to see that it might not be so bad after all. We breathed a sigh of relief!

Stonework in position and pathways formed

Left: Reith and Richard moving one of the holly oak trees into position; right: the first planted bay

Throughout September, the team continued promoting brick orders, spread the word to the parents of the new Year 7 girls and sought more volunteer helpers. We welcomed Varsha Makwana to the team to promote sponsorship of the garden within the local community. She worked with us preparing leaflets, letters and sales pitches in readiness for approaching local businesses. We held more sub-committee meetings to check on finance and agree a delivery schedule of materials for the next big round of activity which was to take place at the October half term.

Foundations for the sphere were constructed during the first weekend of half term and on Monday 26 October the sundial was delivered to site, set into place and aligned so that when the sun shines, it will function. After just a couple of hours work, there it was, taking pride of place and looking as though it had always been there! Engravings were checked and photographs taken to mark the occasion.

In preparation for planting the following weekend, *Bulletin* notices reminded 'foster carers' to return the plants at Halloween which they duly did. Volunteers were requested to come along with gloves, spades and forks, and access arrangements to welfare facilities were laid on with School. Richard and Imogen Sawyer organised the ordering, purchase and collection of 3,500 plants and bulbs from trade suppliers, thereby significantly reducing costs. Imogen's expert knowledge of plant placement within our agreed scheme was invaluable throughout the whole project, but none more so than during this weekend, when she placed each plant in its new location. The weather was extremely pleasant and on Saturday 31 October fabric gazebos were erected for a drinks station and barbecue. Richard explained to the girls about the required spacing of plants, and how deep to plant bulbs. Plants were watered before and after planting and dressings of bark chippings applied. Knees, arms and backs were given a

The sphere takes pride of place

*So much effort from
the girls was wonderful
to see…*

Richard Sawyer inspiring helpers

*Alice and Amy proudly showing off their day's
achievements!*

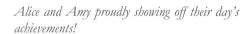

thorough workout and a healthy appetite generated. Barbecue time gave us all the chance to have a break and to take a step back to view the fruits of our labour. The enjoyment written on all faces told us that this was now a real community venture, just as we had hoped for. Everyone worked very hard all day. Girls who came to help began to feel very protective and responsible for the bed they had worked on.

The weather was not as kind on the next day, and fewer volunteers turned out to help. Nevertheless, work continued apace all day and finally the flagged areas were jet-washed. Everyone went home satisfied with their achievements and we, as a team, were thrilled that so many girls and their families took part. Our project photographer, Gary Beal of Vantage Point Photos, came along to record the whole event.

The six segmented planting areas within the hexagonal badge shape and additional large planting areas in front of the staff dining room and facing the West Wing were almost complete. Low box hedging around each segment should knit together over time to provide a seamless border.

Steph and Rachel having fun with the jet washer!

Planting weekend, 31 October and 1 November

The red fruited crab apple tree and day lilies

In order to provide interest for the Food Technology department, and to encourage nature's seasonal visitors, two varieties of crab apples have been planted in the bays. Three have a *Malus* 'Comtesse de Paris' in the centre from which spring blossom produces yellow fruit between October and January. Birds visiting the garden during its construction have already demonstrated that they were keen to sample the fruit so School will have to be quick off the mark if any is to be used by the girls. The other bays have *Malus x robusta* 'Red Sentinel' and this red fruited variety has proved equally as tempting to blackbirds. The inclusion of *Sedum* 'Autumn Joy', with its large flat heads of pink flowers and the small white spring and summer flowering ox-eye daisy *Leucanthemum vulgare* 'Crazy Daisy' together with the blue catmint *Nepeta* 'Six Hills Giant' and the dense spikes of fragrant deep violet flowers of the lavender 'Hidcote' with its aromatic silver grey leaves, will all help to attract bees and butterflies into this outdoor haven.

Within the garden as a whole it seemed obvious to develop a planting scheme that would incorporate the School colours. To create a blue, green and gold effect a wide variety of different shades and forms of foliage will be accentuated by blue and golden flowers from carefully selected species. The dainty flowers of *Salvia* 'Patio Blue', flax *Linum perenne* and the vibrant blue sea holly *Eryngium* with its thistle-like flowers will still be blooming in September at the start of each new academic year. *Hyssopus officinalis* will also add blue highlights over a long-lasting period. The pale lemon-yellow daisy flowers of the golden marguerite *Anthemis* 'E C Buxton' will cheerfully brighten the borders from spring right through to autumn. The early summer flourish of the foliage of golden marjoram and evergreen *Euonymus ovatus aurea* together with the bright heads of *Achillea* 'Gold Plate' and the striking yellow daisy flowers with black centres *Rudbeckia* 'Goldsturm' will ensure a golden glow lasting into the autumn.

In order to fulfil our expectations that the garden should provide interest between September and July in many ways and colours, splashes of hot reds and oranges will help provide vivid variety in two of the segments. Red highlights from the long-lasting tubular flowers of *Penstemon* 'Garnet', and the scarlet poppy petals of *Papaver* 'Allegro' will combine superbly with a sprinkling of the apricot heads of the day lily *Hemerocallis*. The fragile, orange rosette petals on the long wiry stems of the poppy *Papaver atlanticum* should start to appear from late spring whilst the tender, densely packed blooms of the South African twinspur *Diascia* 'Orange Tangerine' will carry strong colour through until October.

Particular attention has also been paid to the provision of plants with textural form such as the beech hedge border. *Phormium* 'Jack Sprat', *Eryngium* and *Miscanthus* 'Morning Light', with its great plumes of frothy heads in the autumn, may all provide form and interest for the art department. More tactile plants include the ornamental woolly-leaved lamb's ears, *Stachys lanata*. Scented plants include lavender 'Munstead' variety, pineapple sage *Salvia elegans* 'Golden Delicious', *Prostanthera cuneata*, an aromatic Australian mint bush, and *Nepeta* 'Six Hills Giant', the blue catmint. Combined with a myriad of bulbs, these will provide a natural, soft fragrance to pathways, beds, borders and seating areas which when brushed against should delicately perfume the air.

November was a really busy month for the team with a flurry of activity in the garden by day and copious amounts of paperwork being completed well into the night. Burning the midnight oil became the norm! The brick order spreadsheet was completed and details for Phase I were sent to EngraveBricks Ltd.

With most planting now in place, focus turned to pathway construction and a need to re-evaluate the finished surface. Quotations for block paving were obtained as the Headmistress had expressed concerns about gravel being walked inside on the soles of the girls' shoes and causing damage to the floorings. Apart from the cost of the materials, sub-committee member Jenny Jeffree, who had been responsible for much of our coordination, administration and finances throughout the project, calculated that this change would take us over our already stretched budget. Luckily, Reith Baines was experienced in this work and generously volunteered to undertake the task. Assistance was also forthcoming from Sailesh Makwana and Bob Blane (parent volunteers).

Some 6,700 buff-coloured plain blocks were delivered to site along with grit sand – now it was just a matter of laying them all into position. From the outset, we knew this was going to be a daunting undertaking, considering such a late starting date as the first week in November. Furthermore it was critical to adopt a 'no noise' work pattern during class time in school. Despite these limitations, and intermittent rain throughout November, the work went well and pathways were completed by mid-December.

Attention was then turned to the provision of benches. Earlier in the year a family concern, the Classic Garden Furniture Company in Lathom near Ormskirk, had been visited by team members, and after lengthy negotiations were commissioned to supply eleven oak benches. We were delighted to learn that the timber came from an approved source of the Forestry Stewardship Commission.

The block paving takes shape

It had been agreed earlier that each bench would be engraved with a unique phrase and an etched image of a feature from the school badge. About sixty suggestions were put forward and eventually eleven phrases were selected by electronic voting. The team allocated a suitable image to each phrase, electing to have three benches with a school badge, three with acorns, three with sheaves of corn, one with the Altrincham Lion and one with the Lamp of Learning. The letters AGGS were also etched on to one leg of each bench.

The following phrases were selected for the benches etched with the badge motif:

'Life is not a having and a getting, but a being and a becoming' – Matthew Arnold, an English poet who once worked as a School Inspector, the son of Thomas Arnold the famed Headmaster of Rugby School.

'Teachers open the door, but you must enter by yourself' – a Chinese proverb chosen to reflect the staff and educational environment and the School's cultural links with China.

'Win as if you are used to it, lose as if you enjoyed it for a change' – Ralph Waldo Emerson, an American poet and philosopher, whose sentiments echo the ethos of how the girls are encouraged to play sport at AGGS.

For benches etched with acorns:

'What is this life if, full of care, we have no time to stand and stare?' – from *Leisure* by William Henry Davies. Hopefully girls and staff will sit or stand in this outdoor space and notice the ever-changing beauty as it is revealed across each season.

'True friends are hard to find, difficult to leave and impossible to forget' – this contemporary statement seems to be most relevant for the location and especially poignant for old school friends.

'Let knowledge grow' – from *In Memoriam* by Alfred, Lord Tennyson. Appropriate text for its location and a link to the English department.

For benches etched with sheaves of corn:

'It's kind of fun to do the impossible' – Walt Disney. It is hoped that this quote might inspire girls to believe they can achieve the impossible.

'The roots of education are bitter, but the fruit is sweet' – Aristotle, the ancient Greek philosopher. This was chosen to represent the hope that girls will realise many things are often difficult to learn, but what and how they learn at AGGS will be a huge benefit for their future.

'I hear, I know. I see, I remember. I do, I understand' – Confucius, born 551 BC. Equally relevant today as in his lifetime.

For the bench etched with the lion:

It's kind of fun to do the impossible

Altrincham en Avant – the motto, in French, on the former Altrincham Borough Council's coat of arms, means 'Altrincham leads the way' and was chosen to reflect that AGGS, a Language College, is a leading light in education and currently the number one school in the North West.

For the bench etched with the lamp:

'All things bright and beautiful' – uplifting words from the hymn by C F Alexander provide a link to the garden for the music department.

In December, tours of the garden were given by members of the sub-committee to visitors at the Christmas Market when families were most interested to see and hear all about the project and a few last-minute brick orders were accepted. The customised oak benches were delivered; the beech hedge running in front of the car park and the West Wing was planted; the last few plants and spring bulbs went in and 350 named bricks arrived from EngraveBricks Ltd.

Just as we were on target to complete the project before the end of term, the frost and ice started to intensify in the prelude to the snow coming, making it impossible to lay the named bricks on schedule. As frustrating as it was, Reith Baines and Bob Blane battled on, striving to finish all work before the start of the spring term, continually being thwarted by freezing conditions. Work progressed slowly throughout January and early February, with time and energy used in fighting the adverse conditions. All the outstanding work, including making plinths for the four lions guarding two entrances to the garden, was gradually achieved by the end of February, when thankfully the thaw had arrived. It is certainly noteworthy to

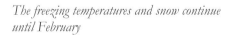

The freezing temperatures and snow continue until February

acknowledge this labour intensive element of the garden had taken over 1,200 man hours to complete by two very dedicated parents over the last four months.

On 1 March after enduring the most prolonged and harshest winter for thirty years and with the pretty little heads of snowdrops and pale yellow primroses in flower, and the tips of spring daffodils just starting to pop up in the borders, the girls were finally invited to use the garden, and our dream was realised. The inquisitiveness of the girls gazing at the sphere, their eagerness to find a particular name on a brick and the smiles on girls' faces as they began to wander around and explore was a delight to witness, which made all the effort and incredible hard work that had been put into this 'once in a lifetime' creation by all parent volunteers so personally rewarding. It was a moment to step back, and to contemplate with pride the enormity of the task that had been undertaken, and physically created in just a little over seven months.

The named brick area is finished

One of the named double bricks

At last, the sight we have all been waiting for – the garden in use

The Parent Teachers Association is delighted to have created this innovative garden for generations of pupils to 'work together, play together and shine as individuals'. Congratulations AGGS on the first one hundred years and we wish you much continued success in the future.

CENTENARY BOOK SUBSCRIBERS
Maiden names where appropriate are shown in brackets.
Subscribers to a further 72 copies of the centenary book wished to remain anonymous.

Susan Abbott (Saunders)
Emily Adams
Edna Adderley (Tetlow)
Zaynah Arub Ahmed
Aylin Akineden
Iwona Akineden
Margaret Aldridge (Hibbert)
Claire Allan
Gay Allen (Osborne)
Billy Amin
Lucy Ashley Armstrong
Vivien Arnold
Gillian R Arnoll (Hamer)
Felicity Ashworth
Barbara Avery
Margaret Bagott (Davies)
Amanda Bailey
Holly Baines
Joan Ball
Sonia Joy Bamford
Sheila M Barker
Christal Barlow-Bates [Christine](Barlow)
Judith Barnard (Noble)
Christine Barnes
Rosie Barrow
Sue Bartram (Acton)
Helen Judith Bateman
The Bates family
Dorothy Beckett (Eaton)
Bridget Beggs (Chadwick)
Elizabeth and Christine Berry
Beryl Joan Bethell (Clark)
Angelica Bhatt
Nichelle Bhatt
Sarah J Blades
Sarah Elizabeth Blane and Sheila Cox
Rachael Bollom (Steeples)
Margaret A Bone (Phillips)
Alexandra Boocock
Hilary Boon (Twiss)
Joyce D Borland (Harris)
Patricia Bottrill (Larsen)
Lesley Boxer (Gill)
Shirley Bradburn (Jones)
Pam Bradshaw
Joan M Brassington (Leather)
Katie Brayzier
Margery Olive Briggs (Wright)
Shelagh Brock (Watt)
Harriet Sandra Brook
Janet Brooman (Kameen)
Cllr Jane Brophy
John Brophy
Kathryn Brown
Alwyn Browne (Rowbottom)
Margaret Brownhill
Michelle Brownhill (Garner)

Jessica Buckingham
Audrie S Burgess
Bethan Burgess
Julie Burgess (Dale)
Jennifer S Burns (Caldwell)
Margaret Burrows (Christianson)
Ruth Callaghan (Moston)
Elizabeth Campion (Bailey)
Lexie Carden
Julie Cardoza (Booth)
Mary Carmichael (Wadsworth)
Flo Carter
Virginia Castick (Whipp)
Kimberley Anne Chambers
Laura Beth Chapman
Christine Margaret Chester
Rosemary Chester
Amy Lap Yee Chiu
Margaret Christie (Hacking)
Mary Clague (Hall)
Jean M Clark (Horner)
Brenda Jean Clarke
Kit Clay (Finn)
Doreen Cliffe (Allsopp)
The Clift family
Shirley Coffey (Smith)
Dr Anne Cohen (Holden)
Helen Cook (Hope)
Lilian A Cooke (Edwards)
Isabella Coolican
Jill Coop
Iris Cooper (McEvoy)
Elizabeth Cottle (Thompson)
Sheila Crane
Becky Crosby
Barbara Mary Crowther (Downes)
Margaret Dale (Hook)
Stanley Dale
Lee Danglidis
Lucy Daynes
Janet S Delgado (Leigh)
Irene De Sanctis (Critchley)
Christine and Helen Disney
Richard and Marilyn Downs
Catherine Drew
Margaret Dunn
Margaret J Dunton (Pybus)
Mary Eastwood (Morris)
Bethany Amber Eaton
Vivien Edge
J C Edwards
Joanna L Edwards
Jennifer Elston (Rampling)
Pamela Emery (Hirst)
Alice Patricia Mary Entwistle (Pat Johnson)
Lizzie Entwistle
Pamela Estcourt (Hart)

Gill Etherington
Doreen Evans (Lucas)
Jacky Evans (Cartwright)
Darcey Ferguson
Emelye Ferguson
The Fielding family
Moira Flanagan
Barbara Jean Fletcher
Barbara L Floyd
Ellie Forrest
Olga Foulkes (Ranson)
Michael Foxford and Sarah Bennett
Caroline Fry
Dr Valerie Fussell (Eccles)
Sophie Kate Gannicott
Zoë Elizabeth Gannicott
Ann Garratt (Critchley)
Margaret Garrett (Wimsett)
Lorna H Gartside (Farquhar-Young)
Joyce Gwyneth Geddes (Taylor)
Ann Geggie (Yates)
Patricia E Gilbert
The Gill family
Karysca Gill
Pashyca Gill
Elizabeth C Gorton (Smithies)
Barbara Gowland
Clare Green
Hilary Green (Cope)
Rachel Greenhalgh
Abbie Greenwood
Jackie and Steve Greenwood
Shirley Gresty (Hart)
Frances and Philippa Griffiths
Ian and Caroline Griffiths
Helena Grimshaw
Ida Grundy
Charlotte Guest
Margery Guest (Blackshaw)
Hale Civic Society, Jabberwocks
Joan E Hall (Bartlett)
Alice Hamer
Rosie Hamer
Delsia Hann (Gowing)
Susan Harden (Swinn)
Alison Harrison (Phasey)
Brenda Harrison (Lawrenson)
Kate Harrison
Olivia Jane Harrison
Kathleen R Hart (Hamer)
Gillian Hartley (Irvine)
Claire L Hatton (Spencer)
Stephanie and Sally Haywood
Gillian Healey (Cranmer)
Nancy Wemyss Healy
Imogen Heaton
Joyce Heaton

Pam Heaton (Brereton)
Wendy Heesom (Evans)
Wendy F Helsby (Lewis)
Ghislaine Hemy
Louise Hepworth
Sheila Hesketh (Huxley)
Norah Hewertson
Peggy Hewitt (Lowe)
Catherine Heys (Baldwin)
Jennifer Hickling (Nuttall)
Marion Hicks (Ferguson)
Shirley Hill
Janice Hitchcock (Jones)
Jon and Vanda Hitchenor
Audrey J Hodson
Emma Hollows
Glenda Hooson
Beryl Hopkins (Rowbotham)
Ruth Horsley (Newton)
Sally Horton
Nancy Houston (Fletcher)
Dorcas Howard
Maggie Hoy
Alice Hughes (Murphy)
Candice Lian Canaveral Hughes
Marlen Hughes (Brine)
Mona Heulwen Hughes
Rowenna Hughes
Pat Hulland
Zoe I Hulme (Burns)
Janet Husbands
Ann M Hutchison
Rosie, Hazel and Bethany Hutchison
Margaret Huzzey (Trodden)
Catherine, Rosie and Lucy Hyde
Lydia Hyde and Charlotte Silva
Pamela Illidge (Hargreave)
Stephanie [Stevie] Ingram
Natalie Innes
Judith Irish (Peake)
Maureen Irwin (Jefferson)
Rachel A Iveson
Sarah H Iveson
Brenda Jackson (Eccles)
Hilary James (Fletcher)
Judith Jarvis (Embleton)
The Jeffree family
Elisabeth Johnson
Grace Johnson
Jane Johnstone (Rose)
The Jolley family
Caitlin M Jones
Carolyn Okell Jones
Faye Alexandra Jones
Jane Jones (Stanbridge)
Jen Jones (Studley)
J Monica Jones (Ferguson)
Pat Jones
Sylvia B Jones (Walton)
Pam Jordan (Jones)
Val Jordan (Rowe)
Lydia Kakabadse
Sara Bianca Kalita

Julie Kavanagh
Adrian Paul Kellett
Claire Louise Kellett
Siobhan Kelly
Margaret Kenna
Winifred Kent (Nuttall)
Marion Ketteridge
Rebecca King
Vera Kinnibrugh
Mary Kirkpatrick (Welch)
Linda Carol Lamb (Rofe)
Anne Lambie
Hannah Lambie
Winifred E Lang
Margaret Lansdell (Morison)
Denise Laver
Katie Laver
Sophie Laver
Julie Leaming (Kershaw)
Julia Lee (Needham)
Eloise Leggett
Kathleen Leigh (Tomlinson)
Dr May Lennie
Joan D Lewis (Hickman)
Rosalind Lewis
Diane Lloyd-Williams (Cocking)
Diana Lockyear (Jordan)
Brenda Lomax (Millet)
Elizabeth Loxton (Lee)
Alina Lyashenko
Hannah and Alice McAuliffe-Hall
Pauline McCabe (Lyle)
Hilary McCormac
Keith McCormac
Pat and Don McCormac
Susan McDonald Williams
Sue McFarland
Elizabeth McGregor
Sue McIntosh (Drinkwater)
Permilla MacLaren (Johnson)
Heather McNaughton
Orla Maguire
Rhianna Krisha Makwana
Ann Malam (Valentine)
Natasha Mann
Joan Mary Marr (Holt)
Jeanette L Marsden (Gray)
June Marshall (Beattie)
Audrey Martin (Jackson)
Sophie Mather
Claire Mathews
Jenny Mathews
Naomi Matthews
Rachel Matthews
Jade Mayers
Christine Medford (Whalley)
Wendy Meniru (Priestner)
Judith Margaret Meredith (Judy Johnson)
Daisy Micklethwait
Mary Missen (Davies)
Maria Mitchenko
Aamna Mohammed
Joyce Molyneux (Ormerod)

Lynne Moran
Ruth Moran
Jane A Morris
Jessica Morris
Anita Mottershead
Lynne and Stephen Mould
Eleanor Frances Myers
Dorothy Nance (Fox)
Julie Napier
Yvonne Navratil (Bertin)
Amy Neild and family
Carol Newbrook
Revd Annette Nixon (Bailey)
Pamela Noar (Harris)
Christine and Hannah Norbury
Sybil Norcott
Hannah Norman
Rebecca Norman
Vivienne Norman (Hiett)
Stephanie North (Chadwick)
Grace Nugent
Dr Catherine O'Doherty (Allerton)
Zoë Olliver
Anita Jane Opie
Dorothy Paddon (Rennison)
Annette Page
Sheila Palmer (Ridley)
Christina and Crete Panayi
Abbie Pardoe
Shereen Farooque Patel
Anne Paton (Hodgkinson)
Mary Pay (Pearson)
Dr Christine Peacock (Leck)
Elizabeth [Betty] Pearse (Ridgway)
Caitlin Peers
Annette Percy
Emma Perkins
Rebecca Perkins
Anne Perrin
Mary Perry (Lewis)
Carolyn Phillips (Edwards)
Dr C L and Mrs K A Poon
Marilyn Portner (Woolf)
Anne Priestner (Mercer)
Lucy Priestner
Hazel Pryor
Diane Pullen
Megan Quigley
Susan Quigley
Ann Quinn (Jago)
Margaret Rathwell
Chloe Ravenscroft
Catherine Rayers (Illidge)
Joy Redfern (Atherton)
Jennifer Reed
Jane Reynolds
Morven Rickwood (Jones)
Sylvia Ridley (Cavanagh)
Susan Ripley
Bev Robinson
Stephen, Denise, Charlotte and Emily Robinson
Janice Robson (Blease)

Hazel Roscoe (Sealey)
Gillian Rose (Lucas)
Lynne A Rose
Dana Ross-Wawrzynski
Nancy Rowbotham
Judyth Rowles (Laver) and Freda Laver
  (Whitehead)
Megan Royle
Marike Jane Rüther
Kate Sadler
Rachel Sadler
Abi Samson
Anna Samson
Amelia Lucy Sandbach
Eliza Jane Sandbach
Carys Santamaria Fox
Madison Schaefer
Janet Schraibman (Woodhead)
Laura Scott
Pat Selby (Evans)
Ellie Seth-Smith
Tina Serb
Ruth Sharp (Horrocks)
Enid M Shaw (Burns)
Helen Shaw
Joan Shaw (Goddard)
Suzanne Shaw
Patricia Sheldon (Clarke)
Eve Shenkman
Eileen Shore
Gabby Shovlin
Gwen Sidebotham (Hallam)
Margaret C C Simpson (Shannon)
Susan J Sinagola
Doreen Sinclair (Lytton)
Eleanor Sinclair
Angela Smith (Munday)
Edna Walton Smith
Emma C M Smith
Heidi Smith (Kennedy)
Jacqueline Smith
Jean Smith
Lydia Smith
Megan L O Smith
Nicky Smith
Helen Soar (Cranmer)
Emma Soper
Mrs M Speakman
Naomi K Spencer (Burns)
Mr and Mrs A Spilsbury
Laura Catherine Stephenson
Rachael Jane Stephenson
Maddie Stewart
A Muriel Stockton (Cheetham)
Dr Barbara Stockton
Martin and Sandra Stone in memory of
  Winifred Rose Noble
Margrit Storrar (Shaw)
Lesley Street
Liz Street
Margaret Street
Audrey Stringer
Patricia Stringer

Clare Stuart (Rhodes)
Katie Stubbs
Sophie Stubbs
Claire E Stuffins
Phyllis E Stuffins
Janet A Stukins (Wilkinson)
Lucille Sumner (Ranson)
Judith Sutherland (Rocca)
Sarah Helen Swallow
Catherine Tait
Patricia [Moore] Tait
Anne Taylor (Cooper)
Liz Temple
Gill Thomas
Jane Thompson (Carter)
Anne Thomson (Kameen)
Hannah Titley
Lydia Titley
Anne and Tom Tomkins
Alison Tonks
Barbara Torrington (Clarke)
Ronald Trenbath
Barbara Tristram (Venables)
Gay Tustin
Amy Unwin
Jean Usher (Murray)
Carole Varley
Aakanksha Verma
Christina Vivian (Flashman)
Wendy Wakefield (Holden)
Amy Walker
Carole Walker (Napier)
Caroline Walker
Dorothy Walker (Marsh)
Grace Walker
Pam Walker
Doreen Walmsley (Garner)
Florence Walmsley
Holly Walmsley
Elisabeth Walton (House)
Janet Walton
Pamela Ward
Ruth F Waterfield (Weetman)
Harriet Waters
E Lynne Watson
Isobel Watson (Parker)
Lynne Watson
Jean Wearne (Morton)
Dorothy Webster (Jones)
Weighell family
Anna Welford
David Welsh
Elizabeth Whitelegg
Sophie Louise Whitham
Helen Whitley-Jones (Edwards)
Anthea Whitt (Jones)
Katherine Whyberd (Williamson)
Gillian Wilkes
Betty Wilkinson
Gillian Wilkinson
Joyce Wilkinson (Allsop)
Erica Wilks (Jones)
Christine Willey (Moore)

Beth Frances Williams
Diana Williams
Grace Elspeth Williams
Valerie Williams (Levi)
Eileen Williamson
Eloise Williamson
Emma Williamson
Kathleen Williamson (Byrne)
Pat Williamson (Shaw)
Emma Wilson
Joan Wilson (Wild)
Julia Wilson (Carter)
Natasha E Wilson
Mary Winder (Taylor)
Aileen Winstanley
Winterbottom sisters
Kathleen Witty (Dunn)
Ann E Wood (Robinson)
Becky Wood
Marian Wood
Rebecca [Becky] Wood
Wendy Wood (Welsby)
Gillian L Woodcock (Spencer)
Eleanor R Woods
Joanna Wright
Juliet Wright (Kakabadse)
Angela Yardley (Litchfield)
Kath Yates
Charlotte Young
Susan Younghouse
Hiu Laam Jenny Yuen

CENTENARY GARDEN NAMED BRICKS – PHASE 1

Sarah Abdelrahman
Yasmin Abdelrahman
Chantal Destinee Adams
Aisha Ahmed
Julia Ajayi
Aylin Akineden
Altrincham Court Leet
Altrincham Grammar School Old Girls' Society
Edemanwan Andah
Efioanwan Andah
Elisabeth Andrew
Neave, Lydia, Rowan Anwar-Wright
Tiffany Armitage
Barbara Armstrong
Laura and Gemma Aspinall
Harriet and Alice and Florence Avis
Amanda Bailey Assistant Head
Holly Baines
Sonia Joy Bamford
Lauren Jane Barclay
Christine Barnes
Rosie Barrow
The Bass family
Dani Bass
Jessica Baxter-Brown and family
Diana Beaumont (nee Lucas), Gillian Rose
    (nee Lucas)
Katharine and Alexandra Bee
Bridget Beggs (nee Chadwick)
Sophie Bell
Imogen Bentham
Sacha Bergmann
Charlotte and Eric Beswick
Sarah Blades
Sarah Elizabeth Blane
Dorothy Boardman
Joyce D Borland (nee Harris)
Kallina Boshnakova
Caroline Bradley
Katie Brayzier
Holly Breedon
Charlotte and Grace Breen
Kate Brodie and Heather Rutter
Julia Broom, Shirley Halman, Julia Hyland
Laura Alice Brophy
Emma Brotherton
Charlotte, Isobel, Rachel Buckingham
Jessica Buckingham
Anne Burnett, Sally-Anne and Lucy J
    Heaford and Hannah Jamal
Kate Lily Butler
Eman Buttar
Lexie Carden
Emily Chan
Trini Chan
Laura Beth Chapman
Zainab Chaudhri
Samia Chaudry
Faye Chen
Amy Lap Yee Chiu
Sophia Chiu
Aniesha Chowdhury
Monique Clarke

Classic Garden Furniture Co.
Sarah and Anna Clements
Jenny and Vicky Clift
Anne Cohen (nee Holden)
Alice Collins
Victoria Conn
Isabella Coolican
Jess Cooper
Moira Cox
Alex and Jayne Craig
Anna Crossley
Alex Cupples
April Curtin and family
Chloe Curtis
Katie Dean, Sophie Diss
Stephanie Dean, Amy Carter
Mrs D Delides Headmistress
Ellie Donovan
Rachel Downs
Richard and Marilyn Downs
Anika Dutta
Valerie Eccles
Helen Edwards, Nina W-Jones
Jane Edwards
John Edwards B&E Manager
Hafsa Ehsan
Hannah and Alia El-Kholy
Jennifer Elston (nee Rampling)
Pamela Emery (nee Hirst)
EngraveBricks Ltd
Sarah Entwistle
Jane Eppleston, Lesley Gill, Valerie Levi
    ACGS
Hannah and Olivia, Nick and Jacky Evans
Kate Isobel Evans
Ruth Faulkner
Eleanor Fethers
Beth, Katie, Rosie and Becky Fielding
Firewall Landscape Consultants Ltd
Abigail Foan
Colette Foan Chair of Governors
Carys S Fox
Catherine and Deborah Frost
Naomi Garside (nee Patchett) and family
Sinéad E Gavin and family
Annie Germain
Jean B Gill OBE
Lizy Gill
The Parents and Grandparents of Pashyca
    and Karysca Gill
Frankie and Fiona Glarvey
Nuala and Aoife Godfrey
Carole Goodsell (nee Crowther)
The Governing Body
Lucy and Zoë Grainge
Annabel and Lizzie Green
Rachel Greenhalgh
Abbie Greenwood and family
Frances and Philippa Griffiths and family
Ursula Ruth Griffiths
Jane Groom
Charlotte Guest
Denise Haddad Governor

Hale Civic Society
Melissa Halliwell
Alice and Rosie Hamer
Rach Hampar
Hand Crafted Armillary Sphere Created By
    David Harber
Mia Hanlon
Molly Harrison
Olivia Jane Harrison
Rachel Harrop and Norma (nee Jay)
Kathleen Hart (nee Hamer), Gillian Arnoll
    (nee Hamer)
Grace and Liza Hartley
Faith Hastings-Long
Sally Haywood, Chair of PTA
Stephanie Haywood
Vicky and Olivia Healey
Liz Heap, Dorcas Heap
Francesca and Claudia Heggie
Vivien Hemingway (nee Massey)
Rebecca Henning-Lee
Rebecca Henry
Sarah Hewitt
Jennifer Nuttall Hickling
Lottie Hicks
Chris and Tricia, Jenny and Katie Hilder
Shirley Hill
Marlen Hughes (nee Brine)
Pat Hulland
Bethany Hutchison
Hazel Hutchison
Rosie Hutchison
Catherine, Rosie and Lucy Hyde
Lydia Hyde
Natalie Innes
Maureen Irwin (nee Jefferson)
Nashwah Ismail
Jabberwocks
Maddie Jackson-Wojcik
Ann, Heather and Margaret Jago
Katrina James
Maryam Jawad, Huda Jawad
Jazib
Jenny and Tony Jeffree
Katie Jeffree
Rachel Jeffree
Arwen Jenkins
Carys Jenkins
Wendy Jenkins
Irene and Eden Jia and family
Kim Johal
Alice Poppy Jones
Caitlin M Jones
Faye Alexandra Jones
Monica Jones (nee Ferguson), Marion Hicks
    (nee Ferguson)
Emma Jurkowski
Arsala Kaushal
Prachi Kaushal and family
Katrina and Suzanne Keddie
Claire Louise Kellett
Siobhan Kelly
Winifred Kent (nee Nuttall)

Usarae and Misha Gul Khan
Pam King (nee Jolley)
Jasmin Yan-Ling Lam
Lane End Nursery
Shaheen Latif and family
Denise Laver, Connie Whitehead
James Laver, Charles Laver
Katie Laver, Sophie Laver
L Saville Laver, Jeanne Laver
Marcelle Laver, Marcelle Chevaldin
Harriet and Georgie Lavin
Mandy Lawton, Lucy and Ella Gilbert
Amy Lea
Julie Leaming (nee Kershaw)
Ellie Leggett
Kimberley Leung
Amy Le Vasseur
Shannah Levey
Rosalind Lewis
Beth and Patti Linnett
Millie Littler
Diane Lloyd-Williams (nee Cocking)
Brenda Lomax (nee Millet)
David and Lorraine Lowe
Alina Lyashenko
Amelia Clapson McBride
Patricia McCormac (nee Allbones) and Donald
Kelly May McGuire
Suzie and Isabelle Mahoney
Rhianna Makwana
Natasha Mann and family
Rebecca Markham
Rebecca Martin
Mather & Ellis Ltd Stonemasons
Amy Elizabeth Mather
Sophie Mather and family
Joanna Matthews (nee Wright) and Rachel
 and Naomi and Carlotta
Judith A Mawer (nee Denby)
Pam Maxey (nee Spilsbury)
Eleanor and Bethany Miller
Lauren and Katrina Miller
Rebecca T Mitchell
Joyce Molyneux (nee Ormerod)
Rachel and Shauna Moran
Brendan, Roisin, Enya and Shifra Moriarty
Eli Morris
Jessica Morris
Róisín Kate Éilish Moss
Jennifer Mould
Angela Munday, Lydia Smith
Anna Murray
Eleanor Frances Myers
Dorothy Nance (nee Fox)
Amy Neild
Kay Neild
Shirley Nield (nee Armstrong)
Anna Nightingale
Annette Nixon (nee Bailey)
Grace A R Nugent
Camilla O'Driscoll
Victoria Ogden
Jennifer Ogunmyiwa

Sian O'Kell
Zoë Olliver MB ChB
Phil Osborne Assistant Head
Ruth Owen
Emily Pacey
Sheila Palmer (nee Ridley)
The Parent Teacher Association
The Parfett family
Shereen Farooque Patel
Rosalind Pearson
Caitlin Peers
Helen Peers and Tilly Russel-Fisher
Rebecca and Emma Perkins
Mary Perry (nee Lewis), Wendy Helsby (nee
 Lewis)
Kelly Peters
Ron Pickering Assistant Head
Chaya Pitchon
Ruth Plant
Ellia J K Pogson
Jonathan Poole
Alison Wing Yin Poon
Sheila Quinn (nee Barker)
Rumaysa Alvi Quraishi
Tara H Qureshi
Danielle Rainford
Sara Rasul
Caroline E Raven
Chloe Ravenscroft
Caitlin Rea
Rosie Orla Reid and family
Jane Reynolds Religious Studies
Alison, Emily and Caroline Richardson
Sara and Neville Richardson
Jennifer Roberts (nee Shaw)
Lydia Roberts and family
Dana Ross-Wawrzynski Headmistress
Nancy Rowbotham School Secretary
Olivia and Phoebe Rudgard
Marike Jane Rüther
Jessica Sandy
Maidah Sardar
Zainab Sardar
Kat Linnaea Sawyer
Madison Schaefer
Jess and Libby Selwood
Ellie Seth-Smith
Iqra Shafi
Hannah Shakespeare
Helen Shaw
Eve Shenkman
Gaby Shovlin
Susan and Isabel Sinagola
Eleanor Sinclair
Charlotte Slaughter
Judith Smith
Megan and Emma Smith
Ella Southern
Phoebe Southern
Mrs M Speakman Deputy Head
Cerys Spilsbury, Ffion Spilsbury
Dianne Sproston (nee Maddocks), Angela
 Sproston, Joanne Sproston

Daisy Stacey and family
Maddie Stewart
Sandra Stone Governor
Katherine Stubbs
Sophie Stubbs
Phyllis Stuffins, Claire Stuffins
Alisha Syal
Serena Tam and family
Isobel and Holly Till
Amy and Ella Timmins
Lynn Tipper
Hannah Titley
Lydia Titley
Maddie Toal
Grace Tomlinson
Nelly Tomlinson
Wendy Tribley (nee Coulson)
Thea Trollope
Sadie Tully
The Turner family
Vantage Point Photos
Aakanksha Verma
Aneesha Verma
Apoorva Verma
Eleanor Vickers
Martha and Connie Vickers
Sophie Vickers
Judith Wade (nee Burdett)
Alysia Wakefield
Grace Walker
Rebecca Walker
Amelia Wallis
Holly and Florence Walmsley
Elizabeth Grace Walsh
Becky Ward
Harriet, Ellen and Lucy Waters
Rebecca Webb
Dorothy Webster (nee Jones), Pam Jordan
 (nee Jones)
Anna Welford and family
Laura and Emma Whalley and family
Freda Whitehead, Judyth Laver
Corin and Maya Whitfield
Sophie Louise Whitham
Victoria and Olivia Whittaker
Heather Whyte (nee Walton)
Gail Wickstead Assistant Head
Joyce Wilkinson (nee Allsop) and Christine,
 Janet, Gillian and Barbara
Hannah Williams
Emma and Vicky Williamson
Aileen Winstanley (nee Littler)
Gillian Winter Assistant Head
Ann E Wood (nee Robinson)
Chris and Becky Wood
Eleanor and Isabel Wright and family
Lillie Wright
Chloe and Matilda Yates
Charlotte Young
Louisa Yung
Bakhtawar Zaffar
Alina Zoya Abeeha Zaidi and family